The Spirituality
of the Future

Other books by K. D. SETHNA

The Spirituality
of the Future

A Search apropos of R. C. Zaehner's Study
in Sri Aurobindo and Teilhard de Chardin

K. D. Sethna

Fairleigh Dickinson

Rutherford • Madison • Teaneck
Fairleigh Dickinson University Press
London and Toronto: Associated University Presses

© 1981 by Associated University Presses, Inc.

Associated University Presses, Inc.
4 Cornwall Drive
East Brunswick, New Jersey 08816

Associated University Presses
69 Fleet Street
London EC4Y 1EU, England

Associated University Press
Toronto ME 1A7 Canada

Library of Congress Cataloging in Publication Data

Sethna, Kaikhushru Dhunjibhoy, 1904-
    The spirituality of the future.

    Bibliography: p.
    Includes index.
    1. Zaehner, Robert Charles. Evolution in religion.
2. Ghose, Aurobindo, 1872-1950. 3. Teilhard de
Chardin, Pierre.   I. Title.
BL1270.G4Z337   200'.1   76-14764
ISBN 0-8386-2028-0

Contents

Note to the Reader

† is used for substantive notes by the author
* indicates notes in the text quoted
Author's notes on the text appear at the ends of chapters, numbered consecutively.

Preface

The Setting and the Scheme

Dr. R. C. Zaehner, well-known specialist in Zoroastrianism, keen scholar of comparative religion and, later, stimulating commentator on the Bhagavad-Gītā, paid a flying visit in December 1969 to the Sri Aurobindo Ashram, Pondicherry. He came after delivering the Westcott Lectures—three in number—under the Teape Foundation in Delhi, Calcutta, and Madras. They were on Sri Aurobindo and Teilhard de Chardin within the general framework of a thesis on religion taking its stand on modern science's discovery of universal evolution, and itself evolving toward a worldwide unity of progressive spiritual outlook.

Zaehner was kind enough to drop in at my place. He had heard of my interest in Teilhard. We had a short pleasant conversation, swapping thoughts on the fundamentals of the French priest-scientist's vision of life. A convert to Roman Catholicism but versed in various scriptures, Zaehner could speak knowledgeably in several respects from both inside and outside the church to which Teilhard was born. On my side also there were a few advantages. Originally a Zoroastrian educated at a Roman Catholic school and college and later a follower of Sri Aurobindo, I could talk of Teilhard with some understanding as well as with a degree of detachment. As for Sri Aurobindo, Zaehner seemed to have read a fair amount of him with fine sympathy. But we hardly entered into any particulars of the Aurobindonian vision, for I was more eager to explore my distinguished visitor's comprehension of Teilhardism than he to make the most of whatever acquaintance I might have with the spiritual light that lay behind Sri Aurobindo's "Integral Yoga."

About two years later his three lectures, "Religions and Religion," "A World in Travail," and "The Communion of Saints," along with a fourth, "Unity in Diversity — Vedantin and Christian," and an appendix, "Commemoration Day Address Delivered at St. Stephen's College, Delhi," were brought out in book form[1] and sent to me for review. I at once launched on my job in the pages of *Mother India*, a monthly review of culture that is published from the Ashram and whose editor I am. But I soon found myself writing, instead of a review, a book occupied with independent exploration no less than with Zaehner's specific research. At times the articles in my series had nothing at all to do with his "study," for other volumes on Teilhard came into my hands and started me off on a discussion of their contents. Even though my themes were sometimes affined to those selected by Zaehner, the articles mainly turned out to constitute a treatment that could very well make a book quite apart from the one stimulated into being by Zaehner. It was only after I had completed my survey of them that I could return to my original scheme. But what happened in a month-by-month comment need not stand in the way of a comparatively more compact dealing with Zaehnerian themes when the writing of a book is in view. So I have decided to save the long interruption for a separate volume and, with a few changes, to put together in this work all that would be more in keeping with the initial intention of my series. The result is that, in spite of my digressions here and there, I come back to the principal points raised by Zaehner.

Before carrying the reader through my "search" apropos of his "study," I would like to say a few introductory words on the latter. I find Zaehner well-grounded in Sri Aurobindo on many topics, but seriously slipping up in some. The mistakes, except for factual ones, do not quite surprise me: they are just what one might expect face-to-face with something that is so revolutionary in its revelation of the heart of our evolutionary universe. Partly they stem from a common Western shortcoming — namely, a difficulty in getting to the real sense of the Eastern mystical attitude. A missing now and then of the revolutionary implications of Teilhardism has also been a frequent phenomenon in the West, and even this, I believe, has something to do with that difficulty; for, in my opinion, Teilhard was Eastern much more than his co-religionists have thought, much more than he himself liked to think or was equipped to realize. Zaehner, too, stops short of certain Teilhardian truths, misled by their discoverer's own blurring of them because of their foreignness in a Roman Catholic context. But, by and large, he sees with a calm clarity and competently appraises Teilhard's insights within the religious field of the modern West, as well as Teilhard's blind spots toward religions other than his own, especially the spirituality of India that is Sri Aurobindo's background.

Note

1. R. C. Zaehner, *Evolution in Religion: A Study in Sri Aurobindo and Pierre Teilhard de Chardin* (Oxford: Clarendon Press, 1971). Subsequent references to this work appear in the text.

Acknowledgments

I wish to thank the following publishers for having given me permission to quote from published works:

Burns & Oates, for permission to quote from Donald B. Gray, *The One and the Many: Teilhard de Chardin's Vision of Unity*, 1969, and from Férnand Prat, *The Theology of Saint Paul*, 1945.

Georges Borchardt, Inc., for permission to quote from Teilhard de Chardin, *Letters to Léontine Zanta*, 1969.

Collins Publishers, for permission to quote from Pierre Teilhard de Chardin, *Activation of Energy*, 1972; *Christianity and Evolution*, 1971; *The Divine Milieu*, 1960; *The Future of Man*, 1964; *Human Energy*, 1969; *Hymn of the Universe*, 1965; *Let Me Explain*, 1970; *Letters to Léontine Zanta*, 1969; *The Making of a Mind: Letters from a Soldier-Priest*, 1965; *The Phenomenon of Man*, 1960; *Science and Christ*, 1968; *The Vision of the Past*, 1966; and *Writings in Time of War*, 1968. Also for permission to quote from Henri de Lubac, *The Religion of Teilhard de Chardin*, 1967; Christopher Mooney, *Teilhard de Chardin and the Mystery of Christ*, 1966; Emile Rideau, *Teilhard de Chardin: A Guide to His Thought*, 1967; Robert Speaight, *Teilhard de Chardin: A Biography*, 1968; H. M. Wildiers, *An Introduction to Teilhard de Chardin*, 1968; and R. C. Zaehner, *Drugs, Mysticism, and Make Believe*, 1972.

Harcourt Brace Jovanovich, Inc., for permission to quote from Pierre Teilhard de Chardin, *Activation of Energy; Christianity and Evolution;* and *Human Energy;* © 1962, 1963, 1969 by Editions du Seuil; © 1969, 1970 by William Collins Sons & Co., Ltd.; © 1971 by William Collins Sons & Co., Ltd. and Harcourt Brace Jovanovich, Inc.

13

Harper & Row Publishers, Inc., for permission to quote from Pierre Teilhard de Chardin, *The Divine Milieu*, 1960; *The Future of Man*, 1964; *Hymn of the Universe*, 1965; *Let Me Explain*, 1972; *The Making of a Mind*, 1965; *The Phenomenon of Man*, 1960; *Science and Christ*, 1968; *The Vision of the Past*, 1966; and *Writings in Time of War*, 1973. Also for permission to quote from H. M. Wildiers, *An Introduction to Teilhard de Chardin*, 1968, and from R. C. Zaehner, *Drugs, Mysticism, and Make Believe*, 1972.

Humanities Press, Inc., for permission to quote from Claude Cuénot, *Science and Faith in Teilhard de Chardin*, 1967.

Oxford University Press, for permission to quote from R. C. Zaehner, *Evolution in Religion*, © Oxford University Press 1971. By Permission of the Oxford University Press.

Sheed & Ward, Inc., for permission to quote from George A. Maloney, *The Cosmic Christ*, © 1968 Sheed & Ward, Inc., New York, New York, and from Olivier Rabut, *Dialogue with Teilhard de Chardin*, © 1961 Sheed & Ward, Inc., New York, New York.

Sri Aurobindo Ashram Trust for permission to quote from Sri Aurobindo and the Mother.

The Spirituality
of the Future

1

Zaehner's Main Comparisons

Zaehner's objective and preoccupation in his book may be summed up in his own words. It is also possible to string together, for convenience's sake, his most important comparative pronouncements, as well as a few general reflections. This stringing together may at times result in too close repetitions, in addition to causing a certain jumpiness. As a rule, Zaehner has a good sequence and, though he is prone to repeat himself here and there, he does so mostly to keep some *leitmotiv*s ringing and usually manages a sufficient spacing out of the reiterations. But my method of massing the major comparisons that are relevant to areas of special interest has the advantage of projecting some sort of total picture that, provided one knows of its having been considerably simplified, does the best justice to Zaehner's overall view.

After writing that Sri Aurobindo and Teilhard "are between them the excuse and the main theme of these lectures," he continues with an explanation of his choice of them and with a stress on the novelty of their outlook:

> The reason why I have chosen them is that, in their separate traditions, they represent something totally new in mystical religion. And the reason is not far to seek. Both, not only accepted the theory of evolution, but enthusiastically acclaimed it, indeed were almost obsessed by it. Both were, it seems, profoundly influenced by Bergson, both were deeply dissatisfied with organized religion, and both were vitally concerned not only with individual salvation or "liberation" but also with the *collective* salvation of mankind. Hence their sympathetic interest in Marxian socialism, for it was the hope of each of them that the unity in

17

diversity which the mystic finds in himself would be reflected in a socialized and free society in which, as Marx had prophesied, "we shall have an association in which the free development of each is the condition for the free development of all."

The reality, as we know, has turned out to be very different from the prophecy both in the Soviet Union and in China . . . [pp. 3, 4]. However, there is always room for hope, and hope is a Christian virtue. It was also recognized as a virtue by Aurobindo though it seems to have faded from his vision towards the end of his life. For, Aurobindo, though he had started as a left-wing politician, had also been the subject of a mystical revelation, and this even so Anglicized a Bengali as Aurobindo could not lightly brush aside. . . ."Cosmic consciousness," as he called it following R. M. Bucke, in which the ego is annihilated and all is seen as One and One as all in a perfect and marvellous harmony, is the "Truth" which the mystic experiences in his own being; it must therefore be true of the cosmos as a whole. Hence evil must either be illusory or a necessary stepping-stone on the way to the good. This is the common experience of all so-called "nature mystics," and it has also the scriptural authority of the Upanishads . . . [pp. 4,5].

Aurobindo . . . too had experienced the omnipresence of God "in every man moving before me, even in every tree, wall, bird, and beast. . . .God is in every metal, and in the earth and mud."* But unlike Bucke he did not suppose that this one experience was in itself typical or complete, although he is not always consistent about this. . . .

Teilhard de Chardin too was a pantheist by nature, and throughout the first World War, during which he acted as a stretcher-bearer, he seems to have lived in an almost permanent state of "cosmic consciousness." It was not he who had sought it out any more than had Bucke. "It was not I," he writes, "who laboriously discovered the All; it was the All which showed itself to me, imposed itself on me through a kind of 'cosmic consciousness.' It is the attraction of the All that has set everything in motion in me, brought it to life and given it organic form. . . . [Hence] I can never aspire to a reward which is less than the All itself."** And this cosmic consciousness if it is to be truly cosmic, must be realized not only in individual men but also in the whole of mankind. Only so can humanity be spiritually unified and collectively redeemed.

---

* A. B. Purani, *Life of Sri Aurobindo,* Pondicherry, 1964, p. 125.

** Pierre Teilhard de Chardin, *Oeuvres* (Paris, Edition du Seuil), 9, p. 72; cf. E.T. *Science and Christ,* London, 1968, pp. 43-44. (E.T. = English Translation, all the volumes of which are published by Messrs Collins.)

Aurobindo and Teilhard de Chardin had these two things in common, the repeated experience of cosmic consciousness, and a profound belief in evolution, the goal of which they saw to be the divinization of man. Both produced their most significant work during and directly after the first World War. Teilhard was prevented by his superiors from publishing anything during his lifetime; hence it would have been impossible for Aurobindo to have become acquainted with his thought. It is, however, strange that Teilhard never came to hear of Aurobindo — or perhaps not so strange, for though he had formed his own ideas about Eastern mysticism, he had quite clearly not read the basic texts in any kind of depth. Had he done so, he would scarcely have dismissed Eastern mysticism out of hand as being *périmé,* "dated,"* how much less Aurobindo whose thought so closely resembled his own. For what was the ideal of both men? "The hope of the kingdom of heaven within us and the city of God upon earth,"** as Aurobindo said, or in the words of Teilhard, "to promote in equal measure the mastery of the world and the kingdom of God."*** [pp. 6, 7]

Having read some basic resemblances in spiritual experience and practical outlook between the two thinkers, Zaehner touches on a difference in their life situations, adjudges the relationship of each to his doctrinal background, and comments on their attitudes towards the future:

Teilhard de Chardin was profoundly dissatisfied with what he considered to be the excessive legalism of the Roman Catholic Church of his time. . . .Yet despite occasional bitterness it never seriously occurred to him to leave the Society of Jesus, let alone the Roman Church, for despite all its defects it was for him the only possible centre of unity in the frame of which the collective salvation of mankind could one day be realized. . . .

For Aurobindo the problem was quite different. Though born in Calcutta, he was sent to England when he was seven. Educated at St. Paul's School in London and King's College, Cambridge, proving himself to be a classical scholar of note, he was thoroughly steeped in the classical humanism of his time: by upbringing he was an English gentleman. . . .It was only on his return to India . . . that he discovered the Hindu religion and the Vedānta. But he could not accept the Vedānta in its classic non-dualist formulation, for in England he had come to accept Dar-

---

* *Oeuvres* 7, p. 236.
** *The Human Cycle,* etc., Pondicherry, 1962, ch. 13, p. 165.
*** *Écrits du temps de la guerre,* Paris, Grasset, 1965, p. 84: E. T. *Writings in Time of War,* Collins, London, 1968, p. 91.

winism and Bergson's idea of *creative* evolution. If the One were totally static and unfractionable, then there could be no room for evolution, creativity, or development of any kind. This could not be. Rather, the One, though absolutely self-sufficient unto itself, must also be the source of multiplicity and not only of change, but of progressive, evolutionary change, an ascent the culmination of which was to be re-united with the One in a new richness and a new glory. Aurobindo knew that his "integral Yoga" which not only aimed at the discovery of the immortal and timeless within oneself but also sought to harmonize the total human being in and around this immortal core and then to concentrate all immortal cores or centres around the core and centre of all things — this integral Yoga was an innovation and constituted a clear break with the traditional Sankhya-Yoga which had made the sharpest distinction between Spirit and matter, the Imperishable and the perishable, Eternity and time. For Hinduism as a social structure he had no use at all, and the Vedānta of Śankara and Theravāda Buddhism he regarded as *hīnayāna*, a "defective way" at the best; but, having once discovered Hinduism, the national religion of India, he had no intention of leaving it. Indeed, he had no incentive to do so, for Hinduism has no central authority to lay down what you should believe nor is it committed to any particular form of religious expression. Moreover, just as Teilhard found the justification for his radical re-interpretation of Christianity in certain of the writings of St. Paul and St. John, so did Aurobindo find the justification for his dynamic interpretation of the Vedānta in the Hindu scriptures themselves, particularly in the Bhagavad-Gītā and (less justifiably) in the Vedic Samhitās. He thus reversed the current monistic trend in Hindu mysticism by appealing to the sacred texts themselves. Though he re-interpreted the Vedas along his own lines, he did in fact bring out their essential concern with *this* world which was a necessary corrective to the dominant inwardness of the later Upanishads. The *Katha* Upanishad (4.1) had diverted man's eyes from the contemplation of the outside world to his own hidden depths. . . .But the full teaching of the Upanishads is that "without" and "within" are one, the infinite and the infinitesimal blend in the human heart, and both are pervaded and ruled by a "Lord" . . . [pp. 9-11].

The essence of Aurobindo's thought is perhaps to be found in his *Thoughts and Aphorisms* compiled, apparently, in his old age. These derive almost entirely from Hindu tradition, particularly the Bhagavad-Gītā and the *Bhāgavata* Purāna. Gone are the European influences, as are Aurobindo's own typical concepts of Supermind, Overmind and so on which appear to be central to his *magnum opus, The Life Divine,* but which in fact only duplicate the more traditional terminology, thereby creating unnecessary confusion. The same might be said about Teilhard with his Omega-point, noosphere, super-humanity, super-Christ and so on—none of which is calculated to endear him to modern secular and scientific man (for whom the terminology was presumably designed), let alone to more traditional Christians.

Despite all this Teilhard, quite as much as Aurobindo, can point to scriptural authority in support of his views. Taking his stand on the assumption that the law of increasing entropy which must finally mean the death of the universe *must* be counter-balanced by a complementary law of continually increasing complexity-consciousness (the highest example of which is up till now the human brain), he goes on to say (as does Aurobindo) that the next stage of the evolution of this planet will be the convergence of humanity upon itself, the development, then, of a *collective* mind the nature of which can be dimly inferred from the experience of cosmic consciousness. All this is to be found in St. Paul, "not," he admits, "in the Sermon on the Mount or even in the gesture of the Cross",*—that is to say, in an aspect of Christianity with which Hindus on the whole are unfamiliar and which Aurobindo himself, despite his English education, either did not know or preferred to ignore. This is St. Paul's vision of the mystical body of Christ in the Church and of the cosmic Christ he reveals in Philippians, Colossians and Ephesians. Through Christ and his Church the human race is destined to grow together until "everything is subjected to him, [and] then the Son himself will be subject in his turn to the One who subjected all things to him, so that God may be all in all."** This consummation of the whole human race through the God-man into God was God's purpose from the beginning . . . [pp. 11,12].

. . .This aspect of Christianity had been neglected and only through this approach, Teilhard thought, could Christianity be made meaningful to modern man. He saw Christ and Christianity in and through evolution—from individuality through collectivity to a unity in diversity centred on the cosmic Christ. This was precisely the vision of Sri Aurobindo in his *The Life Divine.* Substitute the Hindu Trinity *sac-cid-ānada* (Being-Logos-Joy) for Christ, and the parallelism is exact. The difference is that, whereas Teilhard saw the instrument of human unity ready to hand in the Church, Aurobindo could find no such principle of unity within Hinduism since, socially, Hinduism has hitherto been based on caste. . . .Even if we are able to see merit in the caste system, its function is to divide, not to unite, and what divides is, in the eyes of both Teilhard and Aurobindo, evil.

* *Oeuvres* 6, p. 193.
** I Corinthians, 15:28.

Acting on his own principle that even a single soul fully integrated in the divine life must, sooner or later, make its attraction felt throughout the entire world, Aurobindo collected a few disciples around himself in his Pondicherry Ashram in the hope that, with the assistance of a French lady whom he was bold enough to hail as the Divine Mother and the eternal Śakti, he, the utterly perfected Siddha, would draw all things to himself. Since evolution works in units of millions rather than hundreds of years, it is obviously very much too early to say whether he was right . . . [p. 13].

Aurobindo . . . was right to condemn the rigidities of organized religion but wrong to imagine that his vision of the cosmos transformed and re-integrated into the Divine could be realized except in the framework of a religious organization capable of transforming itself into a living organism in which the individual parts would depend for their life on the whole, each contributing its own special excellence to the well-being of the total body which one day would embrace all mankind . . . [pp. 24,25].

To the very last Teilhard, against all the evidence of two world wars and an armistice only maintained by a balance of terror, believed that the spirit of man was on the verge of a breakthrough to a new form of socialized and "totalized" existence. Aurobindo could not entirely share this optimism to the end, for his Ashram in Pondicherry had not yet given birth to new centres in which what he called Supermind could manifest itself. This was perhaps a disappointment to him since, unlike Teilhard, he saw himself as the divine centre from which the transformation of man into "super-manhood" was to radiate. During the thirty years in which he had been engaged in "bringing down the Supramental" nothing much had happened outwardly: the Ashram was indeed and still is going and expanding concern, but its impact on the world has so far been slight and is not yet comparable to that of the widely diffused Ramakrishna Mission. But then Aurobindo, like Teilhard, could always fall back on the theory of evolution itself and the prodigious periods of time that it presupposes . . . [p. 27].

The earth had, indeed, not proved responsive to the divine transformation that was to have become manifest through him. Hence he had no alternative but to give up his body quite voluntarily—or so his disciples believe—"in an act of supreme unselfishness . . . to hasten the hour of collective realization."* In 1915 he had said: "Heaven we have possessed, but not the earth; but the fullness of the Yoga is to make . . . Heaven and earth equal and one."** But it needs more than one lifetime to do this . . . [p. 28].

* *A Practical Guide to Integral Yoga*, Pondicherry, 1955, p. 389.
** A. B. Purani, op. cit., p. 167.

And was it not a sign of an inner despair that Aurobindo retreated into himself during the last twenty years of his life? Despite the theoretical dynamism of his philosophy which was to have transformed Hinduism, when he died he had still not succeeded in "making Heaven and earth equal and one." Perhaps he has left behind in his Ashram not only the "kingdom of God within us" but also, however small it may be, a "city of God upon earth."

And yet he realized that without an inner transformation of the individual there could be no outer transformation of the collectivity. . . ."It is a spiritual, an inner freedom that can alone create a perfect human order. . . .A deeper brotherhood, a yet unfound law of love is the only true foundation possible for a perfect social evolution . . . a love which is founded upon a deeper truth of our being, the brotherhood or, let us say, . . .the spiritual comradeship which is the expression of an inner realization of oneness. For only so can egoism disappear and the true individualism of the unique godhead in each man found itself on the true communism of the equal godhead in the race; for the Spirit, the inmost Self, the universal Godhead in every being is that whose very nature of divine oneness it is to realize the perfection of its individual life and nature in the existence of all."*

This was the hope of Aurobindo, but he was usually clear-sighted enough to see that there was always a chance that it might fail, and in any case things had to be seen in terms of evolutionary time, and not in terms of human generations . . . [pp. 33-35].

Usually, however, Aurobindo is little given to pessimism; for he regards the evolutionary process as inevitably leading back to the supreme *sac-cid-ānanda,* the triune God who is not only the static God of the philosophers but also a *living* God who operates in time. More concretely he sees evolution both in political terms and in terms of ever greater awareness—a progression from apparently inanimate matter to life, from life to consciousness and mind, from mind to what he calls Overmind, and from Overmind to Supermind which, if I understand him aright, is pure *cit,* pure consciousness, operating in the world as *śakti* or power. This ascent from matter to Spirit he sometimes sees as a return to the insights already "given" in the Upanishads and Veda. "We have then to *return* to the pursuit of an ancient secret which man, as a race, has seen only obscurely and followed after lamely, has indeed understood only with his surface mind and not in its heart of meaning—and yet in following it lies his social no less than his individual salvation—the ideal of the Kingdom of God, the secret of the reign of the Spirit over mind and life body."** [pp. 35-36]

* *The Human Cycle,* etc., ch. 20, pp. 295-6.
** Ibid., ch. 22, p. 322.

Next, Zaehner notes in passing how his two subjects relate dissimilarly to science, and discerns, for all their dissimilarity, a world view common to both:

> It must be remembered that there is Aurobindo the socialist and Aurobindo the mystic. The first is typified in *The Human Cycle* and *The Ideal of Human Unity*, while the second unfolds himself at enormous length in *The Life Divine*. Though he continually speaks of his "integral Yoga" which is supposed to contain both, the two aspects of him, the exoteric concerned with the building of the city of God on earth and the esoteric struggling to realize the kingdom of God within you, tend to fall apart, the latter tending to assume greater importance in his later work. Unlike Teilhard his background was literary, not scientific, and his attitude towards science remains ambivalent. Very occasionally he sees science as the great unifier of the human race. . . .His tribute to it, such as it is, seems to be only lip-service paid to a fashionable idol. In this he differs widely from Teilhard for whom scientific research was akin to adoration* and who could say: "Neither in its impetus nor in its achievement can science go to its limits without becoming tinged with mysticism and charged with faith."**
>
> Yet despite the differences between the two men they share a common view of the universe. First, Spirit takes precedence over matter. Secondly, since this is so, it follows that Spirit must always have been in matter in a rudimentary form. Third, evolution is a progressive unification, an ever-increasing spiritualization of matter. Fourth, the goal of evolution must be the integration of matter in a final harmony and its convergence on to a centre of attraction which is supramental and divine. Fifthly, the only conceivable agent of such a convergence is a "yet unfound law of love." Both men again were profoundly dissatisfied with their own religions as currently practised and interpreted and sought to re-construct them in an evolutionary mould. Both again regarded suffering and strife as being of the very stuff of evolutionary progress . . . [pp. 37-38].
>
> Both might be regarded as Gnostics, for both, in their different ways, interpreted the "Fall" in a cosmic sense: Spirit "falls" into matter and its true nature is thereby "veiled" from itself. On the nature of this "Fall" Sri Aurobindo is confused; but in *The Life Divine* his thought seems to be nearest to Neo-Platonism among the philosophies of the West. The supreme Absolute which in itself must be beyond change is the classic *Sac-cid-ānanda* — Being, Consciousness, and Joy . . . — absolutely One in

---

* Teilhard de Chardin, *The Phenomenon of Man*, E.T. p, 250.
** Ibid., p. 284.

itself but nonetheless containing the seed of multiplicity. From
this Trinity, or more specifically from Consciousness in-dwelt by
Joy proceeds Supermind which he also calls Consciousness-Force;
in Christian terminology we might say the Logos in its creative action. From this proceeds Overmind which is the boundary between the "pleroma" of pure Being and the world of becoming,
the universe, that is, in which we live. Thus "Overmind stands at
the top of the lower hemisphere;"* below is what Sri Aurobindo
calls the world of the Ignorance which consists of mind, life, and
finally matter. This descent of the spirit into matter he calls
devolution, the necessary obverse of evolution. In "inconscient"
matter as he calls it Spirit has become totally submerged; it is not
aware of itself, or, if you prefer it, it is playing hide-and-seek with
itself, the divine "game" so loved of the Hindus. . . [pp. 38,39].

God is One: on this the higher religions are in some degree
united: but in Christianity he is also three, and this is a mystery
which the Christians themselves have never been able to explain.
And yet this Christian Trinity is reflected in Hindu theology too,
not in the highly artificial trinity of Brahma, the creator, Vishnu,
the preserver, and Śiva, the destroyer, which is not comparable to
the Christian Trinity at all, but in the standard Vedāntin formula *sac-cid-ānanda*, which all Vedāntins and not least
Aurobindo accept, Being-Consciousness-Joy, or without stretching the formula too much, Being-Logos-Love . . . [p. 55].

On the one hand . . . you have heaven, the realm of spirit
where all is but one, on the other you have the earth organizing
itself at first through the mysterious power of evolution and then
being consciously organized in these "last days" by scientific man.
. . .What . . . is the link between them? In China it is man, in the
Book of Genesis it is God.

"In the beginning God created the heavens and the earth. Now
the earth was a formless void, there was darkness over the deep,
and God's spirit hovered over the water."

We hear no more about the heavens, as is proper, for, as
Teilhard says, "in heaven all is but one." But the earth is very different; it is *tohu* and *bohu*, a "trackless waste and emptiness,"
dark and fluid, having no shape or form, coherence or consistency.
Call it "nothing" or "no thing," say with 2 Maccabees (7:28)
that "God made them out of things that did not exist . . . "; it
doesn't matter very much since even theologians are not very clear
as to what creation *ex nihilo* means. Teilhard did his best to
describe the "nothing" from which God created the earth, and his
account which tries to square evolution with Genesis rather than
the dogmatic creation *ex nihilo* is intriguing if not very convinc-

---

* *A Practical Guide to Integral Yoga*, p. 385.

ing to the rational mind. . . . This is how Teilhard put it in one of
his earlier works:

"In the beginning there were, at the two poles of existence, God
and pure multiplicity (*la multitude*). Even so God was all alone,
because the pure multiplicity which was in a state of absolute
dissociation did not exist. For all eternity God saw the shadow of
his unity in a diffused state of disarray (*éparpillé*) beneath his
feet; and this shadow, fraught as it was with every possibility of
producing something, was not another God because, in itself, it
did not exist, nor had it ever existed, nor could it ever have existed because its essence was to be infinitely divided in itself, that
is to say, to tend towards nothingness. Infinite in extension, infinitely rarefied, this pure multiplicity, annihilated as to its
essence, slept at the antipodes of Being which is One and concentrated.

"It was then that Unity, overflowing with life, joined battle
through [the proces of] creation with the multiple which, though
non-existent [in itself], opposed it as a contrast and a challenge.
To create, as it appears to me, means to condense, concentrate,
organize, unite."*

"God was all alone," Teilhard says. But how could he be alone
if, as the Christians (and the Vedāntins) will have it, he is a Trinity? And what was his "Spirit" which hovered over the water? It
can scarcely be other than the Holy Spirit commonly accounted
as being the third "Person" of the Christian Trinity. It "hovered
over the water" and, presumably, entered into the water, the
symbol of the ever-moving, the unstable, perpetually changing
thing which is chaos—matter in its most embryonic and, if you
like, its most non-existent form. The Spirit, the principle of unity
in the Godhead since it eternally binds the Father to the Son,
descends into matter, descends into the dead, dark waters. Or as
the Rig-Veda (10.129.2) puts it:

> In the beginning was darkness swathed in darkness;
> All was but unmanifested water.
> Whatever was, that One, coming into being,
> Hidden by the Void,
> Was generated by the power of heat.

"Hidden by the Void": this is essential in the thought of Sri
Aurobindo. Spirit or, as he more often calls it, Consciousness-
Force descends into matter and there becomes veiled and
alienated from itself. Though remaining in eternity unfettered
and free in the triune Godhead it, so to speak, loses itself in the

---

* *Écrits du temps de in guerre*, p. 114: E.T. in *Writings in Time of War*, p. 95.

dark, dead waters of matter, but in so doing it stirs them into life
. . . [pp. 54-57].

This means that there is no such thing as really "dead" matter;
all matter is instinct with life and consciousness. What Teilhard
calls the "Soul of the world" and Sri Aurobindo calls
"Supermind" is already there in embryo, just as the soul of an individual is already there, though unconscious, in the human
foetus. It is there but it has not yet developed; yet it develops slowly but inexorably until we arrive at the simple consciousness of the
animal, and then in the first human beings or rather groups of
human beings at a kind of collective consciousness which seems to
precede full self-consciousness. For, as Teilhard says, "in the
opinion of the best observers a kind of collective co-consciousness
can still be distinguished among tribes classified by ethnologists as
primitive which in the most natural way in the world enables the
group to stick together and to function harmoniously as a
group."* This is a primitive form of cosmic consciousness . . .
[pp. 60, 61].

Cosmic consciousness, says R. M. Bucke who invented the
term, appearing in individuals, is the guarantee of a future
cosmic consciousness that must one day be born and which will
mean the transformation of the human race and its unification in
and around a central focus of attraction, the *Sac-cid-ānanda* of
Aurobindo, the Christ-Omega of Teilhard de Chardin . . . [p.
48].

Christ, because he is both God and man, is the Centre to which
all human "centres," all human "selves" as "parts of God," as the
Gītā (15.7) puts it, must look. He is the mid-point in human
evolution, midway between the "beginning" when "God's Spirit
hovered over the water" and the final Parousia when "God will be
all in all."** [p. 81].

I may stop quoting here. These passages, culled from separate
places, cannot give a totally adequate idea of the richness of
Zaehner's book or of the trouble that he has taken over the exposition of several aspects of the Aurobindonian or the Teilhardian
outlook. Some statements about Sri Aurobindo in the foregoing
sound very odd: they should not suggest any hostility on Zaehner's
part, for he is sufficiently eulogistic of Sri Aurobindo. However,
while one or two—such as those on Sri Aurobindo's being
"confused" or "inconsistent"—are rather hasty and childish by being
unconscious of differing contexts and need no further attention, a
good number require correction because of their importance, and,

* *Oeuvres* 8, p. 135: cf. E.T. *Man's Place in Nature*, p. 93.
** Corinthians, 15.28.

in many instances, in correcting them it is possible to alight on significant dissimilarities between Sri Aurobindo and Teilhard in spite of several convergences. The corrections will also serve a wider purpose, to which some of my comments on several sides of Teilhard and on a few of Zaehner's assertions about Hinduism and about Sri Aurobindo's links with it will contribute as well. This purpose is to right Zaehner's tilting of the balance on the whole in the direction of Teilhard as if Sri Aurobindo were an admirable and valuable mystic only inasmuch as he points toward the completeness, in a general sense, of the vision that is Teilhardian.

2

A Few Initial Misconceptions about Sri Aurobindo

Before I launch on a doctrinal study in some depth I may dispose at once of what may be dubbed Zaehner's most glaring gaffes concerning Sri Aurobindo. Two of them relate to doctrine itself or, rather, to a question of doctrinal posture.

One touches twice on intellectual influences in the early part of Sri Aurobindo's life. Zaehner holds Bergson to have been a seminal factor in the development of Sri Aurobindo's world outlook just as he was in Teilhard's. He traces this factor to Sri Aurobindo's period in England and refers in particular to the thesis of Bergson's *Creative Evolution*. Sri Aurobindo left England in 1893. Before that year Bergson had written only his first major work, *Essai sur les données immédiates de la conscience,* in 1888, whose English translation as *Time and Free Will* came out in 1910. His next work, *Matière et mémoire (Matter and Memory)*, appeared eight years later, in 1896. Neither of these compositions concerns itself appreciably with the theory of evolution that, according to Zaehner, is the foundation stone of the Aurobindonian system. *L'Évolution créatrice (Creative Evolution)* saw the light in French in 1907 and was Englished only in 1911. The possibility of Bergson's having made an impact as an evolutionary philosopher on Sri Aurobindo during his early days is utterly ruled out. Of course, Sri Aurobindo had accepted from those days the general idea of evolution. But by 1911 he had already passed through the stupendous experience of

29

Nirvana in 1908 at Baroda and the no less sweeping one in Alipore Jail, 1909, of Sri Krishna as the cosmic Personal Divine. Even the inner sense, in a broad manner, of what he has designated as *Supermind* had developed. Thus evolution as a process of the spirit had already figured in his mind. Actually, some notes on Bergson survive from the time that the English version of the Frenchman's masterpiece was published, but they bear on his philosophy of "becoming" rather than on his scientific thought. And much later, in answer to a disciple's queries, Sri Aurobindo wrote briefly of Bergson's "intuition" as well as of his "élan vital," but in doing so he said: "I have not read him sufficiently to pronounce."[1] Bergson's having been a seminal factor in the development of Sri Aurobindo's world outlook is quite out of the question, and to imagine him profoundly influential on Sri Aurobindo in England is an amazing anachronism.

A much worse mistake on Zaehner's part concerns the last years of Sri Aurobindo. He takes his book *Thoughts and Aphorisms* and finds in this group of pithy and spirited sayings no trace of "European influences" and of "Aurobindo's typical concepts of Supermind, Overmind and so on." But he does not pause to reason that if what is typically Aurobindonian, filling volume after volume, is absent, this comparatively short work cannot belong to the author's most mature period. Instead, he leaps to the conclusion that in this work where he thinks he sees "the Hindu tradition, particularly the Bhagavad-Gītā and the *Bhāgavata* Purāna," is found "the essence of Sri Aurobindo's thought" and that the book was "compiled, apparently, in his old age." Doubtless, the compilation was first published in 1955, half a decade after Sri Aurobindo had passed away. But the publisher's note gives a clear clue to the chronology of its composition. The note explains that this is the full collection of sayings, of which the book published as *Thoughts and Glimpses* was only a portion. *Thoughts and Glimpses* first came out in book form in 1920, but it dates to a period still earlier because its debut was in a series of installments in Sri Aurobindo's philosophical monthly, *Arya*, which ran from 15 August 1914 to January 1921, and the installments appeared in 1915 and 1917.

Possibly such a gross misunderstanding of the place of *Thoughts and Aphorisms* in the history of Sri Aurobindo's philosophical-spiritual outlook has contributed to Zaehner's belief that "Supermind, Overmind and so on" are a matter of unusual terminology alone and do not indicate any really new departure in Yogic experience. Old realizations applied to a modern master idea, evolution, sum up Sri Aurobindo's inspiring novelty for Zaehner. I shall analyze this opinion at a later stage. Here it will suffice to quote some words of Sri Aurobindo in 1935 explaining why, in spite of the presence of several old elements, he calls his Yoga new as compared to the old ones:

(1) Because it aims not at a departure out of world and life into Heaven or Nirvana, but at a change of life and existence, not as something subordinate or incidental but as a distinct and central object. . . .

(2) Because the object sought after is not an individual achievement of divine realisation for the sake of the individual, but something to be gained for the earth-consciousness here, a cosmic, not only a supra-cosmic achievement. The thing to be gained also is the bringing in of a Power of Consciousness (the Supramental) not yet organised or active directly in earth-nature, even in the spiritual life, but yet to be organised and made directly active.

(3) Because a method has been preconised† for achieving this purpose, which is as total and integral as the aim set before it, viz., the total and integral change of the consciousness and nature, taking up old methods but only as a part action and present aid to others that are distinctive. I have not found this method (as a whole) or anything like it professed or realised in the old Yogas. If I had, I should not have wasted my time in hewing out paths and in thirty years of search and inner creation when I could have hastened home safely to my goal in an easy canter over paths already blazed out, laid down, perfectly mapped, macadamised, made secure and public. Our Yoga is not a retreading of old walks, but a spiritual adventure.[2]

I may draw attention to the reference to the Supramental Consciousness and the bringing in of it as a new power. On the change, the transformation, it is meant to effect, Sri Aurobindo says:

By transformation I do not mean some change of the nature — I do not mean, for instance, sainthood or ethical perfection or yogic siddhi (like the Tantrics) or a transcendental (chinmaya) body. I use transformation in a special sense, a change of consciousness radical and complete and of a certain specific kind which is so conceived as to bring about a strong and assured step

† *Webster's New International Dictionary of the English Language,* 2d ed. s.v. "preconize": (1) To proclaim publicly; to publish; also, to commend publicly; (2) To summon publicly or by name; (3) *Roman Catholic Church* of the Pope, to approve by preconization.

forward in the spiritual evolution of the being of a greater and higher kind and of a larger sweep and completeness than what took place when a mentalised being first appeared in a vital and material animal world. If anything short of that takes place or at least if a real beginning is not made on that basis, a fundamental progress towards this fulfilment, then my object is not accomplished. A partial realisation, something mixed and inconclusive, does not meet the demand I make on life and yoga.[3]

Right up to the end, 1950, Sri Aurobindo kept up his new and radical demand. The articles he dictated in the last two years of his life for the Ashram's *Bulletin of Physical Education* ring incessantly with the word *Supermind*. And there was not, as Zaehner suggests, a giving up of "hope" and "optimism" at the end because the Supermind had not been collectively realized in the twenty-four years since 1926 when the organized Ashram came into existence. Every Yoga—particularly one that is "a spiritual adventure"—is fraught with ups and downs, outbursts of light and vigils in the dark. Sri Aurobindo minced no words on this theme: "This Yoga is a spiritual battle, its very attempt raises all sorts of adverse forces and one must be ready to face difficulties, sufferings, reverses of all sorts in a calm unflinching spirit."[4] About his own personal burden of spiritual work, too, he made no secret, but the spirit in which he bore it is also unmistakable in a letter of April 1934: "It is only divine Love which can bear the burden I have to bear, that all have to bear who have sacrificed everything else to the one aim of uplifting earth out of its darkness towards the Divine. The Gallio-like 'Je m'en fiche'-ism (I do not care) would not carry me one step; it would certainly not be divine. It is quite another thing that enables me to walk unweeping and unlamenting towards the goal."[5] Some months earlier—December 1933—found him writing:

As for faith, you write as if I never had a doubt or any difficulty. I have had worse than any human mind can think of. It is not because I have ignored difficulties, but because I have seen them more clearly, experienced them on a larger scale than anyone living now or before me that, having faced and measured them, I am sure of the results of my work. But even if I still saw the chance that it might come to nothing (which is impossible), I would go on unperturbed, because I would still have done to the best of my power the work that I had to do, and what is so done always counts in the economy of the universe. But why should I feel that all this may come to nothing when I see each step and where it is leading and every week and day—once it was every month and year and hereafter it will be every day and hour— brings me so much nearer to my goal? In the way that one treads with the greater Light above, even every difficulty gives its help and has its value and Night itself carries in it the burden of the Light that has to be.[6]

Here is a positive statement of a lifelong attitude and resolve and a flaming certitude. In the same year, on 10 August he wrote in a similar vein. And in this letter there is a reference to the question of giving up the ghost in a mood of disappointment. Apropos of the clamoring by intellectuals like Tagore, Russell, and Rolland for the end of an age in which misery was rampant everywhere, he was asked by a disciple: "How is it that things should be marching headlong into a quagmire such as this? I sometimes fear that eventually you and the Mother will retire into an extra-cosmic Samadhi leaving the wicked world to sink or swim as best it can. Perhaps that would be the wisest course—who knows?" Sri Aurobindo replied:

"I have no intention of doing so—even if all smashed, I would look beyond the smash to the new creation. As for what is happening in the world, it does not upset me because I knew all along that things would happen in that fashion, and as for the hopes of the intellectual idealists I have not shared them, so I am not disappointed."[7]

One realizes that the appearance of things going contrary would have no effect on Sri Aurobindo and would never induce him "to give up his body voluntarily." Zaehner is rather mixed-up here. He quotes some words from the Ashram—they are the Mother's, in fact, but in a somewhat garbled form—declaring that the earth's unresponsiveness led Sri Aurobindo to give up his body. The Mother was far from suggesting any sense of frustration in Sri Aurobindo. What she definitely indicated was that, as Zaehner himself discloses, Sri Aurobindo's departure was "an act of supreme unselfishness . . . to hasten the hour of collective realisation." What the unselfishness consisted of is not mentioned by Zaehner. The Mother said that it lay in his "renouncing the realisation in his body." This implies an occult strategy whereby the leader's death spells a violent breakthrough accomplished for the followers. Only such a death can be envisaged for a Yogi with a spirit in him like Sri Aurobindo's.

Perhaps one may object on the basis that the spirit spoken of is expressed in letters of 1933 and 1934 and that surely they are a far cry from the year 1950, when Sri Aurobindo left this "wicked world." One may voice the doubt whether there are any letters close to 1950 to show the same spirit.

First of all, Zaehner cannot logically want late letters rather than early ones. For he writes: "And was it not a sign of inner despair that Aurobindo retreated into himself during the last twenty years of his life?" The allusion is to the so-called retirement of Sri Aurobindo on 24 November 1926, giving the Ashram and its work into the Mother's hands. So anything after 24 November 1926 disproving "inner despair" would be appropriate and cogent against Zaehner.

Actually, however, there are letters of a late period also breathing the same indomitable spirit and conviction of success. On 2 June 1946 Sri Aurobindo observed: "I know that this is a time of trouble for you and everybody. It is so for the whole world. Confusion, trouble, disorder and upset everywhere is the general state of things. The better things that are to come are preparing or growing under a veil and the worse are prominent everywhere. The one thing is to hold on and hold out till the hour of light has come."[8] On 19 October 1946 Sri Aurobindo asserted: "I have not been discouraged by what is happening, because I know and have experienced hundreds of times that beyond the blackest darkness there lies for one who is a divine instrument the light of God's victory. I have never had a strong and persistent will for anything to happen in the world — I am not speaking of personal things — which did not eventually happen even after delay, defeat or even disaster."[9] On 9 April 1947 he once more said: "I am not discouraged. I know what is preparing behind the veil and can feel and see the first signs of its coming."[10] When a disciple discussed with Sri Aurobindo the implications of modern physics and Sri Aurobindo thought that the disciple was urging on him some writings that could place again "a dogmatism from materialistic science on its throne of half a century ago from which it could victoriously ban all thought surpassing its narrow bounds as mere wordy metaphysics and mysticism and moonshine" so that "there can be no possibility of a divine life on earth," Sri Aurobindo in a powerful letter affirmed, with superb irony and sweeping determination, about those "writings": "I dare say these . . . may be entirely convincing and I would find after reading them that my own position was wrong and that only an obstinate mystic could still believe in such a conquest of Matter by the Spirit as I had dared to think possible. But I am just such an obstinate mystic."[11] This was penned in May 1949. And as late as 4 April 1950, in connection with "the present darkness in the world round us," he pronounced:

> For myself, the dark conditions do not discourage me or con-
> vince me of the vanity of my will to "help the world," for I knew
> they had to come; they were there in the world-nature and had to
> rise up so that they might be exhausted or expelled so that a bet-
> ter world freed from them might be there. After all, something
> has been done in the outer field and that may help or prepare for
> getting something done in the inner field also. For instance, India
> is free, and her freedom was necessary if the divine work was to be
> done. The difficulties that surround her now and may increase
> for a time, especially with regard to the Pakistan imbroglio, were
> also things that had to come and to be cleared out. . . .Here too
> there is sure to be a full clearance, though unfortunately a con-
> siderable amount of suffering in the process is inevitable. After-
> wards the work for the Divine will become more possible and it
> may well be that the dream, if it is a dream, of leading the world
> towards the spiritual light, may even become a reality. So I am
> not disposed even now, in these dark conditions, to consider my
> will to help the world as condemned to failure.[12]

It is surprising that Zaehner, studying Sri Aurobindo, could miss articulations that would give the lie in an absolute manner to all suspicions of despair in Sri Aurobindo at any time. And indeed to link "an inner despair" with the sequel to 24 November 1926 is the height of absurdity. For that day is regarded in the Ashram as the Day of Siddhi, Victory. Sri Aurobindo's own words on it are: "24th November 1926 was the descent of Krishna into the physical. Krishna is not the Supramental Light. The descent of Krishna would mean the descent of the Overmind Godhead, preparing, though not itself actually, the descent of Supermind and Ananda."[13]

A most momentous event with an extremely positive spiritual con-sequence for Sri Aurobindo's Integral Yoga is evident here. And if it led to his retirement, the latter must be construed as an extremely positive move, a secret victorious march forward and not at all a despairing retreat by him into himself because of disappointment in world work. Even on the retirement there are some direct words from him. When asked on 25 August 1933 when he would come out, he answered: "That is a thing of which nothing can be said at present. My retirement had a purpose and that purpose must first be fulfilled."[14] Nor was the withdrawal from common contact total. Sri

Aurobindo wrote practically thousands of letters during his period of "seclusion" on all kinds of topics — Yoga, philosophy, science, literature, life-problems — and sometimes at enormous length. During World War II he made public his complete support of the anti-Hitler cause and repeatedly averred in private that he was using his spiritual force for it. A radio was installed in his room for hour-to-hour information of the war's progress. When during Sri Aurobindo's last two years the present writer was editing *Mother India,* then a fortnightly, from Bombay, no editorial of his on national or international politics as viewed from a higher nonpolitical standpoint was published unless it had first been read out to Sri Aurobindo and fully approved by him. In addition, from 1938 — after an accident to his right leg — to 1950 he had daily talks on a variety of subjects with a small circle that was in attendance on him. Surely, even the term *retirement* is a bit of a misnomer in Sri Aurobindo's case. And whatever withdrawal was present was said by him explicitly to have advanced the work on which he had been bent. He wrote on 14 August 1945: "My retirement . . . was indispensable; otherwise I could not be now where I am, that is, personally, near the goal."[15]

I may close on this triumphant note — a note natural to a supreme Yogi, a master mystic. Contrary to Zaehner's contention, it was not Sri Aurobindo but Teilhard who in his last year (1955) bewailed his complete isolation and his spiritual ineffectivity:

> How does it happen that, still intoxicated by my vision, I look around me and find myself practically alone? . . .And . . . how can it be that, "having come down from the mountain," and notwithstanding the splendour of my vision, I find myself so little better, so little pacified, so incapable of communicating to my own actions, and therefore to others, the marvellous unity in which I feel myself plunged? The universal Christ? The divine Milieu? May I not after all be simply the victim of some mental delusion? That is what I often ask myself.[16]

And it was Teilhard who, in the midstream of his career (1934) of reasoned scientific optimism and ardent religious devotion, could yet sadly confess:

> After what I have just said of my conviction that a term exists for cosmic evolution which is divine and personal, one could imagine that I look forward in future years to a life that is luminous and serene. . . .Nothing could be further from the truth. Though

I am certain, more and more certain, that I must continue to live as if Christ were waiting for me at the goal of the universe, I experience no special assurance at all that he is there. To believe is not to see. As much as anyone, I think, I walk in the darkness of faith.[17]

Not that a lofty visionary like Teilhard could ever quite lose his inner glow of joy—and, actually, in the last year of his life he seeks out evidence to reassure him and counter his doubts—but one cannot expect of him the Aurobindonian heroism and certitude and imperturbable poise born of a manifold realization of the Eternal Spirit's working out for man a supramental destiny in time. And this very difference should provide an initial clue to the direction in which lies the spirituality of the future.

Notes

1. Sri Aurobindo *On Yoga,* part 2 (Pondicherry: Sri Aurobindo International University Centre Collection, 1958), 6:231.

2. Ibid., pp. 107-8.

3. Ibid., p. 105.

4. Ibid., 7:717.

5. Sri Aurobindo, *Sri Aurobindo on Himself and on the Mother* (Pondicherry: Sri Aurobindo International University Centre Collection, 1953), 1:221.

6. Ibid., pp. 223-24.

7. Ibid., p. 231.

8. Ibid., p. 241.

9. Ibid., p. 242.

10. Ibid., p. 244.

11. Sri Aurobindo, *Letters of Sri Aurobindo,* 4th ser. (Bombay: Sri Aurobindo Circle, 1951), p. 70.

12. Sri Aurobindo, *Sri Aurobindo on Himself,* pp. 247-48.

13. Ibid., p. 208.

14. Ibid., p. 270.

15. Ibid., p. 288.

16. Pierre Teilhard de Chardin, *"Le Christique,"* as quoted in Christopher Mooney, *Teilhard de Chardin and the Mystery of Christ* (London: Collins; New York: Harper & Row, 1966), p. 196.

17. Ibid., p. 197.

3

The Role of the Church; Christian Orthodoxy and Teilhard's "New Religion"

It is not unnatural for Zaehner, a Roman Catholic, to favor Teilhard and to see, along with him, the Church of Rome as the one great gathering force of the superhumanity to which Teilhard looked forward. One must have respect for him because he is no blind partisan. He refers to the Church's "pettifogging legalism and a sacramental system that had so often degenerated into an almost mechanical device by which salvation might be obtained" (p. 9). About brother killing brother and brotherhood slaughtering and persecuting brotherhood, he remarks: "In this particular form of beastliness Christianity has won for itself a unique distinction" (p. 11). Weighing the chances of what evolution will achieve by way of drawing humankind together, he opines that there may result a "civilization" of the anthill, or "by a miracle (and a real miracle is needed) the Catholic Church, re-invigorated and transformed once again by the power of the Holy Spirit, will, purged at last of the miserable legalism that has cramped and stunted her so long, grow inwardly into a superconsciousness manifesting itself in spontaneous love and joy" (p. 85). The same thought recurs:

> But—and it is an enormous "but"—if—and it is an enormous "if"—if the Church is indeed the "mystical" body of Christ, living by the breath of the Holy Spirit, how are we to account for its

disgraceful, blood-stained history? We have already suggested that the root-sin of the Church has, ever since the conversion of Constantine, been its betrayal of its spiritual mission in the interest of worldly power, and its total loss of Christ's gift of love which was made manifest in its mad and criminal career of persecution and intolerance. (p. 112)

Zaehner levels the identical charge elsewhere too. After approving of Gandhi's condemnation of the Indian caste system with its institution of "untouchableness," he writes: "Substitute the word 'persecution' for 'untouchableness,' and the same must hold good for the Catholic Church. It has been the 'ineffaceable blot' and the 'curse' that Western Christianity has carried with it ever since Augustine of Hippo gave the full weight of his authority to the persecution of heretics — persecution, that is, in the name of Catholicity and unity, no matter at what cost to the real organic unity that St. Paul had called the body of Christ" (p. 89). And, of course, Zaehner is fully aware of the crass suppression of Teilhard himself by the Church during his whole lifetime: "At every stage of his life his ideas and writings were suppressed not only by his own superiors but also by the curial authorities in Rome" (p. 9).

Yes, Zaehner has no illusions about his own Church, but there are some counterbalancing factors in its favor: the sense of its origin in Jesus, the host of mystics and saints it has produced, its long and widespread persistence as the guardian of a great tradition, and the living touch it brings of a collective religious experience. Zaehner even claims that Sri Aurobindo grants Catholicism "a tendency towards some conservation of the original plastic character of religion and a many-sidedness and appeal to the whole nature of the human being" (p. 24). True, Sri Aurobindo does speak of "two tendencies, catholic and protestant," but he uses the adjectives to denote a pair of recurrent categories applying to the religious phenomenon in general; one may also note that the noun that he makes from the former is *catholicity*,[1] not *Catholicism*, and the outstanding example he adduces of "catholic" religion, "with its pristine wholeness of movement", is "religion in India."[2] Zaehner is hardly justified in declaring of Sri Aurobindo: "When he thought of it at all, he realized that the Catholic principle in Christianity was the nearest approximation in the history of religions to his own vision of a humanity redeemed and divinized" (p. 25). Nevertheless, one may attribute something to Catholicism, as contrasted with Protestantism, to have suggested those two specific adjectives to Sri Aurobindo. Evidently, this strain and the other factors lead Zaehner, as they did Teilhard, to regard the Roman Church as "the only possible focus of unity" (p. 9).

Expressed by so honest and broad-minded an adherent, this view should not be attacked with acrimony. And a superficial survey of world institutions is likely to support the impression of uniqueness voiced by the word *only*. Besides, the recent championship of Teilhard by a number of highly qualified Churchmen is a healthy sign, very encouraging to liberal thinkers like Zaehner. Perhaps this championship and the ecumenical movement have been the two most pleasing aspects of the Church's orientation today. Surely, Zaehner has his eye on both when he attests: "The tug-of-war between the conservatives and progressives has ever since the truly miraculous pontificate of good Pope John testified to the renewed vitality of the Roman Catholic Church" (p. 15). A student of comparative religion, Zaehner cannot but be affected by the new ecumenism, with its tolerance and understanding. He is also bound to see a great light in the pro-Teilhard enthusiasm frequently evinced by both Jesuits and Dominicans and, above all else, in the tribute Pope Paul VI has himself paid to Teilhard. For pro-Teilhardism shows the perception, as Zaehner puts it, of "a point of union in time to be — the cosmic Christ of Teilhard's vision 'through whom and for whom God wanted all things to be reconciled' " — a point of union about which Zaehner says: "Most Christians before Teilhard had long forgotten they ever had it" (p. 16). However, the tilt toward Teilhard on the Church's part is a phenomenon worth a little attention and analysis.

One may pertinently ask whether the Church is really turning Teilhardian rather than watering Teilhard down to its own dogmas. The aim of his champions is to prove him orthodox under a novel nomenclature. Zaehner himself has suggested, as has already been observed, that "Teilhard with Omega-point, noosphere, superhumanity, super-Christ and so on" was in the same case as Sri Aurobindo with his "typical concepts . . . which . . . only duplicate the more traditional terminology, thereby creating unnecessary confusion" (pp. 11,12). I shall contest the thesis concerning Sri Aurobindo and may at once assert that Teilhard, in his most natural and transparent moments, was, to say the least, very far from including himself in the fold of orthodoxy, however generously spread out.

I shall begin with a text of June 1926 quoted by Zaehner (p. 9). There, Teilhard, for all his seeing in Christianity the sole "axis" providing "any guarantee or way out for the world," categorically said: "Around this axis, I can glimpse an immense quantity of truths and attitudes for which orthodoxy has not made room." And he added with decisive frankness: "If I dared use a word which could be given unacceptable meanings, I feel myself irreducibly 'hyper-Catholic.' "[3]

What is the drift here? Granted that in Teilhard's vocabulary words like *hyper, ultra, super* do not, as a rule, indicate transcendence of a thing, but only its expanded, heightened, intensified form, and granted that, as the phrase "unacceptable meanings" shows, Teilhard had no desire to renounce the Roman Church, so deeply attached was he to its collective presence as being the one sure path to the future, still the irreducibleness of his hyper-Catholicism entails that he would never dilute those convictions of his which rendered him suspect in the eyes of the Vatican. His position was: To be really faithful to Christ the Church must change, not Teilhard; the Church must realize the Teilhardian way to fulfill its august mission. Clearly, to his mind, Christian orthodoxy, as history knows it, was incapable of containing him; it was not what Christianity should be. Christianity must become quite new, incorporate "attitudes" and even "truths" for which it has had no room so far; it must let itself be expanded, heightened, intensified beyond its established formulas in order to fulfill its original genius, its primal Catholic seed. It must grow Teilhardian and not seek to absorb Teilhard into those fixities. Not historical Catholicism, but something it has never dreamed of being, yet ought to be, alone can do justice to Teilhard.

As early as May 1916, when he had composed his first characteristic essay, "Cosmic Life" he wrote in a retrospective *nota:* "If one tries to bring out the presuppositions and principles it is based on, one finds that it introduces a completely new orientation into Christian ascetical teaching."[4] As late as July 1950, in concluding "A Clarification: Some Reflections on Two Converse Forms of Spirit," he reflected on the new religion toward which, as a representative of the modern world, he had moved by fusing mysticism with evolutionism: "It is still impossible at the present moment to find a single printed work which affirms the existence and describes the specific properties of an interior attitude (the *centric* cosmic sense) which, through force of circumstances, is coming to be the hidden mainspring of the life of each one of us."[5] July 1952 found Teilhard practically reiterating in "The Stuff of the Universe" the text of June 1926: "A whole series of adjustments must be made, I am well aware (if we wish frankly to Christify evolution), in a number of representations or attitudes which seem to us to be definitively fixed in Christian dogma."[6] And at the very close of his life, in 1955, while he recognized in "Le Christique" "the pulsation of countless people who are all—ranging from the borderline of unbelief to the depths of the cloister—thinking and feeling, or at least beginning to feel, just as I do,"[7] he set against such unofficial religious modernism in sympathy with his own vision the fact, already stressed in July 1950, of his utter isolation in the midst of contemporary Catholic authorities: "I cannot, when asked, quote a single writer, a single work, that gives a clearly expressed description of the wonderful 'diaphany' that has transfigured everything for me . . . .It would be impossible for me, as I admitted earlier, to quote a single 'authority' (religious or lay) of whom I could claim that in it I can fully recognize myself, whether in relation to my 'cosmic' or my 'Christique' vision."[8]

No, Teilhard cannot be "orthodoxised" in any manner without being essentially violated. To be Teilhardian, Roman Catholicism has to be as he conceived it instead of what it is: "Christianity now appears to me much less a closed and established whole than an axis of progression and assimilation."[9] What the phrase "progression and assimilation" connotes is not simply that orthodox Christianity can remain basically the same but assume new modes of expression in tune with modern evolutionary concepts. Henri de Lubac reports, though without giving any reference, that Teilhard wrote to a friend: "I am convinced that a more traditional expression of my views is possible"[10] De Lubac also states about the "experience" at the base of Teilhardism: "He was confident . . . that 'substantially, the experience is orthodox.' "[11] Yet nowhere did Teilhard himself succeed in bringing his views or his experience into perfect rapport with tradition and orthodoxy. Something always remained over, in regard to which he appeared to blow hot and cold or to stand with his legs in two camps. For an example some remarks of de Lubac may be studied:

> It is commonly thought today that anthropogenesis has come to a complete halt. . . . This Père Teilhard regarded as an illusion, and a pernicious illusion. . . . After hominization, which was still an "elementary phenomenon", we are advancing towards a

"second critical point of reflection", in this case "collective and higher": "the critical point of socialization" or "co-reflection", which will ultimately bring with it full "humanization".

We should not attach too much importance to what we are told about this "super-organism", that it will be made up of all human individuals just as the biological individual is made up of cells. . . The individuals that enter into the composition of such a super-organism are not conceived as ceasing to be so many reflective, personal centres. . . .Here, however, we meet with a question that cannot be evaded: is it possible to conceive a "critical point" of collective reflection, which possesses so extraordinary a property and nevertheless allows the whole effect of the first "critical point" to remain operative? . . .We may wonder whether, to express the envisaged "planetization of man", such expressions as "second critical point" or "second hominization", if taken in the literal sense that Père Teilhard sometimes seems to give them, are not too strong, or whether they are not even self-contradictory. . .

What could be meant by an "ultra-reflection" that was specifically a "consciousness raised to the power of two"? . . .Is it really consistent, in the same sentence, to define an "evolutionary neo-humanism" as "dominated by the conviction that there is an ultra-human", and as being simply "a humanism of fully evolved man"? From the fact that man is "destined to synthesis" can one conclude that "something greater, more complex, more centred than man is taking shape before our eyes . . . "? Some expressions of this type might have reflected their author's deliberate intention. But does not Père Teilhard betray the indecision of his thought or its lack of accuracy when, in language that contrasts with his normal assurance, he speaks of a "harmonized collectivity of consciousnesses *equivalent to a sort of* super-consciousness", "a sort of common personality", or again when he says that he is coming to see that "under the influence of co-reflection" the "multiple reflective centres" represented by human individuals will be totalized in a "still nameless something", in which every difference will vanish at the boundary between universe and person?[12]

The general situation is best put in de Lubac's own admission: "Père Teilhard's personal interior experience was too authentic and too deep, it was (to use his word) too *innate,* for it ever to be possible to be left out of account in his formed thought and his teachings. It had been 'developed,' 'extended,' 'transformed,' into knowledge and love of God. Even so, in spite of his persistent efforts, he was not always able to find ways of expressing it which, without doing violence to it — 'without distorting and weakening it'—would both clarify it for him and harmonize it with the most sensitive demands of faith."[13] It was this recurring inability on Teilhard's part to effect a complete harmony between faith and his "innate" experience that rendered his hyper-Catholicism irreducible. Moreover, it was not his perpetual preoccupation to reconcile himself with faith's most sensitive demands. To quote de Lubac once more: "Père Teilhard attacked this problem with patience and loyalty, but he always kept his eyes fixed firmly on his vision."[14] And that vision struck him as considerably novel and worth propagating: "In truth (without, I think, the least touch of conceit) I do believe that I can see something, and I would like that something to be seen."[15] No wonder he was mostly all out to "modernize" Christianity in order to make it "get off to a completely new start."[16]

From the very beginning of his reflective life the task faced him of bringing his point of view into accord with orthodoxy. In his *nota* to "Cosmic Life" in 1916 he observes:

> In the "classical" interpretation, suffering is *first and foremost* a punishment, an expiation; . . .it is born of a *sin* and makes reparation for the sin. . . .In contrast with this view, suffering, according to the general line followed by *Cosmic Life* and the ideas it puts forward, is primarily the consequence of a *work of development* and the price that has to be paid for it. . . .Physical and moral evil *are produced by the process of Becoming:* everything that evolves has its own sufferings and commits its own faults. The Cross is the symbol of *the arduous labour of Evolution*—rather than the symbol of *expiation.*[17]

Then Teilhard admits that the two points of view can be reconciled if the Fall of Man, which Christianity postulates as the ground of sin and suffering, is taken to have brought about mankind's entry into nature's evolutionary setting for progress and work "by the sweat of its brow." But Teilhard goes on to say that there is no mark left in nature by the postulated Fall, "since its visible penalty is contained in Evolution, with Expiation coinciding with Work." This obviously renders the postulate arbitrary and otiose. Even after its acceptance, "there is a great difference of emphasis between *expiatory ascesis* and the ascesis underlying 'Cosmic Life.' " And Teilhard's last words on this are: "I would have been dishonest not to point this out."

Nor are his contrasts a heresy of his younger days outgrown in the period of maturity. In April 1948, he sent to a colleague in Namur a typed note, "My Intellectual Position," which was later published in *Les Études philosphiques* (vol. 10, Oct.-Nov. 1955) under the title "The thought of Père Teilhard de Chardin in His Own Words."[18] In this note he summarizes his "Physics," shows how upon it his "Apologetics" and "Mysticism" are built, and then refers to the outline of a "Metaphysics" being suggested and formed by the three branches of his system taken together. He says that in this Metaphysics "even the Problem of Evil is given an acceptable intellectual solution (the statistical necessity of disorders within a multitude in process of organization)."[19] Again, in 1953, as one of the readjustments in definitively fixed Christian dogma, he has: "The twofold notion of *statistical evil* and *evolutionary redemption* correcting or completing the idea of catastrophic sin and reparatory expiation."[20] Thus, Teilhard in his old age repeated the "completely new orientation" of his youth vis-à-vis suffering and sin.

And in between his youth and his old age occurs a declaration that is total and that goes to the root of the matter. On 26 January 1936 he wrote in a letter from China:

> What increasingly dominates my interest and my inner preoccupations, as you already know, is the effort to establish within myself, and to diffuse around me, a new religion (let's call it an improved Christianity, if you like) whose personal God is no longer the great "neolithic" landowner of times gone by, but the Soul of the world—as demanded by the cultural and religious stage we have now reached. . . . My road ahead seems clearly marked out; it is a matter not of superimposing Christ on the world, but of "panchristising" the universe. The delicate point (and I touched on part of this in *Christology and Evolution)* is that, if you follow this path, you are led not only to widening your views, but to turning your perspectives upside down; evil (no longer punishment for a fault but "sign and effect" of Progress) and matter (no longer a guilty and lower element, but "the stuff of the Spirit") assume a meaning diametrically opposed to the meaning *customarily* viewed as Christian. Christ emerges from the transformation incredibly enlarged (at least that is my opinion—and all the uneasy contemporaries with whom I have spoken about it think like me). But is this Christ really the Christ of the Gospel? And if not, on what henceforward do we base what we are trying to build? I don't know whether among the many of my colleagues who are in front of me or behind me on the road I am travelling, there are any (or even a single one! . . . that seems incredible) who realise the importance of the step that all are taking. But I am beginning to see it very clearly. One thing reassures

me: it is that, in me, the increase of my light goes hand in hand with love, and with renouncement of myself in the Greater than me. This could not deceive. Thus in an obscure way I fall back on the feelings that Being is infinitely richer and more able to bring renewal than our logic. As all forms of movement, the paradox of the religious change now in progress will resolve itself by its very movement. *"Solvitur eundo."*[21]

This declaration should settle all controversy. Teilhard was after a new religion—one that can stand in its own right. It need not be un-Christian, but it can be Christian only if Christianity undergoes an improvement. The improvement does not lie just in extending, heightening, and intensifying what we have been accustomed to as Christian; it lies basically in a complete revolution, an entire inversion. The head has to be put where the feet were and vice versa: no mere patch-up or expansion along the same line will do. But Christ still remains the core of the new religion, even though the Church's outlook on evil and on matter has to be turned topsy-turvy or taken to a sheer antipodes. And Christ is now the soul of the World, the Cosmic Person who is the animating principle of all matter. He is as wide as the universe; he is the universe itself in its true inner reality, the One Spirit whose outer stuff, as it were, is the world of matter, the sphere of a difficult, often erring yet ever-advancing evolution. There can be no going back on this view, whether or not it agrees with the picture of Christ given by the Gospel. But if one gauges the true temper of the Gospel's Christ—the revealer of love for God's children and of the mystical resort of one's whole self to the Divine Infinite—one may be sure he is not negated by this Panchristism, which the trend and mood of the modern age, with its discovery of universal evolution, demands.

The last portion of the declaration—about the power of Being and that of logic—is not very clear, but a general light is shed on it by some other letters to the same correspondent. "The weaker and less confident you feel in yourself, the more you need to strengthen in yourself the vision of the omnipresent Being to whom you have vowed your effort."[22] "May God preserve within me the deep taste, and the sort of lucid ecstasy, that intoxicate me with the joy of Being—a joy drunk in as though from an everlasting spring . . . . What science or philosophy is comparable to the knowledge of that Reality—and above all to the perception of it, even at the most modest and inchoate level!"[23] The world and its Soul, Matter inwardly one with Spirit and serving as its developing expression—such seems to be "the omnipresent Being." And a broad clarification as well as confirmation of what the whole passage denotes is found in an earlier letter from China:

> In my heart I haven't changed, except along the same lines. One consequence of this movement is that I am gradually finding myself more and more on the fringe of a lot of things. It's only thanks to the exotic life I'm leading that this drift doesn't develop into a break. What rather reassures me and saves me is that, if a whole wall of ecclesiastical concepts and conventions has definitively collapsed around me, I have never, on the other hand, felt nearer to what seem to me the deeper axes of Christianity: the future value of the world, the primacy of the Spirit and the Personality, divine Personality. I can see no way out, nor any strength for me, outside the (theoretical *and* practical) synthesis of passionate faith in the world and passionate faith in God. Being fully human and Christian, one through the other. This leads to situations that appear paradoxical. But I am more and more determined to put my trust in Life, without letting anything surprise me. And then I feel that I haven't the least apprehension about anything that could happen to me, provided that it is "in the service of the world."[24]

A point of particular interest here is a fact that has never been thrown into relief or even brought out into the open. It is known that Teilhard passed through many an inner crisis of "anti-ecclesiasticism, not to say anti-Christianity,"[25] yet came out an obedient child of his order and his Church, letting his books be suppressed and not losing his trust in the institutions of Roman Catholicism. It is known that he perceived the delicate and dangerous situation he was in and once devoutly wished that "loyalty" to himself might not sever him from his Church nor "attachment" to his Church falsify his own truth: he wrote that all that was asked of him and of his correspondent was "to try, ceaselessly, to climb upwards towards more breadth and more light, without letting go of these two threads," and he ended: "Pray that I may never break either of them."[26] He feared the possibility of a recantation or else a revolt—and managed to live on without allowing either alternative to actualize. But now for the first time we are told that the drift of his vision away from "ecclesiastical concepts and conventions" was so great, so decisive that if he had not been leading an "exotic life," living in a place of personal isolation and intellectual distance like China, there would have been a rupture. The conflict would have been of such acuteness and the pressure of such magnitude that Teilhard, to remain himself, would have had to cut himself apart from his order and his Church; a "break" with them would have surely developed round about the period of the letter— June 1934. Furthermore, he was absolutely sure of being most truly Christian in the "faith" he had found for himself for good and all, and he would not shrink from any future "break" if he could live up to his "faith."

The position thrown into relief here is prepared, as it were, by a confession made on 10 January 1925. Robert Speaight pointedly notes that, even while affirming his fidelity to the Church, Teilhard made no attempt to conceal his estrangement from its representatives. Speaight quotes from a letter: "In a kind of a way I *no longer have confidence* in the exterior manifestations of the Church. I believe that through it the divine influence will continue to reach me, but I no longer have much belief in the immediate and tangible value of official directions and decisions. Some people feel happy in the visible Church, but for my own part I think I shall be happy to die in order to be free of it—and to find our Lord outside of it."[27]

The last phrase is radical. It shows Teilhard feeling the actual Church to be unbearable and yearning somehow to get rid of it and to go out of it in order to reach and live in its ideal spirit.

Again, some years later (23 August 1929), in the midst of a deep and cordial attachment to his order, Teilhard, in the correspondence with Léontine Zanta, alluded to a situation in which he would be compelled to abjure his membership of the Church—"the case . . . of my being driven into a corner where I should be faced with intellectual dishonesty."[28] He personally thought such a case "very unlikely," but his words prove that his adherence to institutional Roman Catholicism was not unconditional at all and, as the rest of the letter says, he narrowly had the luck "to have passed the turning-point of last year, which was certainly a critical juncture in my intellectual and emotional life, without a break."

As time passed, Teilhard, for all his sticking on, found himself no better reconciled to the actual Church. One discerns in a letter to Bruno de Solages on 17 January 1954, just a little more than a year before his own death, the same feeling that prompted, nearly twenty-nine years earlier, the death wish for the sake of liberation from the visible institution of his religion: "The sin of Rome (for all its casual benedictions on technique and science) is not to believe in a future, and an achievement (for heaven) of man upon earth. I know it because I have stifled for fifty years in this sub-human atmosphere."[29]

One can now easily see the naturalness of the perception Teilhard once had in China that, had he been anywhere near the active field of orthodoxy, a break would have been inevitable.

The cause of the break, it should go without saying, would have been the too intolerable contrast between established Christianity and his science-activated, humanism-steeped religion of a spiritually evolving physical universe. He had not the slightest inclination to yield on fundamentals to his religious masters.

In a communication of September 1948, in connection with his efforts to secure a *nihil obstat* from Rome for *The Phenomenon of Man,* he told Paul Lamare of his loyalty to his own light: "Absolutely nothing will make me change my mind or hold my tongue on the essential points. They must take me as I am or not at all. I am going to Rome but not to Canossa."[30] The reference to the north Italian village where in 1076 King Henry IV performed the penance required by Pope Gregory VII spotlights the firmly defiant stand taken by Teilhard behind all his good will toward religious authority and his wish to go as far as was in his power before having to drop out.

Born of his sense of the historical associations of Rome was a double desire: the eagerness not only to attempt all the conformity he honestly could but also to endure Rome's irrational asphyxiating atmosphere as much as possible and to reform the Church rather than abandon it to its own devices. If it forgot the truths that he read in Christ and if it failed to realize the high office to which it was called, he conceived it as his duty to illumine it. Now and again one gets a pretty clear picture of his aim in this direction. About this motive for staying within the fold in spite of his "new religion," one learns from Speaight: "To those who begged him to take a freedom always open to him, he would borrow the words of St. Exupéry: 'In order to have an effect upon the house, you have got to live in it.' To all such impulsive well-wishers Teilhard emphasized that . . . a revolutionary attitude . . . would mean 'the killing of everything that I want to liberate, and not destroy.' "[31]

ii

Whatever might be Teilhard's resolution to be true to himself at all times, he could not escape traditional influences coloring his mind on the whole, but his central aim in general to "Teilhardianize" the Church (from within it) instead of letting himself be "Churchianized" is too patent to be denied. And the letters from China provide some sharp, straightforward insights into what I have called his science-activated and humanism-steeped religion, which stood over against established Christianity.

"One single operation is in process of becoming in the world, and it alone can justify our action: The emergence of some spiritual Reality, through and across the efforts of life."[32] "I've reached the point of being unable to imagine the world, even physically, other than in the form of a huge movement of spirit."[33] "I see all the at-tributes that science has accumulated round matter in the last 150 years, whether as regards energy or history, transposing themselves and passing over onto Spirit."[34] "It looks as though mankind will never regain its passion for God until God is presented to it as the term of a movement that extends our worship of the concrete Real (rather than tearing us away from it). Oh, how tremendously power-ful the Real would be for lifting us out of our egoism if only we knew how to see it in its prodigious greatness!"[35] One may note that for Teilhard two realities are bound together for worship: "the concrete Real"—that is, the tangible cosmos in its totality—and the "huge movement of spirit," the emerging Cosmic Person, whose physical aspect or expressive body it is. Both jointly constitute "the great All," which was the object of his most intense meditation in that "most alive region," the "front" of World War I, and in "the vast solitudes of Mongolia."[36]

No doubt, the emerging Cosmic Person was connected by Teilhard with the historical Christ. According to him, through Jesus of Nazareth divinity had been concentrated and organically inserted into the world of matter. As a result of the incarnation of God two thousand years ago, the slow Godward process of the evolving world got its decisive impetus to "divinization" and the certainty of its fulfillment in the final union with the Supreme beyond time and space, which Christianity calls the pleroma, the plenitude, of Christ—the union whose natural support would be effected by the evolution of a totalized and unified humanity functioning as a col-lective Person. In that Person, identical with the Omega Point of evolution, the World Soul will have emerged. Certainly a Christiani-ty is here, with Christ in several roles—transcendent, universal, im-manent, matter-suffusing, evolutionary, incarnate, superanimative,

pleromatic—but an utterly recast Christianity, both in its basic vision and its various derivative implication. That is how Teilhard saw
his religion when he spoke out of the deepest and clearest part of
him.

Against this interpretation some words of Henri de Lubac's may
be pitted:

> Père Teilhard sometimes seemed unnecessarily to exaggerate the
> originality of his teaching in the field of religion. . . . In his en-
> thusiasm for the new prospects opened up by generalized evolu-
> tion, he over-emphasizes, in a way that can even be annoying, the
> contrast between "yesterday" and "tomorrow." He is all the more
> inclined to do this in that his knowledge of Christian thought
> throughout the centuries was never (as is true of many, even bet-
> ter theologians than he) more than elementary . . . . On such oc-
> casions, one would like to be able to say to him, "Why do you
> make it seem as though you wanted to be an innovator, whereas
> all you are really trying to do is to be a rejuvenator? Why are you
> ready to accept, without any distinction, an image of the Chris-
> tian past that is derived from a present that often suffers from
> sclerosis?"[37]

De Lubac imagines Teilhard as answering: "I obtained this image
from recognized theologians. They seem quite satisfied with it. Is it
my fault that I accepted it?"[38]

A less Teilhardian answer can hardly be conceived. His charge
against Christianity's past and present is not confined to a condemnation of what he termed *juridicism* or of an other-worldliness. De
Lubac may be right in saying that juridicism does not describe "the
main stream of theological tradition" and that Teilhard's picture of
Christianity's wanting "to withdraw from the world into the
'beyond'" is "oversimplified."[39] But the heart of the novelty in
Teilhardism lies in a certain sense that could never have been in
fundamental Christianity because this sense is inextricably bound
up in the West with the world view of modern science, which was
impossible when the Christian ground plan was laid out and per-
manently demarcated. Orthodoxy resides in sticking to that ground
plan, and if it gets unstuck it is no longer itself. What the new sense
is—splitting Teilhardism from orthodoxy—may be briefly set forth
in some phrases of Teilhard's own:

> In the space of a century the combined influence of history,
> physics, philosophy and sociology, has shown us that the whole
> universe is carried along in an over-all movement (or ·evolution)

within which the special evolution of consciousness has its determined place. Time now appears to us not as the permanent setting of divergent or circular diversifications but as the axis of a sort of cosmogenesis. Things do not repeat themselves, the world presses on.[40]

From the scientific and philosophical point of view, this way of looking at the universe has consequences of obvious importance: its influence is necessarily felt, and felt effectively (though this has not yet been sufficiently emphasised) even in the religious depths of the soul. By taking on a sort of natural unity in the course of duration, the world does more than acquire an additional dimension in the eyes of intellectual inquiry. It stands out, in an encounter with the human individual, as an object endowed with higher value and dignity, to which, it is clear, he must subordinate and dedicate himself. It arouses in us, with the undeniable appeal of a tangible immensity close to us, the resonance of the chords, ever ready to vibrate, of worship.[41]

As a result of the scientific discovery of the natural unity of the world and its vastness modern man can now recognise God only in the continuation (could one, perhaps, say "under the species"?) of some universal progress of maturing.[42]

It has become a commonplace to designate western civilization as materialist. . . .Nothing could be more unjust. The West has overthrown many idols. But, by its discovery of the *dimensions and forward momentum of the universe,* it has set in motion a powerful mysticism. For we can properly speak of it as a mysticism, in that we have been aroused by physics and history to the consciousness of a tangible immensity, and so can conceive no values, can take delight in nothing, except our arduous identification with the fulfilment of that immensity. The whole problem now is to determine the truth and the name of the presence that we believe we can feel behind the blaze of the universe.[43]

The same spiritual modernism, impossible to connect in toto with accepted Christianity, is evident when Teilhard emphasises his "need to reconcile in a solidly coherent system scientific views on evolution (accepted as, in their essence, definitively established) with the innate urge that has impelled me to look for the Divine not in a cleavage with the physical world but through matter, and, in some sort of way, in union with matter"[44] There is also his description of himself as an "average man of the twentieth century" who "has been unable to find the proper balance for his interior life except in a unitary concept, based upon physics, of the world and Christ."[45]

Christ's entry into this concept depends on the formulation of "a Christology proportionate to the dimensions now attributed to the universe—that means. . .recognising that. . .Christ possesses 'universal' or 'cosmic' attributes in addition to his strictly human and divine attributes (with which theologians have hitherto been primarily concerned): and it is precisely these attributes that make him the personal Centre which the physics and metaphysics of evolution feel must exist and for which they are looking."[46]

Then Teilhard points to the support he finds in Scripture and tradition: "These views show a startling coincidence with the most fundamental Johannine and Pauline texts and with the theology of the Greek Fathers." In those texts Christ is said to be *"he who fills all," "he who consummates," "he who gives its consistence* to the entire edifice of matter and Spirit."[47] These functions of Christ, says Teilhard, are to be taken "physically and literally." And, as a result, the man who has religiously adhered to "God in All" "cannot see which is the more precious grace: that he has found Christ to animate matter, or matter to make Christ tangible."[48] However, it is important to note that by referring to Saint Paul, Saint John, and the Greek Fathers, Teilhard, while validly Christianizing in a general sense his cosmicism, does not merely revive a component of Christianity that was relegated to the background: what he formulates is still a new Christianity, and he was cognizant of many differences from Saint Paul in the very act of claiming that the apostle's line was being followed.

Thus a note during his retreat of 1940 says: "Into the famous text of Romans 8:38, 'Quis separabit nos a caritate Christi'—'Who will separate us from the love of Christ'—I introduce a shade of meaning that differs from St. Paul's (even though it follows his line). For St. Paul charity is the force greater than all forces; for me, it is the dynamic milieu that embraces and super-animates them all."[49] De Lubac himself admits that, putting forward the Cosmic Christ, the Evolutive Christ, Teilhard had "the insight to perceive that this new way of looking at Christ involves more than a new shade of inter-pretation of the Apostle's thought. . .since at that time the world, the 'whole' (with all the organic definition that these words imply for us), were still non-existent for human consciousness."[50]

Thus, Teilhard was justified in speaking of "a new religion," "an improved Christianity"—something that can fit into no Christian orthodoxy of any time. And it is the same sense of a radical innovation, in the midst of whatever adherences in him to his Church and its tradition, that is behind the religious envisagement that de Lubac speaks of in referring to Teilhard's response, in "Le Coeur de la matière" (1950), to God's calling him from both scientific evolutionism and Christian spirituality, "from the depths of the cosmic future, as from the heights of heaven." De Lubac tells us: "He now seems to envisage 'a new Faith, in which are combined the upward striving Faith in a transcendent and the propulsive Faith in an immanent.' "[51]

This conclusion for a Christianity "set off on a completely new start" cannot be controverted simply by showing, as does de Lubac, how Teilhard, in spite of all the novelties of his thought that during his lifetime the Church regarded as dangerous if not heretical, observed the various traditional credos and practices and pieties of his priestly vocation. It must be remembered that Christ's universal or cosmic attributes did not negate for Teilhard his usual human and divine ones: on the contrary all of the three types were intimately linked together in his mind and significantly colored one another. Nothing diminished the essential newness of his religion. Nor are de Lubac and others of his school right to make capital out of certain resemblances between Teilhard's formulations and those of older exegetes and thinkers, as if the latter in part anticipated the former. A few verbal similarities, a few affinities of definition are the utmost that can be demonstrated. Even if they spoke of Christ's being cosmic, their purport would be different: it would not go beyond a stress on "omnipresence" and "immanence," which were orthodox theological ideas, or on a universal, ubiquitous role of Christ in human destiny. Teilhard remained inevitably unorthodox.

Broadly speaking, de Lubac admits as much in his carefully balanced sentence: "If [Teilhard] seemed to go beyond some positions generally adopted by the Church, he would never have been willing to lag behind any one of them."[52] Here his conformities are juxtaposed with his novelties, with his outstrippings of orthodoxy. While the former do not fall short of the Church's interpretations, the latter cross the limit to which these interpretations, whether in the past or in the present, have gone.

From some other statements of de Lubac's one can even infer that following Saint Paul's line in general does not disprove Teilhard's novelty and nonorthodoxy. De Lubac writes:

> It fell to him to explore truths which, without being new, stretched out like continents untrodden by man. "St. Paul and the Greek Fathers speak of a cosmic function of Christ: the exact

content of that phrase has never perhaps been brought out."[53] That is precisely what he liked to find in the theology of his time—more light on "the organic and cosmic splendour contained in the Pauline doctrine of Christ gathering up all things. . . ."[54] Finally, we should remember that, throughout his whole life, Père Teilhard had to struggle to define a spiritual attitude for which there was no adequate model in past centuries. This was because it had for the first time, without distorting the perennial Christian ideal, to make that ideal accept the responsibility towards a developing world or, as he put it, towards Cosmogenesis, that man had newly come to feel.[55]

Even the one reservation made by de Lubac, in the midst of statements that imply Teilhard's novelty and nonorthodoxy despite his following the line of Saint Paul, can be rendered ineffective. He speaks of the Teilhardian truths as having been like "continents" already there, though stretching out "untrodden by man." It is possible to provide an answer from Teilhard himself: "One might say that a hitherto unknown form of religion—one that no one could as yet have imagined or described, for lack of a universe large enough and organic enough to contain it—is burgeoning in the heart of modern man, from a seed sown by the idea of evolution."[56] Surely this means that "the organic and cosmic splendours contained in the Pauline doctrine of Christ gathering up all things" were organic and cosmic in a very different sense.

The "hitherto unknown form of religion" is set off yet more clearly elsewhere by Teilhard with even recognizable allusion to the Pauline doctrine. He says of "the various creeds still commonly accepted": "They were born and grew up in a time when problems of cosmic totalization and maturing did not *exist*. However universal their promises and visions of the beyond might be, they did not explicitly (and with good reason) allow any room to a global and controlled transformation of the whole of life and thought in their entirety. And yet. . .is it not precisely an event of this order (an event that involves the expectation and the advent of some ultra-human) that we are asking them to include, to hallow, and to animate, now and for ever after?"[57] The conclusion that one reaches from this is unmistakable: the "promises and visions" in the Pauline doctrine, no matter how "universal," had a foundation other than Teilhardism. The hope of a reappearance of Christ—the Parousia—for a plenary gathering up—the pleroma—had necessarily a religious core radically dissimiliar to the one that takes shape under the vision of an evolution-conducting cosmic Christ. Without mincing words, Teilhard insists on the radical dissimilarity: "It is impossible to think of Christ as 'evolver' without at the same time having to re-think the whole of Christology."[58]

And he goes on to indicate in a summary the immediate lines of rethinking, one of which I have already spotlighted. They are: "A functional completion of the one and the multiple takes the place of the creative paternalism we habitually envisaged. The twofold notion of *statistical evil* and *evolutionary redemption* correcting or completing the idea of catastrophic sin and reparatory expiation. The final parousia more akin to a maturing than to a destruction."

The first line has found some elaboration in Teilhard elsewhere:

I have no intention of contesting. . .an ontological distinction between the divine Centre and the elementary centres that form the world. . . .Nevertheless, from the point of view of action, I shall note that the Christian solution, if it is not taken further than it actually goes, is certainly unable to fulfil the conditions of activation[†], imposed on the universe by the progress of modern thought. An entirely gratuitous creation, a gesture of pure benevolence, with no other object, for the absolute Being, than to *share* his plenitude with a *corona* of participants of whom he has strictly no need—that could satisfy minds that had not yet awoken to the immensity of space-time, the colossal stores of energy and the unfathomable organic articulation of the phenomenal world; but we who have become conscious (and vividly so) of the majesty, the implacability, and the truly "divine" power of cosmic evolution—we would suffer deeply, in the honour we pay to being, and the respect we have for God would be insulted, if all this great array, with its huge burden of toil and trouble, were no more than a sort of game whose sole aim was to make us supremely happy. We can accept that by ourselves and in ourselves we are initially nothing to the ultimate depths of ourselves. . . .But if we could not somehow consciously feel that we cannot "be of service to God" without God adding something to Himself, that would most certainly destroy, at the heart of our freedom, the intimate driving forces of action. To be happy? But what use have we for the *selfish* happiness of *sharing* the joy of the supreme Being, when we can dream of the infinitely greater happiness of completing that joy?. . . Philosophically we are still living in an antiquated body of

---

† In Teilhard de Chardin. *Science and Christ*, p. 171 n. 5, Teilhard states: "By activance (activating potential) I mean the power an intellectual or mystical outlook possesses of developing spiritual energies in us and super-stimulating them."

thought,. . .now. . .being undermined by physics that is succeeding in abolishing any real distinction, for our reason, between extension and motion, between particles and waves, between matter and light, between space and time. . . .Under the pressure and contagious influence of these revolutionary reappraisals (whose result is in every case to bring out a necessary link between pairs of realities that hitherto seemed to be as independent as they possibly could be), we are inevitably making our way to a completely new concept of *being*: in this the hitherto contradictory attributes of the *"ens ab alio"* ["being by another"] and the *"ens a se"* ["being by itself"], of the world and God, would be combined in a general synthetic function (cf. algebraic functions including an imaginary term): God completely other in nature than the world and yet unable to dispense with it.[59]

The second line of rethinking has already received enough gloss in brief. The third is connected with Teilhard's idea that Christ's Parousia, with its consequent pleroma, will be a supernatural event coinciding with a progression of the human into the ultrahuman by a natural evolution toward Omega point and must indeed depend upon such a consummate maturing of humanity as a single unified being. Not that the ultrahuman natural will compel the divine supernatural, but by a functional relationship through the Cosmic Christ the two logically stand together. In Christian dogma the Parousia has no intrinsically organic relationship with human progress: it can even come *"in rupture* with it."[60] "Whether the terrestrial world achieves its success or ends in failure," the Divine Kingdom will arrive—"even more certainly, maybe, if failure is the answer."[61] Therefore, the Divine Kingdom tarnishes the flower of progress, or kills it completely.[62] Referring to the Christian Revelation, Teilhard writes: "The Parousia, we know, is promised as a dawn that will rise over a supreme onslaught of error."[63] His editors append the footnote: "In later years, Père Teilhard sometimes took a more optimistic view. He still, nonetheless, maintained the dramatic possibility of evil being the final choice." He maintained that possibility because of the loyalty of the Christian in him to the dogma of Revelation, but the whole evolutionist in him rejected the notion of the Parousia's destructiveness, dealing as it would with a paramount evil instead of a luminous and harmonious maturity. Against the supernatural dogma, as well as against the ultimate contempt by religious orthodoxy of a world whose trend is felt to be toward evil, his rethought Christology held:

Of the two or three natural dogmas that mankind, after long centuries of debate and after ceaseless critical examination, is now definitely establishing, the most categorical and the dearest to us is certainly that of the infinite value of the universe and its inexhaustible store of richness. "Our world contains within itself a mysterious promise of the future, implicit in its natural evolution." When the new-born mind surveys the grandeurs of the cosmos, those are the first words it falters; and that is the final assertion of the scientist as he closes his eyes, heavy and weary, from having seen so much that he could not express.[64]

iii

What masks for most minds Teilhard's revolutionary religion is the persistence with which he clung to Christianity and the Roman Church at the same time that he welcomed "with irrepressible hope. . .the inevitable rise of this new mysticism" and anticipated "its equally inevitable triumph."[65] To him Christ is the manifestation of the Divine such as one may logically expect in an evolving universe. Universal evolution rising, by and large, on a tide of increasing complexity and consciousness, proceeds in response to a focus of attraction in the future, representing the maximum of complexity-consciousness, the ultrahuman on a unified global scale. What acts through this focus must be an already existent Divinity, and such a Divinity, bent on evolving its universe toward himself, must send his radiation into it not only through a general religious self-manifestation but also through a direct incarnation serving as redeemer: in other words, he must, according to Teilhard, be "Christified." And the Roman Church, with which Teilhard intimately connected God's "Christification," is to him the logical axis upon which the consummation awaiting humankind in the future can and must be effected. Furthermore, he saw in Roman Catholicism at its most intense not only the finest vision of a world in relation to God, but also the most activating *"experiences of contact with a supreme Inexpressible"*[66] preserved and passed on—experiences that, sustaining and guiding men "along the road of contemplation and prayer", would make them "succeed in entering directly into receptive communication with the very source of all interior drive,"[67] all evolutionary urge. No wonder, then, that he did not wish to break with the "old love" that Catholic

Christianity was to him. Inasmuch as this "old love" was to be retained, he was averse to "a completely fresh faith" — particularly if it would be a religion concentrated only on "some 'evolutionary sense' or 'sense of man' "[68] and lacked the sense of an already existent and attracting God.

But "the consciousness of a deep, ontological drift that embraced the whole of the Universe I lived in," the consciousness of evolution "much less as an abstract notion than as a presence to such a degree as to fill my whole spiritual horizon"[69] made the intuition of a cosmic Inexpressible ahead so strong in Teilhard that to him the already existent God rendered vivid by Roman Catholic Christianity was, first and foremost, the God of evolution: the divinity already existent was to Teilhard the Christ commensurate with the cosmos and most organically linked to all its processes rather than the God who, in Roman Catholic Christianity no less than in every other creed of the past, was associated with a pull toward a Beyond, bearing one away from the concerns of terrestrial life.[70] What such a stance constituted was, by its multitude of novel and unorthodox implications with their call for basic readjustments, "a hitherto unknown form of religion."

Only in the double light of an "old love" retained in essence, yet radically reorientated, can one understand the picture that Étienne Gilson, eminent historian of Christian and medieval philosophy, has painted. Robert Speaight quotes from *Seminarium*, no. 4, where Gilson describes his meeting with Teilhard at a symposium organized by the University of Columbia at Auden Home near New York a year before Teilhard's death:

> He had hardly seen me when he came forward to greet me but his face lit up with a candid smile and grasping my arm with both his hands, said, "Can you tell me who will give us at last the meta-Christiantiy we are all waiting for?" I have hesitated for a long time before reporting these words. They seemed to me incredible, impossible from the lips of a priest. . . .
>
> But on the same day, during the afternoon, in a passage where a crowd of people were incessantly moving to and fro, I happened to pass in front of a priest seated in an arm-chair. He was completely oblivious of what was going on around him and absorbed in the reading of his breviary. It was the Reverend Father Teilhard de Chardin of The Society of Jesus. This double image sums up for me what I call "the case of Teilhard de Chardin." Even if he was waiting for a "meta-

Christianity," it was in Christianity itself that he had already found it."[71]

What is meant by "Christianity itself" is evident from another Gilson quotation of Speaight's about Teilhard from *Seminarium*, No. 4: "Under the continual flow of scientific or other alluvions he kept intact and miraculously preserved the nugget of pure gold which was the piety and faith of his childhood."[72] Fervour for the historical Christ, as kindled at his mother's knees in Auvergne and later kept incandescent by the sense of the Christian mystical life down the centuries, was Teilhard's until the end. But this Christ was aureoled for him by a mysticoscientific humanism that laid bare to Teilhard Christianity in a form quite "meta" to the Church's version, the form in which the cosmos-commensurate Christ, the God guiding evolution and fulfilling himself in it, predominated.

De Lubac tries to offer assurance that this aspect of Teilhardism, emphasising earthly maturation for the pleroma, is not at loggerheads with Roman Catholic Christianity at all: "There is a certain relation, even if we cannot completely succeed in determining it, between the natural, collective and terrestrial future of humanity and its super-natural and eternal end. . . .Whether in the particular form in which Père Teilhard expressed it, or in some other form, this idea, thanks more to him than to any other writer, has become generally accepted. It has ample support in the earliest tradition. It now seems an essential element in the Church's consciousness."[73] De Lubac's assurance immediately becomes suspect by his allusion to "ample support in the earliest tradition." If the Cosmic Christ of Saint Paul and Saint John was not sufficient to prevent Teilhardism from being revolutionary, how would the earliest tradition help?

And what exactly is this tradition? De Lubac asks us to consult a certain writing of Saint Irenaeus, but he does not give the actual words.[74] Luckily, in another place there is a similar harking back to that Greek father. In *Activation of Energy* Teilhard writes: "The supernatural. . .would not exclude but, on the contrary, call for, as a necessary preparation, the complete maturing of an ultra-human."[75] The editorial footnote informs the reader: "Here Père Teilhard reproduces the teaching of St. Irenaeus, of which he was so fond. God raises man up step by step in the course of history. 'It was necessary that man should first be created, then that he should grow up, then that he should become adult man, then that he should multiply, then gain in strength, then attain glory, that he should have the vision of his master' (Demonstration, Bk. IV, ch. 38)."

Can this be a genuine parallel to Teilhardism? Obviously, Saint Irenaeus, with a phrase such as "adult man," is comparing human history with an individual's growth into religious wisdom and presenting a broad ideal picture in which the spiritual turn would be a widespread achievement after mankind had developed from bare primitivism through rich vitalism to adventurous civilization and enlightened culture. Any student of historical humanity could have made Saint Irenaeus's pronouncement. It has nothing to do with the Teilhardian *Weltanschauung*. The "vision of God" spoken of is just what Teilhard, in the very essay containing that editorial footnote, found deficient or incomplete. Modern knowledge "discloses ahead of us the possibility of as yet unknown physico-psychic arrangements": one recognizes "that the universe is moving evolutively towards a peak of consciousness, that it has a 'head.'" This recognition "has more than a great physical importance." It has also "more than a great meta-physical importance," for now "the act of reflection" is not confined to being "an individual operation of mental dialectic": it "assumes the form of an historic process cosmic in scope." "Even—indeed above all—in the field of mysticism the newly acquired perception of a movement of ontological convergence inevitably arouses questionings and necessitates profound reformulations."[76] Saint Irenaeus, surely, demands no challenges to doctrine, no revolutionary changes of outlook.

The reason why may be described as follows in Teilhard's words:

Hitherto, the idea of *spirit* had always, on the whole, been presented to the consciousness of man as linked with an *ascending movement* which carries the soul towards heaven through denial (or at least through *contempt*) of terrestrial values. Thus whatever the form of the divine—personal or impersonal, immanent or transcendent—for the "perfect" it always represented a sort of Above; and to attain it, it was "by definition" necessary to escape from the determinisms and seductions of the corporeal things in which we are involved.

Now it is precisely at right-angles (if I may so put it) to this traditional pole of sublimation and holiness that, as a result of the *cephalization* [the coming to a "head"] of evolution, our baffled minds see the emergence at this moment of a second centre of spiritualization and divinization; spirit no longer in discord, but in *concord*, with a super-arrangement of the phenomenal multiple. The issue, no longer above, into some transcendent supernatural, but ahead, into some ultra-human.

In other words there is now a conflict between two pictures of God, one vertical and the other horizontal.

In that diagrammatic form, I am daily more convinced, we can express the root source of the religious difficulties we are going through.[77]

Then Teilhard suggests his solution: "a synthesis between the above and the ahead in a becoming of the 'Christic' type, in which access to the transcendent hyper-personal would depend, as a condition, on the previous arrival of human consciousness at a critical point of collective reflection."[78]

De Lubac is right in saying that one need not restrict oneself to every "slant" and stress in Teilhard's vision. But to be Teilhardian in the essential connotation one must respond to the conceptual and mystical need set up by modern evolutionism. Saint Irenaeus is quite irrelevant there, and if the Church merely modernizes him, it has missed the Teilhardian "revolution."

iv

Teilhard's "revolution" led him in 1953 to make one more attempt to formulate — in "The Stuff of the Universe" — "the fundamentals of what I feel, of what I see and what I live."[79] He introduces the attempt with the following words:

Without for once being concerned to respect any orthodoxy (whether scientific or religious) in the way I express myself — though at the same time in the consciousness that I am simply acting out of loyalty, carried to its extreme limit, to my two-fold vocation as a man and as a Christian: this is the astounding panorama that, simply by adjuring our vision to what we can all see, I would like to bring out for you with unmistakable clarity.[80]

Then Teilhard states his credo in general terms:

For a long time, just like anybody else, I came close to being bogged down in the antiquated habit of looking on man, in nature, either as an inexplicable and ephemeral anomaly—or as the product of a physico-chemical evolution strictly confined to our planet—or, again, as the result of some miraculous extra-cosmic intervention.

Now, on the other hand, that my eyes have been opened, I have come to understand that in the totality of itself, and at every point within itself, the *Weltstoff* tended to reflect upon itself— now, in other words, that I can no longer regard the terrestrial human except as the natural and local, and for the moment the most advanced, product of a trend that embraces the totality of matter, and time, and space: now that that is so, I can say that I have found my bearings, and I can now breathe freely, in the feeling, vindicated at last, of forming but one with all the rest.[81]

Teilhard goes on to offer a startling formulation of the insight that the universe is "spirit" in a progressive flux of material organization: "The 'spirit' of the philosophers and theologians was seen by me as a direct extension of universal physico-chemism." Next, he adds to "the discovery of this prime relationship" "a further apparent fact: that, on earth, in mankind, the cosmic process of psychogenesis (contrary to what one is told) is far from being halted at this moment: we can only say that it is accelerated." To Teilhard, "twentieth-century mankind. . .presents itself quite clearly to our experience as a system in the full vigour of *co-reflection*, which is exactly the same as saying of *ultra-hominization*." "And this irresistible biological folding-back (planetary in its scope and urgency) suggests to our minds the wild idea and the wild hope that perhaps there really does exist an ultimate centre of reflection (and hence of beatifying consummation) ahead of us, at the upper term of evolution."[82]

Here Teilhard speaks of "the great event of my life"—"the gradual identification in my spiritual heaven of two suns: one of these stars was the cosmic peak postulated by a generalized evolution of the convergent type; and the other was constituted by the risen Christ of the Christian faith." He continues with an emphasis on "the astonishing energetic properties of the *divine Milieu* which is generated in the utmost depths of human consciousness by this truly 'implosive' meeting between a rising flood of co-reflection and a second, descending, flood of revelation."[83]

What the meeting stands for receives from Teilhard its closing description thus: "The final and complete reflection of the universe upon itself in a meeting between the above of heaven and the ahead of earth—in other words, proceeding from the same movement, a God who makes himself cosmic and an evolution which makes itself person."[84]

Where in Saint Irenaeus can one ever find that "same movement" visualised by a fusion of evolutionist modernism and a rethought Christology? And if the Church is simply Saint Irenaeus clothed in a twentieth-century nomenclature, there is certainly no genuine "Teilhardization" of the Church. Teilhard the Roman Catholic still remains "un-Churchianized"—novel, nonorthodox.

One may even take leave to doubt whether the fusion that has been spoken of is the only fundamental difference between Teilhard and Saint Irenaeus and his fellow fathers. Both Teilhard and admirers of him, such as de Lubac, often categorize his thought with that of the theologians of Alexandria, in general. But Speaight records weighty notes of dissent:

> Teilhard had against him some very considerable theologians, and in Gilson the most erudite historian of philosophy. Not an historian in the dry, academic sense, but a mind which had counted for a great deal in the renaissance of Catholic thought; deeply versed in scholasticism, but well able to look beyond it. For Gilson as for St. Augustine whom he quoted in support— *Nobis ad certam regulam loqui fas est*—theology was "the most exact of sciences," and Kant had admired the scholastic method. Gilson criticized Teilhard's transposition of the Christ of the Trinity into the Christ of the cosmos and his generalization of Christ the Redeemer into a motor of evolution. The Alexandrian Fathers to whom Teilhard appealed had assimilated the Logos to the Redeemer—not, as Teilhard claimed, the other way about; just as it had been the error of the Gnostics to "cosmify" the Redeemer at the same time as they "christified" the universe. For St. Irenaeus "the true gnosis" was "the teaching of the twelve apostles." Gilson maintained that the historical Christ was not "the concrete germ of Christ Omega."[85]

According to Speaight, Gilson questions Teilhard's science as well and sets no value—either scientific or religious—on his exposition: "Moreover, the cosmic Christ was a Christ in whom no scientist believed. There was 'too much parascience in Teilhard for too little true Christian wisdom,' and as for his style—'what a fall is there when one deserts the naked rigour of the old masters for the gelatinous prose of our contemporaries.' "[86]

I am afraid that Gilson is too much caught in the traditional religious mode of thinking, the "naked rigour" of the champion logic-choppers, to appreciate what may be termed the intuitively guided argument of insight, a kind of leaping logic that is not just poetic in the pejorative sense but is secretly behind even the fundamental movements of scientific theory no less than behind the basic turns of religion rationalizing itself. But, of course, it is true that science in its common outlook has not yet come to believe in anything like the cosmic Christ. Teilhard is well aware of this fact, and that is why he calls his science "hyper-physics" or "generalised physics." Leave aside Christ Omega, Omega itself without Christ coloring it has no acknowledged place in the scientific world view. Even Julian Huxley, whose evolutionary thinking runs on lines similar to Teilhard's on many large issues, says that Teilhard's vision of Omega is far from clear to him and that Teilhard "appears not to be guarding himself sufficiently against the dangers of personifying the non-personal elements of reality."[87] Like most scientists, Huxley can hardly "follow him in his gallant attempt to reconcile the supernatural elements in Christianity with the facts and implications of evolution."[88] But he adds: "This in no way detracts from the positive value of his naturalistic general approach."[89] And Huxley, apropos of his own phrase that in modern scientific man evolution is at last becoming conscious of itself, writes of Teilhard: "His formulation. . .is more profound and seminal: it implies that we should consider inter-thinking humanity as a new type of organism, whose destiny it is to realize new possibilities for evolving life on this planet."[90] Furthermore, the religion that Teilhard tries to draw out of science has a basic relationship with the greatest experience that Huxley has known independently of science, which he describes in his autobiography. It happened during a dance at Shackleford: "Wandering out into the fragrant night air, the sky crowded with stars, I had a strange cosmic vision — as if I could see right down into the centre of the earth, and embrace the whole of its contents and its animal and plant inhabitants. For a moment I became, in some transcendental way, the whole universe."[91] Here Huxley is a true pantheist, and one may dare say that his experience is not unassimilable to his own scientific sense of the evolutionary process coming to self-awareness in men like himself and pointing to a new collective "psycho-social" development.

Gilson, I feel, tends to exaggerate Teilhard's "parascience." But he hits the bull's-eye when, referring to traditional Christianity, he avers that Teilhard had "too little true Christian wisdom." Teilhard's "meta-Christianity" is an undeniable fact. Nor can I be content, as is Gilson, with his sincerity and piety, while ignoring his thought-structure merely because it misinterprets Alexandrian or other doctrines and employs a different type of expository language from that of the master scholastics. Like Rabut, de Lubac, and Mooney, I have more respect for his religious philosophy than has Gilson, to whom Vernon Sproxton attributes the catty remark: "I see what he believes; but what does he know?"[92] However, I part company with whoever equates him in essence with the Church. He stands out, when most Teilhardian, as novel and nonorthodox.

The sure sign of his novelty and nonorthodoxy is his various lapses into "heretical" utterance despite all his care for what de Lubac has called "the perennial Christian ideal." What I mean is best illustrated by a series of questions raised by de Lubac.

> He tried to show in our Lord Jesus Christ "the synthesis of the created Universe and its Creator"; did he not sometimes seem to establish this synthesis at a too accessible level and thus, in spite of the qualifications and corrections we have noted and against his own unmistakable intention, to some degree naturalize Christ? In some over-hasty expositions, did he not appear, as though *a priori*, to fuse together Cosmogenesis and Christogenesis? Again, he sought to bring out the wonder of the universal "diaphany" of him who, in the first place had effected, at one particular point in time and space, his "epiphany"; though unambiguously affirming the causal link, did he not sometimes seem in practice to overlook it, and so seem to drown the unique datum of faith in the ocean of a natural mysticism?[93]

Apropos of the last lapse, de Lubac adds in a note: "That such an appearance is deceptive, we have as warrant, among others, the explanations he gave to his friend Père Auguste Valensin, who had mentioned to him the doubt referred to."[94] Giving explanations is very well, but where one encounters repeated need to explain one may assume an ineradicable element of novelty and nonorthodoxy calling to be fused with the devotional and credal Christian element, yet failing to be fused because of some radical disparity between the ultimate metaphysical bases of the two. Neither element can be denied its place in Teilhardism. As a Jesuit, Teilhard desired the former to be integrated into the latter, but he could not help again and again going beyond the terms by which this component could be first subordinated to the other and then combined with it. It kept on functioning in its own right and pointed to a transcendence of basic Roman Catholicism by a Christianity set off on a fresh start. Admittedly, Teilhard could not coherently work out in full his hyper-Catholicism, but the essential newness of it insists on shining out on occasion and takes on its most self-aware avatar in the letters from China to Léontine Zanta.

NOTES

1. Sri Aurobindo. *The Life Divine* (New York: The Sri Aurobindo Library, 1949), pp. 775, 776.

2. Ibid., p. 775.

3. Teilhard de Chardin, *Letters to Léontine Zanta* (London: Collins; New York: Georges Borchart, 1969), p. 36.

4. Teilhard de Chardin, *Writings in Time of War*, trans. René Hague (London: Collins, 1968; New York: Harper & Row, 1973), pp. 70–71.

5. Teilhard de Chardin, *Activation of Energy* (London: Collins; New York: Harcourt Brace Jovanovich, 1972), p. 227.

6. Ibid., pp. 382–83.

7. Teilhard de Chardin, *Let Me Explain*. Texts selected and arranged by Jean-Pierre Demoulin, trans. René Hague et al. (London: Collins, 1970; New York: Harper & Row, 1972), pp. 157–58.

8. Ibid., pp. 156, 157.

9. Teilhard de Chardin, *Letters to Léontine Zanta*, p. 36.

10. de Lubac, *Religion of Teilhard de Chardin* (London: Collins; New York: Desclee, 1967), p. 185.

11. Ibid., p. 364, note 55. The reference is Letter of 3 October 1918 in *The Making of a Mind: Letters from a Soldier-Priest* (London: Collins; New York: Harper & Tow, 1965), p. 244.

12. Ibid., pp. 208, 209, 211.

13. Ibid., p. 229. The quotation is from "Mon univers" (14 April 1918).

14. Ibid.

15. Letter of 13 December 1918 in *The Making of a Mind: Letters from a Soldier-Priest*, p. 269.

16. Teilhard de Chardin, Introduction à la vie chrétienne (1944), p. 11. Quoted by de Lubac, op. cit.

17. Teilhard de Chardin, *Writings in Time of War*, p. 73.

18. *Let Me Explain*, p. 12.

19. Ibid., p. 146.

20. Teilhard de Chardin. *Activation of Energy*, p. 382.

21. Teilhard de Chardin. *Letters to Léontine Zanta*, pp. 114–15.

22. Ibid., p. 60.

23. Ibid., p. 72–73.

24. Ibid., pp. 110–11.

25. Ibid., p. 91.

26. Ibid., pp. 79–80.

27. Robert Speaight, *Teilhard de Chardin: A Biography* (London: Collins; New York: Harper & Row, 1968), p. 140.

28. Ibid., p. 174.
29. Ibid., p. 320.
30. Ibid., p. 282.
31. Ibid., p. 323.
32. Teilhard de Chardin. *Letters to Léontine Zanta*, p. 52.
33. Ibid., p. 89.
34. Ibid., p. 87.
35. Ibid., p. 72.
36. Ibid., p. 52.
37. de Lubac, *Religion of Teilhard de Chardin*, pp. 186-87.
38. Ibid., p. 187.
39. Ibid., p. 186.
40. Pierre Teilhard de Chardin, *Science and Christ* (London: Collins; New York: Harper & Row, 1968), p. 102.
41. Ibid., p. 114.
42. Ibid., p. 115
43. Ibid., p. 103.
44. Ibid., pp. 44-£.
45. Ibid., p. 37.
46. Ibid., p. 119.
47. Ibid., p. 167.
48. Ibid., p. 78.
49. Henri de Lubac, Teilhard de Chardin: The Man and His Meaning, trans. René Hague (New York: New American Library, A Mentor Omega Book, 1967), p. 28 n.
50. Ibid., p. 43.
51. de Lubac, *Religion of Teilhard de Chardin*, p. 104.
52. Ibid., p. 139.
53. O. Rabut, *Dialogue with Teilhard de Chardin* (London and New York: Sheed & Ward, Stagebooks, 1961), p. 187. The translation in de Lubac's book is different.
54. Pierre Teilhard de Chardin, "La Crise présente," Études. 20 October 1937.
55. de Lubac, *Religion of Teilhard de Chardin*, p. 203.
56. Teilhard de Chardin, *Activation of Energy*, p. 383.
57. Ibid., p. 240.
58. Ibid.
59. Ibid., pp. 180-82.
60. Teilhard de Chardin, *Writing in Time of War*, p. 55.
61. Ibid.
62. Ibid.
63. Ibid., p. 51.
64. Ibid., pp. 55-56.
65. Teilhard de Chardin, *Activation of Energy*, p. 383.
66. Ibid., p. 242.
67. Ibid.
68. Ibid., p. 241.
69. Pierre Teilhard de Chardin, "Le Coeur de la manère as quoted in idem. *Writing in Time of War*, p. 78 n. 4.
70. Cf. Teilhard de Chardin, *Activation of Energy*, pp. 262-64, 276.
71. Speaight, *Teilhard de Chardin*, p. 224.
72. Ibid. p. 326; Cf. Teilhard de Chardin, *Activation of Energy*, pp. 262-64, 278.
73. de Lubac, *Religion of Teilhard de Chardin*, p. 219.
74. Ibid., p. 358 n. 78.
75. Teilhard de Chardin, *Activation of Energy*, p. 279.

76. Ibid., pp. 277-78.

77. Ibid., p. 278.

78. Ibid., p. 279.

79. Ibid., p. 375.

80. Ibid., p. 376.

81. Ibid., p. 378.

82. Ibid., pp. 378-81.

83. Ibid., p. 381.

84. Ibid.

85. Speaight. *Teilhard de Chardin, p. 326.*

86. *Ibid.*

87. *Julian Huxley, Intoduction to The Phenomenon of Man*, by Pierre Teilhard de Chardin (London: Collins: New York: Harper & Row, 1960), p. 19.

88. Ibid.

89. Ibid.

90. Ibid., p. 20.

91. Julian Huxley, *Memories* (London: George Allen & Unwin, 1973.).

92. Vernon Sproxton, *Teilhard de Chardin* (London: SCM Press; Naperville, Ill.: Allenson, 1971), p. 73.

93. de Lubac, *Religion of Teilhard de Chardin*, pp. 202-3. Quoted words are from Teilhard de Chardin, "Mon univers."

94. Ibid., p. 354 n. 31.

4

Sri Aurobindo's Ashram; Spirituality and Religion; Sri Aurobindo's General Philosophical Position; His Attitude and Teilhard's to Science

Realizing the impossibility of the Church's assimilating Teilhard by mere readjustments of nomenclature, and recognizing in Teilhardism an entirely reoriented Christianity of universal evolution, which has an affinity though not an identity with the cosmic vision of Christ in Saint Paul and a few others, one cannot but feel at a loss to comprehend how Zaehner can subscribe to Teilhard's belief as Zaehner states it: "The Roman Church, with the supreme Pontiff as Vicar of Christ at its head, was still the only possible focus of unity which, acting as the axis of evolution itself, could mould mankind together into a unified and forward-looking collectivity destined ultimately to converge upon God as its true and predestined Centre" (p. 9). Besides, he grants: "The Christian Church even now represents only a fraction of mankind, but ideally the body of Christ should encompass the whole human race — how and in what form we have not the slightest idea" (p. 112). Further, after affirming that "without love there can be no Christianity," he confesses: "Whatever we have advertised as Christianity has rarely been more than a caricature — make-believe, which makes fewer and fewer believe" (p. 113). Even about the ideal of "unity in diversity suffused by love," he says that very few Christians feel it as a living reality, and he characterizes it as one that "not only Christianity proclaims but also the Śaiva Siddhanta and the Vedānta of Rāmānuja which have grown independently on Indian soil" (p. 113). Finally, there is the fact, the raison d'être of Zaehner's comparative study, that Sri Aurobindo, no less than Teilhard, has the vision of an evolution "from individuality through collectivity to a unity in diversity," though here the diversified union would be, in Zaehner's view, love-centered not on "the cosmic Christ" but on "the Hindu Trinity *sac-cid-ānanda* (Being-Logos-Joy)," a substitute whose "parallelism is exact" (p. 13). Hence, where is the need to fall back on the Roman Church as "the instrument of unity ready to hand"? With all the rest given, would not the Ashram of Pondicherry suffice as the instrument?

Zaehner's argument that "Aurobindo could find no such principle of unity in Hinduism" is irrelevant (p. 13). There was no call for Sri Aurobindo to look for it outside his own Ashram, which not only is growing apace in Pondicherry but also has, contrary to Zaehner's belief, a large number of centers both in India and abroad and has now extended its work in the project, supported by UNESCO as well as by the Indian Government, of a model international "city of dawn" with the Aurobindonian vision as its guiding light: "Auroville." Moreover, this "instrument of unity," the Ashram, has sprung up around a figure recognized more and more in the whole world as what, according to Zaehner, he saw himself to be—"the divine centre from which the transformation of man into 'super-manhood' was to radiate" (p. 27). I may add that the unique distinction of this instrument did not diminish in any manner with the passing away of the master par excellence of the Integral Yoga. Even apart from his spiritual presence persisting as a living force, there was at the Ashram's core the radiant personality whom Zaehner, with a tinge of incredulity, calls "a French lady whom [Aurobindo] was bold enough to hail as the Divine Mother and the eternal Śakti" (p. 13). If Sri Aurobindo was anything like "the utterly perfected Siddha" (Zaehner's words), surely he could be trusted to put at the very heart of his world work a worthy fount of spirituality.

Here a point often forgotten is worth emphasizing. When people make comparisons between Sri Aurobindo and Teilhard, they mostly think of two men with a spiritual vision of the world's future,

and they start assessing whether one or the other was a greater and
truer visionary. But actually, there is no real comparison possible
between the men. Would anyone dream of classifying Teilhard
along with the figure to whom he linked his scientific-religious
message and whom he regarded as the sole incarnation of God in all
history? Would one set Teilhard even in the lesser company of Saint
Paul, Saint John of the Cross, or Saint Angela of Foligno—mystics
he particularly extolled? Sri Aurobindo is precisely one who would
have to be brought into relation not only with the group of
Teilhard's favorite saints, but also with whoever would be considered
as incarnations or avatars. All evidence portrays him as a being of
the highest spiritual consciousness, a summation of all time's
achievement of inner light, a God-realized guide to an achievement
beyond any in the past. If a comparison in the Teilhardian context
were to be made, it would have to be not with Teilhard but with his
Christ. Even there one would have to hesitate in view of the plenary
spiritual knowledge revealed by Sri Aurobindo. No Divine
Messenger has come with such an intimate and masterful possession
of the secret of existence and such a gigantic embodiment in his own
person of the illumined states described and explained in his
writings. Many a reader of Sri Aurobindo's *Life Divine* has felt on
putting it down that the author of this book must be the author of
the universe! And all who have known him would agree with the
Mother's declaration: "What Sri Aurobindo represents in the
world's history is not a teaching, not even a revelation; it is a decisive
action direct from the Supreme." To talk, in the same breath, of
him and Teilhard as men with a world-enlightening or world-saving
mission is to fumble in the proper assessment of divine vision and
work. Some parallelism between certain aspects of their thought and
some comparative estimate of their immediate impact on the
modern mind are the only things one can attempt. To pass beyond
them to balance the living sources of the thought or the impact is to
risk floundering in a sea of incommensurables.

Once the avataric status of Sri Aurobindo is perceived, all that
has been said of him must apply to the personality whom he set by
his side at the center of his Ashram. If there is a tinge of incredulity
in Zaehner's mention of the importance that Sri Aurobindo
accorded to the Mother, it is just because of his insufficient
appraisal of Sri Aurobindo the avatar.

And the momentous companionate arrangement Sri Aurobindo

instituted for his Ashram throws into relief a point that Zaehner, though not lacking a clue to it, tends often to ignore. The clue is in his observation: "Hinduism has no central authority to lay down what you should believe nor is it committed to any particular form of religious expression" (p. 10). This means that basically Hindusim is not at all a religion, but for all its characteristic moods and modes historically and geographically cultivated, a many-sided synthesis of spiritual experience, which has a possibility of assimilating every existing kind of Godward movement as well as of developing new kinds, because of an extremely broad basis, a true "catholicity" or universality of essential mysticism. So it is rather inapt to term Hinduism "the national religion of India": it is actually a multi-tudinously single essence of spirituality explored under certain national conditions. This really is what is known as "Vedanta" and what Sri Aurobindo accepted as both his background and point de départ. Consequently—in the sense in which Teilhard wanted to change and expand his religion and his Church—Sri Aurobindo cannot be said, as Zaehner suggests, to have wanted to transform Hinduism by his dynamic philosophy (p. 34). In fact, Sri Aurobindo explicitly declared that his Yoga and his Ashram had nothing to do with any religion as such. Does not Zaehner himself record: "The religions, Aurobindo thought, had served their purpose" (p. 33)? Although all of them have certain contributions to make to the coming culture, none of them had for Sri Aurobindo an inevitable utility any longer. There has been no religion practiced in the Ashram. The disciples do not follow even Hinduism in distinction from Buddhism or Islam, Judaism or Christianity, or Zoroastri-anism. And the Mother, coming from the West and put by Sri Aurobindo at the head of his Ashram, proved to the world that for him the age of religion, whether Indian or any other, was utterly past and that we have to move forward into a new epoch of spiritual truth going beyond even the vast synthesis of God-realizations associated with historical and geographical India.

The Ashram of Sri Aurobindo and the Mother, therefore, is above all such rivalries as Christianity must face—still more the Roman Catholic brand of it, which stands over against the Protestant within the same religion. It is the most natural locus of a future world union in a progressive spiritualization. Zaehner, in a very fair moment, said in passing: "Perhaps [Sri Aurobindo] has left behind in his Ashram not only the 'kingdom of God within us' but also, however small it may be, a 'city of God upon earth' " (p. 34). It would be too tall a claim that the ideal combination, seed of the entire world's unified spiritual evolution, has been actualized in embryo here. But, by all tokens, Zaehner has rightly divined the Ashram's destiny.

This destiny does not essentially change just because two years after the publication of Zaehner's book the Mother departed from her body at the age of nearly ninety-six. Even as she declared that the truth manifested by Sri Aurobindo went on working after he had passed away, one may affirm that this truth is still active, although she too is no longer physically present. In fact, the affirmation can be all the stronger, since in the interval of twenty-three years between the two withdrawals from embodied life, the establishment of that truth was naturally deeper and wider. Hardly anyone visiting the Ashram today can fail to feel the tremendous concentration there of a new consciousness radiating out to create a finer world.

On the general trend of Sri Aurobindo's thought, which is the ultimate foundation of his Ashram, it is possible to throw some light from what he wrote on the completion of the fourth year of his philosophical monthly, *Arya*, which ran from 1914 to 1921. The novel temper of this thought in spite of its relation to ancient India's spirituality, as well as to the modern world vision, comes out here very clearly in a brief compass. Sri Aurobindo did not intend "at any time a review or magazine in the ordinary sense of the word, that is to say, a popular presentation or criticism of current thought on philosophical questions." Nor was the *Arya*, like some philosophical and religious magazines in India, "the restatement of an existing school or position of philosophical thought cut out in its lines and needing only to be popularised and supported." Sri Aurobindo's work was "the thinking out of a synthetic philosophy which might be a contribution to the thought of the new age that was coming upon the world." He expatiates on this theme:

We start from the idea that humanity is moving to a new life of the race—in all countries where men think, there is now in various forms that idea and that hope—and our aim was to search for the spiritual, religious and other truth which can enlighten and guide the race in this movement and endeavour. The spiritual experience and the general truths on which such an attempt could be based, were already present to us, otherwise we should have had no right to make the endeavour at all; but

the complete intellectual statement of them and their results and
issues had to be found. This meant a continuous thinking, a high
and subtle and difficult thinking on several lines.

After this introduction Sri Aurobindo dwelt a little on the series of
essays standing first in the *Arya*, *The Life Divine*, and sharply distinguished their thesis from Shankara's Mayavada, illusionism:

> Here we start from the Vedantic position, its ideas of the Self
> and mind and life, of Sachchidananda and the world, of
> Knowledge and Ignorance, of rebirth and the Spirit. But Vedanta
> is popularly supposed to be a denial of life, and this is no
> doubt a dominant trend it has taken. Though starting from the
> original truth that all is the Brahman, the Self, it has insisted
> in the end that the world is simply not-Brahman, not-Self; it has
> ended in a paradox. We have shown that mind and life and
> matter are derivations from the Self through a sort of spiritual
> mind or Supermind which is the real support of cosmic existence
> and, by developing mind into that, man can arrive at the
> real truth of the spirit in the world and the real truth and
> highest law of life. The Self is Sachchidananda and there is no
> incurable antinomy between that and the world; only we see the
> world through the eyes of the Ignorance and we have to see it
> through the eyes of Knowledge. Our Ignorance itself is only
> Knowledge developing out of its involution in the apparent
> nescience of Matter and on its way to a return to its conscious
> integrality. To accomplish that return and manifest the spiritual
> life in the human existence is the opportunity given by the
> successions of rebirth. We accept the truth of evolution, not so
> much in the physical form given to it by the West as in its
> philosophical truth, the involution of life and mind and spirit in
> matter and their progressive manifestation. At the summit of this
> evolution is the spiritual life, the life divine.

The point about evolution is worth an elucidatory comment.
Having actually possessed "the spiritual experience and the general
truths" by which the evolution of the life divine could be essayed, Sri
Aurobindo cannot be expected to look to science for a foundational
revelation. Teilhard based on physics his reconciliation of the God
above with the God ahead: apart from a strong feeling of evolution
as a universal "presence," a spirit at secret work behind or within the
terms stressed by materialistic science, he had no substantial
mystical realization to fall back upon. The Christian Scripture he
deeply revered, and in portions of it he discerned a kind of grand

analogue to what science, pressed to its ultimate and enlarged into
"hyper-physics," laid bare to his researching eyes, but, with his
rational mind the main leader available on the way to truth, he
could not but describe himself as he once did: "I am neither a
philosopher nor a theologian, but a student of the 'phenomenon,' a
physicist (natural philosopher) in the old Greek sense."[1] Inevitably
he would differ from Sri Aurobindo, as Zaehner has remarked, in
his fundamental attitude toward science (pp. 36-37). The attitude
he took was natural to him. Sri Aurobindo did not need it at all. But
this does not connote any neglect by Sri Aurobindo of science. Even
to the most materialist, most secularist epoch of it he has paid a
tremendous tribute, and there was never any Tolstoyan or
Gandhian cry by him toward a premachinery primitivism, a pre-
scientific simplicity. At the conclusion of a long examination of the
debit and the credit sides of Materialism he writes:

> Three things will remain from the labour of the secularist
> centuries: truth of the physical world and its importance, the
> scientific method of knowledge — which is to induce Nature and
> Being to reveal their own way of being and proceeding, not
> hastening to put upon them our own impositions of idea and
> imagination, *adhyāropa* — and last, though very far from least,
> the truth and importance of the earth life and the human
> endeavour, its evolutionary meaning.[2]

The importance of the earth life and of the human endeavor was
not unknown to ancient Indian spirituality. In the *Arya* Sri Aurobindo demonstrated by a close study of the Gītā, the Upanishads,
and the Rig-Veda how the concept of a divine life is consistent with
the old Vedantic truth. But the "evolutionary meaning" of
terrestrial existence and of man's agelong odyssey could not be there
in the past to a plenary extent: the vistas of natural progress, which
the scientific theory of evolution discloses when plumbed to its
depths, were very fitfully open to the ancient eye. Modern science
alone could make them an organic part of man's world vision. But
modern science by itself is unable to provide the total possible
content of progress or the master means to achieve it. Evolution has
to be spiritually probed, and a new spiritual verity corresponding to
the new scientific discovery has to operate. This verity,
automatically luminous with the profoundest secrets of the human
body's potentiality, as well as with the largest powers for a material

fulfillment not only individual but also collective, is what Sri Aurobindo designates *Supermind*, a level of consciousness that Zaehner
fails to assess properly and about which I shall have more to say
later. Suffice it here to note that Sri Aurobindo has called it a
greater truth than any realized up to now, and demanding, as I have
already observed, a new Yoga, synthesising the past Yogas but
carrying them further into an integrality of aim and process oriented
toward an all-round perfection.

The modern theory of evolution, therefore, is in its essence the
right background for the Aurobindonian spirituality. But it cannot
in its purely physical form be of primary moment to Sri Aurobindo.
One aspect of its vital philosophical truth, anticipated in the
Vedanta, though without being fully exploited, he has expressed:
"The involution of life and mind and spirit in matter and their
progressive manifestation." The other aspect, also already in general
in the Vedanta and hinted at in the *Arya*'s fourth-year self-review,
may be summed up for Aurobindonian purposes:

> If there is an evolution of consciousness in an evolutionary
> matter taking various individual forms and if there is an
> individual soul with a developed consciousness inhabiting each of
> the highest developed of these forms, namely, the human, then
> this soul too must have an evolutionary past as well as future and
> it is the progressive experience of this soul which constitutes
> the evolution of consciousness in an evolving physical Nature.
> But how can that experience take place except through the
> soul's rebirth? Thus rebirth is self-evidently a necessary function
> of the consciousness undergoing evolution—the only possible
> machinery of such a process.

Teilhard, radical evolutionist though he was, no less than believer
in the individual human soul, could not take any step in the
direction of the theory of rebirth. Involution in the Aurobindonian
meaning he did envisage, even if he did not employ that word in a
similar context and even though he actually gave a different
meaning to it as a rule and was not always clear as to the state in
which life and mind and spirit were involved in matter. Roman
Catholicism so far has not subscribed to involution, yet Teilhard was
not stopped by this oversight. But as regards rebirth, he seems
completely at one with orthodox Christianity. Rather an anomaly
for one who subscribed to "spiritual evolutionism" and said of the
man deeply convinced of the evolutionary viewpoint: "Body and

soul, he is the product of a huge creative work with which the totality of things has collaborated from the beginning."[3] And again, "His true being is not limited to the narrow boundaries of his limbs and his historic existence but. . .he forms part, body and soul, of the process that drives the universe."[4] Zaehner too, for all his detached and impartial outlook on the Roman Church and his openness at several points to non-Christian religions, has no "hyper-Catholic" inkling at this particular point. Nor does he touch on the subject in relation to Teilhardism, science, and evolution.

Notes

1.   *Nouvelles Littéraires*, 11 January 1951.

2.   Sri Aurobindo, *Evolution*, 5th ed. (Pondicherry: Sri Aurobindo Ashram, 1950), p. 52.

3.   Pierre Teilhard de Chardin, *The Vision of the Past*, trans. J. M. Cohen (London: Collins, 1966), p. 137.

4.   Ibid., p. 140.

5

Zaehner's Interpretation of Teilhard; The Question of Teilhard's Pantheism

i

Apart from the subject of rebirth, Zaehner's broad-mindedness, getting naturally infused into his survey of Sri Aurobindo and Teilhard, has most interestingly brought in some shades that his fellow religionists would repudiate and that he himself does not appear to have properly gauged. His view of Teilhardism creates a picture that slants it toward Sri Aurobindo rather than the Roman Church.

Equating the pantheistic experience with "cosmic consciousness," he not only says that Teilhard was a pantheist by nature and that his temperament was thoroughly pantheistic (pp. 6, 20); he also says that Teilhard was never ashamed of having such a temperament and that he considered the pantheistic experience as the necessary first step toward realizing a universe finally converging onto a personal Center that is God (pp. 20-21). Absolutely anathema to Roman Catholicism is "cosmic consciousness" in the pantheistic sense that the whole universe can be experienced by the mystic as an interconnectedness of being, which is one substance with God, not a creation out of nothing and substantially other than he. But pantheism — the secret identity of the cosmos with God — as a part of a total spiritual realization, in which God is more than Pantheos, is welcome to Sri Aurobindo.

Even outside the question of cosmic consciousness, Zaehner

inclines Teilhard toward Sri Aurobindo and not Roman Catholicism. Does he not say, as if both Teilhard and Sri Aurobindo meant the same thing on a basis of common spiritual metaphysics, that what Teilhard calls the "Soul of the World" and Sri Aurobindo "Supermind" is already in matter in an embryonic form (pp. 60-61)? Again, he brings Teilhardism and the Gītā into a common focus when he writes: "Christ, because he is both God and man, is the Centre to which all human 'centres,' human 'selves' or 'parts of God,' as the Gītā (15.7) puts it, must look" (p. 60). To make the human self a part of God instead of a created entity is to assimilate pantheism into one's philosophy, as does the Gītā as well as Sri Aurobindo. Expounding the latter's view on the divisive "ego" born of ignorance and preventing us "from seeing the whole universe as an interconnected and harmonious whole centred through the channel of Supermind onto the undivided Trinity from which it proceeds," Zaehner rounds off with the words: "Original Ignorance or original sin consists in identifying oneself with the body and mind rather than with the immortal 'person' which is eternal and a 'part' of God as the Gītā (15.7) puts it" (pp. 39-40). The Gītā is quite in place in relation to Sri Aurobindo: if it is deemed equally in place in reference to Teilhard, Teilhardism is certainly unfrocked of its Jesuit priesthood and given an Aurobindonian garb.

In my opinion, in the last analysis, Zaehner is right in regarding pantheism as an ingredient of Teilhard's worldview. But the way in which he shows him to be a pantheist is an oversimplification. Teilhard could never really reject the label *pantheism* for his own religion, but he tried hard to distinguish false from true pantheism and called himself a Christian pantheist as opposed to a pagan one. Zaehner explains what pagan pantheism is in Teilhard's eyes: "The vision of the inter-connectedness of all things in matter which does away with all that is conscious and personal, sacrificing it all to 'the rudimentary and diffused modes of being' characteristic of emergent life" (p. 20). A serious complication in this context is that *paganism* is a term, as Zaehner tells us, "by which Teilhard means Hinduism and Buddhism as well as nature mysticism in general" (p. 18). I shall touch on the complication later. At the moment I am concerned only with Teilhard's notion of non-Christian pantheism — namely, in Zaehner's words, the merging back "into the diffused state of primal matter, a state in which neither self-consciousness nor conscience has yet appeared" (pp. 18-19). While referring to Hinduism and Buddhism, as envisaged by Teilhard, in terms of pagan pantheism, Zaehner informs us of what Teilhard saw to be their revelation: "It is not a broadening of consciousness directed towards a universal Centre which is for him the cosmic Christ but a merging and dissipation of the infant ego into the unconscious matter from which it had so laboriously evolved. It is essentially retrograde and the enemy of all progress" (p. 18). How then can a revelation leading definitely away from the universal Center that is the Cosmic Christ be considered by Teilhard the sole possible beginning of a movement converging onto a personal Center that is God? Surely Zaehner has tripped up here and landed in self-contradiction.

The cause of the mischance is Zaehner's idea that for Teilhard *cosmic consciousness* (or its equivalent, *cosmic sense*) and *pantheism* are interchangeable terms. So far as explicit statement is concerned, the exact opposite is the case. Teilhard uses several expressions in treating the theme. *Cosmic mind* is one of them, and he has the phrase "the cosmic mind (of which the pantheist mind is *only one particular form*)."[1] He goes on to say that, facing the plurality of things,

> the cosmic mind (which enjoys a cosmic vision) is primarily aware of *their common basis*. This basis seems to it to become continuously more luminous, real and individual—so much so that the particular determinations of concrete things tend to interest the soul less and less, as though they were dissolving into a higher entity. This transformation (or manifestation) of the universal stuff of the world, we should note, is an experienced psychological fact; in other words, it is an intuition, pre-intellectual in order and is not the fruit of a chain of reasoning. It is basically, therefore, beyond the reach of criticism: *it exists*. However, when we try to explain this—when the man who has that intuition tries to interpret and rationalize his feelings—we find ourselves at a loss. However the explanation may be expressed, it is generally wrong because the terms it uses are pantheist. In the language of pantheism the "universal element" we glimpse is sought for in the direction of matter, or is, at least, conceived by *analogy with matter*.

In another place Teilhard observes: "Thus there develops in souls that have an unusual capacity for this special intuition a specifically characteristic psychic state—'cosmic consciousness. . . .' The pantheist universal element. . .does not meet the demands of cosmic consciousness, even though it is nevertheless presented as alone capable of satisfying its desires" (pp. 22-23). In this context, too, he concludes: "Pantheism cannot satisfy a truly cosmic mind."

Thus, just because "Teilhard himself admits that only a greater diffusion of the 'cosmic sense' can point the way to the cosmic Christ whom he sees at the end of our heavenward journey" (p. 6), Zaehner is not justified in dubbing Teilhard an open pantheist. And his mistake seems to have arisen from his own uncertain understanding of "cosmic consciousness." On the one hand, besides describing it in the words I have already cited, he quotes Bucke as saying: "Cosmic consciousness shows the cosmos to consist not of dead matter governed by unconscious, rigid, and unintending law; it shows it on the contrary as entirely immaterial, entirely spiritual and entirely alive; it shows that death is an absurdity, that everyone and every-thing has eternal life" (p. 5). And he also says: "What the mystic experiences in cosmic consciousness transcends time—he sees all things in one all-comprehensive sweep, in eternity, as God sees them" (p. 8). Then he makes the criticism that cosmic consciousness bypasses the problem of evil, since for this consciousness—to quote Bucke again—no evil ever did or ever will enter the universe. "For the mystic," Zaehner tells us, "the Absolute transcends all opposites; and it must therefore transcend good and evil too, fusing and unifying them in a higher synthesis" (p. 291). The bypassing of evil is done "either by writing it off as illusory or at most an appearance, as with Śankara, or by subsuming it and 'negating' it into that all-comprehensiveness which cosmic consciousness reveals" (p. 8). From this notice of what he calls "the great defect of mysticism" (p. 8), Zaehner proceeds to assert that cosmic consciousness destroys the distinction between good and evil because this consciousness is "the reflexion of the totality of matter within us" (p. 51). Thus, Bucke's experience of the entirely immaterial, spiritual, and alive is turned into its antipodes. What is still more alarming, Zaehner attributes to the Upanishads and to Sri Aurobindo the view that to have the cosmic consciousness is "to merge back into the diffused state of primal matter" (pp. 51, 18-19), and he declares that "for the man who is merged in cosmic consciousness, in Brahman, good and evil no longer have any meaning," so that he is free to do anything, "for matter is not concerned with morals" (p. 21). Quite a tangled skein exists here. The immediate thread that one has to catch is that the cosmic consciousness that transcends good and evil in a higher synthesis is identified with the state of matter in which, because "neither self-consciousness nor conscience has yet appeared," "there is no sense of good and evil" (p. 19). So this consciousness is made to coincide with pantheism as Teilhard conceives it — a seeking of the "universal element" in "the direction of matter."

An additional inducement to paint Teilhard as an open pantheist is found in his bipolar attitude to matter, and Zaehner appears to have succumbed to the snare. For Teilhard does not stop with telling us how — prompted by "the cosmic awakening" — he yielded to the enchantment of matter "in its most simple and unevolved state," "tried to extend myself throughout the universe — boundlessly and without discernment," but found "that the light of life was being darkened within me" (pp. 20-22). He goes beyond the conclusion of his experiment: "To grow in the truth we must travel with our backs turned to matter and not try to make contact with it once more so as to merge into it" (p. 22). Being too much in love with matter to look down on it altogether, Teilhard, as Zaehner observes, shows "with astonishing power in his little parable entitled *The Spiritual Power of Matter*" how worship of matter can "be pressed into the service of the new evolutionary mysticism which he calls the 'mysticism of the West' " (p. 21). By employing a new approach to matter — an approach that at once grapples with it and gives way to it and draws upon its forces — Teilhard discovered a secret living intensity in its depths: "A Being was taking shape in the totality of space, a Being with the attractive power of a soul, palpable like a body, vast as the sky; a Being which mingled with things yet remained distinct from them; a Being of a higher order than the substance of things with which it was adorned, yet taking shape within them."[2] Zaehner (pp. 22-23), though not unaware of the change involved, is still disposed to see a play of the "cosmic sense," and consequently of pantheism, as a stepping-stone to the Cosmic Christ when Teilhard says in "The Spiritual Power of Matter": "Son of man, bathe yourself in Matter. Dive into it where it is at its most violent and deep. Struggle in its current and drink of its waves. It is she who cradled you when you were yet unconscious; and it is she who will carry you right up to God."[3]

Unlike his careful and perspicacious self in several parts of his book, Zaehner in this context is rather badly mixed-up. However, the impetus to such a condition must be traced to a subtle ambivalence in Teilhard himself.

ii

Intellectually, Teilhard defined non-Christian pantheism in the most pejorative style and thus could not but condemn it. Yet his whole nature, with its innate pantheistic trend, felt a rich and exalted impulse in the heart of pantheists. In 1916 he wrote to Père Victor Fontoynont: "I shall put the intoxication of pagan pantheism to a Christian use."[4] And he connected this intoxication with the question most prominent in his mind: "Cannot *the object, the actual matter* of our human passions be transformed, transformed into the Absolute, the definitive, the divine?" In the same letter he expressed his " 'cosmic' aspiration": "I should like to be able to love Christ passionately (by loving) *in the very act of loving the universe*. Is it a wild dream or a blasphemy? Besides communion with God and communion with the Earth, is there communion with God through the Earth — the Earth becoming like a great Host in which God would be contained for us?"[5] The urge to such love would be "a blasphemy" only if it were pantheistic. And yet this pantheism would seem to lie at the very root of Teilhard. And in unguarded moments it sprouts up into the open, as in the declaration: "I love the universe too dearly not to have confidence in it."[6] A packed pantheistic confessio fidei is here. Not only to love but also to have confidence in the object of the love can mean just one thing: the universe in its true aspect is, to Teilhard, an infinite Being that is loving and lovable at the same time. The declaration is pregnant with Wordsworth's "nature-mysticism" in the Tintern Abbey poem, his pantheism

> Knowing that Nature never did betray
> The heart that loved her,
>
> (Lines 122-123)

and that she can so "inform the mind that is within us" that, in spite of every appearance of adverse circumstance, nothing

> Shall e'er prevail against us, or disturb
> Our cheerful faith, that all which we behold
> Is full of blessings.
>
> (Lines 132-134)

And in connection with Wordsworth one may draw upon a letter of Teilhard's to Léontine Zanta: "I have often told you: the secret of having peace and never getting stifled (even in the worst commonplace circumstances) lies in managing, with God's help, to perceive the One Element Needful which circulates in all things, which can give itself to us (with its joy and freedom) through any object provided that object is brought before us by *fidelity* to life, and that it is transformed by *faith* in the divine presence and operation."[7] This is not what may be termed pure pantheism: God is there in addition to "the One Element Needful which circulates in all things," but that Universal Element is capable of response and is full of joy and freedom; it is a spirit of world life continuous with the divine presence and operation. It is as though God himself were concretely projected into nature and meeting man through any object if the human approach is confident and consecrated. This Element recalls the Wordsworthian experience in the Tintern Abbey poem:

> And I have felt
> A presence that disturbs me with the joy
> Of elevated thoughts; a sense sublime
> Of something far more deeply interfused,. . .
> A motion and a spirit, that impels
> All thinking things, all objects of all thoughts,
> And rolls through all things.
>
> (Lines 93-96, 100-2)

Teilhard, even in his guarded moments, let out, time and again, his sense of the spiritual fervor inseparable from pantheism. Thus, he put the question: "Has any evolutionist pantheism, in fact, ever spoken more magnificently of the Whole than St. Paul did in the words he addressed to the first Christians?"[8] The intention toward the pantheist is negative, but a positive stir to his mighty enthusiasm and eloquence about the All comes through. Once more, when Teilhard wrote against false pantheism's aspiring to "a centre of intellectual dissociation" and "of unconsciousness," he said: "The danger of false pantheism has been removed, and yet we retain the irreplaceable strength of the religious life that the pantheists unjustly claim as their own."[9] How could pantheists claim anything so necessary to genuine religion if they were impelled to become intellectually dissociated and grow unconscious? The very idea is absurd, and at the back of it there is a cleavage between Teilhard's mental figuration of pantheism and his inner feeling of its authentic, precious, spiritual drive. Again, there is the unacknowledged sympathetic note, a sort of admiring shudder of joy, in: "Many non-Christian mystics have not hesitated, trusting to their desires and natural predilection, to cast themselves into the delectable abyss of belief in a soul of the world."[10] At another place too one finds a deep-seated appreciative response: it passes through his vision of the world's end in the pleroma of Christ: "Like a vast tide, Being will have engulfed the shifting sands of beings. Within a now tranquil ocean each drop of which, nevertheless, will be conscious of remaining itself, the astonishing adventure of the world will have ended. The dream of every mystic, the eternal pantheistic ideal, will have found their full and legitimate satisfaction."[11] Even in clear conceptual language the intuition of the true character of pantheism shines forth: "Throughout history wherever man (either in isolated cases or collectively) has effected a sufficiently deep breakthrough into the domain of religious forces (whether among the Vedantists, the Taoists, the Sufis or the Christians)—in each case he has felt that he is drifting towards a mysticism of the monist or pantheist type."[12] Doubtless, Teilhard follows up with a sharp distinction between the pantheism to be rejected and the one to be accepted, but his sweeping testimony, that the ne plus ultra of religious realization has to be pantheism of some kind or other, makes one question whether the two pantheisms that he has diametrically opposed are not, after all, complementary rather than contradictory. And the very sweepingness of the testimony carries an undertone as of rejoicing in an unescapable single thing, whatever its form.

Evidently, quite unlike the whole mass of Catholic thinkers, Teilhard had no wish to disclaim pantheism in general, and it was still so when he spoke à la Blondel of pan-Christism and used such expressions as: "Christ is loved as a person; he compels recognition as a world."[13] "No one, I think, will understand the great mystics, St. Francis and Blessed Angela, and the others, unless he understands the full depth of the truth that *Jesus must be loved as a world*."[14] "Lord Jesus,. . .I love you as a world, as *this* world which has captivated my heart and it is you, I now realise, that my brother-men, even those who do not believe, sense and seek throughout the magic immensities of the cosmos."[15]

In the passage about the world's end in the Cosmic Christ's pleroma, there is even the classic pantheistic metaphor: God is an infinite ocean and individual souls are the innumerable drops of it. It is the metaphor that Teilhard elsewhere employed disparagingly:

"Many a system of pantheism has led us astray in the cult of a great All in which individuals were supposed to be merged like a drop in the ocean."[16] He refers again unfavorably to these systems with practically the same metaphor when, regretting the common neglect of nonunderstanding of what he terms *cosmic sense*, he adds: "Or else, among those who appreciate and foster it, its promptings are interpreted. . .as an invitation to anonymous dissolution in the cosmic ocean."[17] But now, in this passage, Teilhard approvingly sees everything as one element, an essential homogeneity of substance: God is All and All is God — the typical pantheistic experience.

Of course, Teilhard would play down the sameness of the metaphor and speak, as he actually does, of "making a distinction between two entirely opposite sorts of union: union by dissolution and union by differentiation."[18] Surely, there are two sorts of union, yet to talk of dissolution by union is fairly meaningless. How can anyone experience a union by getting dissolved and growing anonymous? Can any sane mystic desire to do what Teilhard imagines him as doing? If "anonymous dissolution" of any kind is desired, why not just kill oneself as painlessly as possible, effect a euthanasia, in the hope of ceasing to exist? Really, what is desired is, on the negative side, a forgetfulness of the feverish little self in some universal vastness; on the positive side, the longed-for state is the realization of a self of selves that is not individual but cosmic. It is never "anonymous dissolution" that is sought but the "cosmic ocean" itself. The former is a misleading label for a psychological act by which one desires to *be* that ocean or at least to get enveloped concretely by it, penetrated by it so that one is not bound to one's all-too-human personality. Nothing except this was basically in the mind of Spinoza, whom de Lubac sets in direct opposition to Teilhard, saying: "Spinoza, that supreme pantheist, who dreamt of 'absorption in the immense calm in which is swallowed up all personality.' "[19] In pantheism the drops that are conscious individuals join a sea of consciousness, where their small limited being finds liberation in an immensity whose constituent stuff is the same as their own, namely, water. In other words, water limited loses its boundaries and partakes of a water infinity. Water does not cease to be water; from its confinement in drops it only enters into a vast wateriness that is the true Being of its being. What is lost is "drophood" — what the Upanishads designate "name and form."

There is no dissolution at all: there is an infinitization of the essence. There would be dissolution if one were to be absorbed into something that is "other" than one: in pantheism there is no ultimate "other": the cosmic ocean is the full final Self of each drop: each drop realizes there its own plenitude. There is, for pantheism, merely the Single multiplied or diversified, merely the Universal particularized. And in the so-called dissolution, the multiple or diverse attains its own Singleness; the particular becomes conscious of its own Universality.

Here a pertinent question is: Even in being Single and Universal, can the multiple and particular keep a sense of multiplicity and particularity? When Teilhard, contrary to his usual practice, describes his own summum bonum in terms of the "tranquil ocean" and "each drop," the only difference that he suggests between "the eternal pantheistic ideal" and the "full and legitimate satisfaction" offered for it by his summum bonum, is related to this question. It amounts to: "Each drop will be conscious of remaining itself" within the "tranquil ocean" of the One Being. And naturally, since the drops are consummated "persons" — souls conscious of themselves and interiorly centered to perfection — the ocean must be an infinite self-aware Center, a Superperson. This is to say that the Center of centers must be at the same time immanent and transcendent, cosmic and personal, uniform within all and yet distinct in its own right, essentially identical but having also a relationship of the One to the Many, simultaneously the single Self of all and their divine Lord.

All this is precisely what, according to the quotations from Zaehner, the spirituality, in its fullness, of the Indian Upanishads and the Integral Yoga of Sri Aurobindo aim at, and they do so without excluding pantheism from their vision and their discipline. In another place Zaehner makes the same point, expounding Sri Aurobindo and Indian spirituality together:

> How. . .is the human race to emerge from "this perpetual cycle of failure?"* In *The Life Divine* Aurobindo sees the solution in a descent of "Supermind" which will reveal to the world that it has a common soul, present and the same in all but differentiated in each. . . .
> . . .Each individual realizes that he is not an independent ego

---

* Sri Aurobindo, *The Human Cycle*, p. 272, n. 1.

acting of his own free will, but an interdependent person deriving his personality from God, wholly indwelt by God, possessed of his eternal Being, his eternal Consciousness, and his eternal Joy, and through this "sameness" of nature which all beings derive from God, at one with all created things, and so acting and knowing that he acts not on his own account but entirely in accordance with the will of God. But before this stage can be reached the ego must be destroyed;. . .we must depersonalize ourselves, give up self as the Buddhists are bidden to do and enter the timeless bliss of Nirvāna,. . ."isolated" and "unconditioned" as are the *purushas* of the Sānkhya-Yoga. . .But, as Aurobindo points out again and again, this is not the end as Sankara had supposed, identifying the "oneness" of each "part" of God with the totality of God himself: for this is to realize Being only, beyond Becoming. God, however, is not just a static monad but a *living* and therefore dynamic reality: for does not the Iśa Upanishad (5) say:

It moves. It does not move.
It is far, yet it is near.
It is within this whole universe,
And yet it is without it.

To attain to Nirvāna is to become Brahman, to pass beyond space and time into an unconditioned form of existence. From this vantage-point the Yogin sees his "self in all things standing, all things in the self: the same in everything he sees."* But one must then go on to the further realization that this interconnectedness, though deriving from the same impersonal One, nevertheless does not mean complete identity of absorption, but leads on to the discovery of a new relationship with a personal God on whom the impersonal Absolute itself depends.

Who, standing firm on unity communes in love with me as abiding in all beings, in whatever state he be, that integrated man abides in me.**
So says the Gītā, and, as Aurobindo points out, this depersonalizing process, this loss of all sense of self in the still waters of eternity in which all passion is quenched, love quite as much as hate — this depersonalizing process is only the necessary prelude to the resurrection in God and for God in love. (pp. 31, 40-41)

If pantheism can be included in a spiritual outlook and practice, without its shutting off the transcendent Personal Divine and the

*Bhagavad Gītā, 6.29.
** *Ibid.*, 6.31.

persistent human soul in relation with him, why does Teilhard shy away from it? He should be the last person to disavow it. His entire nature moves toward "a mysticism of the monist or pantheist type," not only by inner instinct but also by his modern evolutionism. This evolutionism, taking the universe as one immense developing entity, is seen by Teilhard to be, in its religious mood, pantheistic. What he has himself tried to do is to interpret this evolutionism in Christian terms so that a Christ whose attributes are made proportionate to the dimensions now attributed to the universe "takes over, correcting and completing them, the energies that undoubtedly lie hidden in modern forms of pantheism."[20] In short, a universal or cosmic Christ is necessarily posited: "To 'universalise' Christ is the only way we have of retaining his essential attributes (alpha and omega) in a fantastically enlarged Creation."[21] And Teilhard, eager to seize the truth, which he thinks pantheism seeks but distorts, concludes: "If Christianity is to keep its place at the head of mankind, it must make itself explicitly recognisable as a sort of 'pan-Christism.' "[22] In other words, Christianity must become a new, a true pantheism, agreeing with yet differing from "modern forms" of the doctrine in one central point: Christ must be as concretely universal as the God of pantheism, but "in taking on universality, Christ is not lost in the heart of the universe:. . .he dominates and assimilates the universe by imposing upon it the. . .essential characteristics of his traditional truth."[23]

I need not go into the details of Christ's "traditional truth." My concern is crucially with that in Teilhardism that is *pan* on the one hand, *Christ* on the other. *Christ* stands for the God who is personal, *pan* for the God who is universal.

And the question of questions is: In making the two coincide, can Teilhard escape making the universe and the human soul fundamentally one substance with his Universal Person?

Repeatedly, by envisaging the coincidence of the two, he is led into undeniable pantheistic language. Every reader of Teilhard is likely to notice the phenomenon. Some may do it rather cautiously, seeing it in terms of either careless thinking or linguistic disproportion, but the upshot is the same. Thus de Lubac admits: "We believe, as Père Rabut does, that the elliptical form and the emphasis of some of Père Teilhard's expressions would seem to suggest a sort of natural identity of Christ and the Universe."[24] To quote de Lubac again, "In 'Comment je crois' (1934), p. 21, we may note, as an example of awkward or over-condensed expression, the phrase 'the world, around me, becomes divine.' "[25] And one does not find pantheistic language only in locutions such as "To this faith, Jesus, I hold. . . that you do more than stand apart from things as their Master, you are more than the incommunicable splendour of the universe; you are, too, the dominating influence that penetrates us, and draws us, through the inmost core of our most imperative and most deep-rooted desires; you are the cosmic Being who envelops us and fulfills us in the perfection of his Unity."[26] Or else the sentences: "The world is still being created, and it is Christ who is reaching his fulfillment in it. When I had heard and understood that saying, I looked around and I saw, as though in an ecstasy, that *through Nature I was immersed in God.*"[27] Or again the phrases: "The saint. . .loses his materiality. Everything is God for him, God is everything for him, and for him Christ is at once God and everything."[28] One discovers pantheistic language also in formulations like the following: "We twentieth-century humans are, indeed, scientifically speaking, nothing but the elements of a soul seeking itself through the cosmos."[29] Perhaps an example extremely apt to the theme of Teilhard's "tranquil ocean" whose "drops" remain themselves is to be found in the passage in which he says that men are called one day to become, without being lost in it, "one and the same someone."[30] Here is a turn of language that, free from any resorting to metaphor on the part of Teilhard, plainly voices an aspect of Vedantic pantheism. To bring out the full content of his cosmically mystic Christianity, Teilhard must use words that, if they are to have a real meaning and not be vain mouthings, accord with that aspect. Pan-Christism constantly passes into and out of pantheism and makes this accord for a moment every now and then.

Such merging and separating was inevitable by the very nature of Teilhard's personality. He was "by temperament a pantheist"; "the pantheist's yearnings" were "native" to him.[31] He openly admitted his "own profound tendencies towards pantheism";[32] he even declared: "I believe that I was born with a 'naturally pantheist' soul."[33] And the preoccupation of his life may be discerned in his statement: "The pantheist tendency is so universal and so persistent that it must have in it a soul of naturally Christian truth that we must baptise."[34] Can a born pantheist ever cease to be so? He may become something more, he may find a greater vision in which

pantheism—that is, the vision of the universe as God's own being
under a multitudinous spatiotemporal aspect through which we
have to pierce to the eternal reality—may be taken up as one
element in the midst of many, but he cannot become something that
essentially alters the pantheistic vision, diminishes it by means of a
vision running counter to it. If by some need discovered in himself
he accepts a vision that he cannot reconcile with his native
pantheism, and if he tries to give different meanings to pantheistic
terms such as *the All, Universal Element, Soul of the World* and
Cosmic Consciousness, he will never succeed in being consistent.
The different meanings will somehow fall short of his innate understanding of the terms, and to keep the terms alive and packed with
the fullest significance possible he will be driven to exceed the limits
set to the formulas under which others, whose temperament is not
pantheistic, approach the "truth," with which those different
meanings attempt to accord. In carrying out his self-appointed
mission to "baptize," to Christianize, the reality toward which the
universal and persistent attraction to pantheism moves, he is bound
again and again to pantheize the baptizing and Christianizing
mood. The Christology of one whose urge toward pantheism is
profound can never be the same as that of a Christian who has no
such urge: the two Christologies must be fundamentally at variance.
The Christian may see the necessity of widening his traditional
evolution. He may say, as does Olivier Rabut, about Teilhard's
cosmic Christology: "We can distinguish some extremely sound
seminal intuitions that can introduce new vigour into Christian
thought."[35] But, like Rabut, he will be obliged to add: "There is no
doubt on some important points Teilhard needs to be completed
. . . .Sometimes the vocabulary is ambiguous, some expressions are
unfortunate, and sometimes the development is insufficient."[36] Or
he may echo de Lubac:

> The least. . . we can do is to recognize that he will have done more
> than any other man of our time to open up a vast field of
> inquiry for theologians, and that they must make it their
> business to apply themselves to it. It is hardly to be wondered
> at that we can find some indecision in his writings, or things
> that are awkwardly expressed, or some lack of precision in his
> thought, or some verbal inconsistencies. He raised problems of
> great importance that urgently needed to be attacked but that
> he could not by himself solve completely. He opened up some

wide avenues of research. He brought out a capital idea, the analysis of which he could not by himself carry further.[37]

Yes, broad and enlightened but basically noninnovative minds like Rabut's and de Lubac's will always know where they stand. In doctrinal matters they will not be ambiguous in vocabulary, unfortunate in expression, insufficient in development. Their writings will not be indecisive, their thought imprecise, their words awkward or inconsistent. But Teilhard simply could not help any of these things. By whatever standard, he was mentally head and shoulders above every one of his Christian commentators, highly gifted and finely acute though several of them are. It is absurd to suggest that in some respects Teilhard was inadequately equipped in intellect to deal with the issues he raised or that he was not master enough of the proper language to tackle them. The faults found in him — conflicts of idea, contradictions of speech — were due only to the fact that the pantheism born with him was sought to be suppressed by the considerably strong and wholly sincere call in him to be a Roman Catholic, but could not be quite put down: it kept surging up ever and anon. It refused to let Pan-Christism suffice in the shape Teilhard tried to give it; it merged Pan-Christism, time and again, with a non-Christian cosmic sense. Occasionally, it even showed clearly its own face and urged him toward a greater synthesis. At times he appeared to recognize the real features and gazed vaguely beyond both pantheism and Catholic Christianity.

iii

Nothing else than the inner pantheistic pressure is responsible for those traits in Teilhard's system which Christopher Mooney, an admiring fellow Jesuit of a caliber equal to Rabut and de Lubac, is inclined to criticize.

First of all, there is Teilhard's "uncompromising 'evolutionism,' "[38] I have already pointed out the fact that he bases everything on physics — the physics of the universe as a single evolutionary process. The same point occurs in the declaration that, while affirming

Christianity, gives primacy to the sense of this process: "An apologetic based on evolution yet whose spirit seems to be to be truly and equally Christian."[39] To hold that "an evolutionary world-view is the *only* world-view, the sole framework, the sole mode of approach to reality, the sole criterion for solving all problems, whether scientific, philosophical, theological or sprititual,"[40] carries in its deepest attitude overtones that Teilhard indicated when he referred to "our generation, essentially pantheist because evolutionist."[41] It is not in the temper of Christianity to insist, as Mooney finds Teilhard doing: "That others must continue to work within the same evolutionary framework, this was a fact beyond discussion."[42]

The pantheistic pressure may be discerned also in the way in which Teilhard's evolutionism went against his Christian conception of the human person. In pantheism, although the individual is not neglected or denied, he is not made too much of: it is the whole that is primarily important. or, rather, the individual in his true ultimate being, his basic whole self, his universal selfhood, is stressed. Now, Teilhard's often vaunted spirituality of the personal unit lacks, according to Mooney, the real Christian attitude. Mooney explains:

> A constant emphasis on the destiny of the human race as a whole risks losing sight of the supreme importance which each individual possesses in his own right. God's plan for mankind does not subordinate the person to the species. . . .Even love energy . . .tends in [Teilhard's] system to be treated exclusively in the context of its function for the species. This fact is most evident in regard to personal sin, whose central character as a refusal of love is never explicitly treated at all. In the end, therefore, Teilhard's strong emphasis on the role of the human person involves an ironic tendency towards the impersonal, and this must be recognized as a real danger in his evolutionary system of thought.[43]

Actuated by the pantheistic pressure again is "his key-concept of Christ as physical Center." This concept "tends to distract one's attention from the fact that Christ gives meaning to evolution not through his passive physical omnipresence but primarily through the exercise of his freedom and love. This is in no way denied by Teilhard. . . .Nevertheless, the strong dichotomy he sets up between the physical and the juridical in Christology somehow manages to throw into the shade an all-important third element, the personal initiative of Christ."[44] Similarly, reparation for sin through the relationship of love between persons is ignored and is absorbed into a cosmic mystery of redemption, the forward-moving evolutionary building up of the universal Body of Christ: "We must recognize that in Teilhard's treatment of the Body of Christ as a living organism, there is present once again that strange inclination towards the necessary and the impersonal."[45] Teilhard admits as much "when he says that by 'progress' he means not that man is becoming morally better but that as a species he is moving towards a higher state of complexity and consciousness."[46]

The "series of equal terms" that Teilhard formulates — "cosmogenesis-biogenesis-individual anthropogenesis-collective anthropogenesis-Christogenesis" — shows further the pantheistic pressure. It tends to render evolution an intrinsically natural and unavoidable movement. The risk here to Christianity "consists in the fact that [Teilhard's] explanations so emphasise the immanence of the divine action in the evolutionary process itself that a *sense* of transcendence gets lost, even though the concept of transcendence itself is never absent."[47] A case in point is his approach to the mystery of the Cross and to personal sin: both appear in his system "as something understandable, made inevitable, in a certain sense, by a world undergoing *genèse*."[48]

Mooney then drives his point home from another direction:

> A lack of this sense of transcendence may also be seen in Teilhard's unqualified insistence on the "Christian" commitment, and consequently the Church's commitment, to human values. . . . It is dangerous to state categorically that for the Christian it is "a matter of life and death that the earth should flourish to the uttermost of its natural powers." Neither the Christian nor the Church can conceive their mission chiefly in terms of fostering evolution, even when this is seen to be growth in spirit and personal fulfilment in the realm of knowledge and love. . . .Teilhard's desire to give a sacred character to all things profane without exception is a natural expression of his own mystical bent, as well as an understandable reaction against the severe dichotomy he encountered between sacred and profane in the lives of many Christians. Yet such a desire also involves risk, since its instinctive tendency is to suppress altogether a distinction which must never be too far from the Christian consciousness.[49]

The mystical bent that Mooney regards as typically Teilhardian is best described as evolutionist pantheism. This kind of pantheism has a special shade to it and its penchant is more to seize God's eternal cosmic reality within his multitudinous spatiotemporal aspect than to pierce through this aspect to that reality. But the ultimate identity of the two remains the basic datum. Such a datum falls outside Christianity. That this should be so was a misfortune for Teilhard and occasioned the conflicts of ideas and the contradictions of speech that no student of him can miss. The underlying and sometimes even emergent push in him is toward their resolution. But, failing to move definitely beyond pantheism and Catholic Christianity alike, he exhibits no proper sign of achieving it.

Perhaps the most curious complication into which Teilhard was driven by his divided spiritual vision is one touched on by Zaehner when he gives us a glimpse of Teilhard's tussle with the dogma of God's creation of the world out of nothing, *ex nihilo* (pp. 55-56). De Lubac also deals with the subject and briefly reviews Teilhard's several efforts to be himself and yet be accounted orthodox. After looking at his last effort, de Lubac ends on a note of satisfaction, saying: "Since he so explicitly rejects any idea of a 'pre-existing substratum,' we cannot say that he rejects or compromises creation *ex nihilo*, even in this last form of his speculation on the matter."[50] How premature really de Lubac's satisfaction is can be gathered at once from his own next sentence, which runs: "We must, nevertheless, admit that he did not achieve a perfectly clear and coherent formulation of his thought."

De Lubac attempts to provide an excuse: "It may be—in fact there can be no doubt about it—that he started by trying to unite everything in a synthesis that was too simplified and too what one might call physically attainable." The words are not particularly transparent, but the fact that Teilhard was doing something quite new and not following the orthodox theological line does come through. No doubt, the line of orthodox theology is itself hardly a matter of concrete comprehension. As Zaehner tells us: "Even the theologians are not very clear as to what creation *ex nihilo* means" (p. 55). But there is a core of the dogma that, if accepted uncompromisingly and without any reservations, would make for the clarity and coherence that de Lubac misses in Teilhard and that can be found in the orthodox line for all the difficulty in concrete comprehension that the latter entails. De Lubac pinpoints the core: there should be no pre-existing substratum for God to work upon. And the questions crucial to this discussion are: When Teilhard subscribes to this core, does he do so uncompromisingly and without any reservations? If he means the same thing as does orthodoxy, why is his thought not formulated with perfect clarity and coherence? Could it be that the "nothing" that he accepts has a meaning that refuses to fall in step with the orthodox theological one?

The clue to a proper understanding here occurs in the words of Teilhard quoted by Zaehner: "to be infinitely divided. . . .is to tend towards nothingness" (p. 56). What Teilhard offers is not nothingness itself but what he conceives to be an approximation, a tending to it. He knows this very well, but he would like somehow to identify the two. The process of the identification is clearly revealed in the same essay on which Zaehner has drawn. Teilhard writes: "If, along the lines of its essential capacities and natural 'planes of cleavage,' the stuff of things were to become infinitely loose-textured, infinitely dissociated, it would be as though it had ceased to exist. Dissolved in non-activity and non-reaction, it would be indistinguishable from nothingness; it would be tantamount to, and so identical with, nothingness."[51] There is a progressive slide of sophistry: from "as though" to "indistinguishable," and then, through "tantamount," to "identical." What Teilhard has actually done is not at all to posit nothingness as such but to essay a new definition of it and put a positive content into what should be an absolute negative. What he says soon after makes no attempt to camouflage this legerdemain: "No-being coincides, and is one, with completely realised plurality. Pure nothingness is an empty concept, a pseudo-idea. True nothingness, physical nothingness, the nothingness found on the threshold of being, that on which at their lowest levels, all possible worlds converge, is pure Multiple, is Multitude."[52]

Orthodox theology is left miles behind. "Pure nothingness" is the demand of that theology. Teilhard rejects it as a pseudo idea and consequently throws orthodoxy to the winds, as may be confirmed from the sour remark of his ecclesiastical editors at this point: "This questionable proposition is to be found in Bergson, too."[53] What Teilhard puts in the place of orthodoxy's concept is a pseudo-nothingness.

And this unorthodox redefinition is necessary because his notion of creation is "slanted" in a particular way. Zaehner quotes him: "To create, as it appears to me, means to condense, concentrate, organize, unite" (p. 56). So the nothingness preceding creation has

to be a Teilhardianly creatable nothingness: it has totally to lack
unity and represent "completely realised plurality." But as it must
have the potentiality of being united, it has to be the pure multiple
that is also the pure unifiable. And this double character argues all
the more for some species of substratum, be it ever so phantasmal.
Can there be—to use one of Teilhard's favorite terms—*creative
union*, can there be a creativity on God's part bringing about
synthesis on greater synthesis in the evolutionary process, without a
subject (as the Scholastics would phrase it) already existing in a state
of dissociation capable of progressive unification?

The essential import of Teilhard's redefinition glares out still
more when, after saying that the initial "negative" that precedes
creation is "in its real form. . .pure Multiple," he calls this negative
"a sort of positive nonbeing"[54] and adds from the orthodox angle
that such a concept "raises grave difficulties."[55] The reason is:
"However closely tied to non-being we may suppose it to be, the
Thing, dissociated by its nature, required for the operation of
creative union, implies that the creator found outside himself a
purchase-point, or at least a reaction."[56] But Teilhard accepts the
difficulties as unavoidable, since the traditional explanations would
be "purely *verbal*."[57] Piqued by this jibe at orthodoxy, the editors
again sourly remark: "A metaphysician would comment that it is
more the expression 'positive non-being' that is a 'purely verbal
explanation.' "[58] Thus Teilhard's unorthodoxy characterizes his
nothingness to be such that God's creativity is not altogether unconditioned. it is unconditioned inasmuch as God may or may not
create, but when he chooses to create he can do so only from
nothingness of a particular kind that would give him some response
if not even a leverage. Without this kind of nothingness, no creation
will result. From orthodoxy's nothing, which is pure and undefined,
nothing can be made; creation, as understood by Teilhard, cannot
occur at all. That is inevitably his basic stand, holding as he does
that the history of the created world is one of an increasingly
complex synthesis of divided materials.

Zaehner rightly notes that Teilhard's "account. . .tries to square
evolution with Genesis rather than the dogmatic creation *ex nihilo*."
For the first chapter of Genesis speaks of "a formless void" and of
there being "darkness over the deep" and finally it says: "God's spirit

hovered over the water" (p. 55). Zaehner glosses the term *water*: "Water, the symbol of the ever-moving, the unstable, perpetually changing thing which is chaos—matter in its most embryonic and, if you like, its most non-existent form." Matter, therefore, is implicit in the Teilhardian picture of creation. Matter existing in a chaotic state is what Teilhard means when, in a visual phrase, he writes (as cited by Zaehner): "For all eternity God saw the shadow of his unity in a diffused state of disarray (*éparpillée*) beneath his feet" (p. 56).

Teilhard shows an aversion to accepting matter "at the beginning of things," and de Lubac is willing to take him at his word and approvingly quotes him: "Where there is a complete disunity of the cosmic stuff (at an infinite distance from Omega) there is *nothing*."[59] De Lubac, like Teilhard himself, seems to be either unaware of or else determined to slur over the self-contradiction in the sentence. In the very act of affirming *"nothing"* Teilhard affirms "the cosmic stuff," even if in "complete disunity"! Indeed, one cannot give nothingness a certain specific nature as distinguished from all other natures and at the same time take it to be the sheer absence of all existence, all "cosmic stuff," and therefore that which has no kind of nature at all.

De Lubac tries to escape this conclusion by arguing: "Before there is any unification we can speak only of the negative. Pure multiple must be thought of as a pure 'potentiality of dispersion' and creation would consist in 'reversing' this."[60] My comment must be that here is word-jugglery. One may legitimately talk of nothingness as a pure potentiality, but to talk of a pure potentiality of *dispersion* is to introduce a positive content. It already amounts to qualifying *nothingness*, particularizing it, giving it a certain specific nature. One is going beyond the mere negative.

How particular, how specific Teilhard's nothingness is may be seen from the fact that, as de Lubac must know, Teilhard has even spoken of "the very structure of nothingness," which rules that "God, in order to create, can proceed in only one way: by arranging, by gradually unifying, a multitude of elements."[61] Orthodox nothingness imposes no conditions on God: it is structureless and so he is free to bring about either a slowly built evolutionary world or an instantaneously created full-formed world. Teilhard's pure multiple makes it impossible for God to bring about the latter. Hence, to equate "complete disunity" or "pure 'potentiality of dispersion' " with "non-existence" is an ingenious fallacy.

In light of all this, it is pertinent to hark back to de Lubac's satisfaction over Teilhard's subscribing to the core of the *ex nihilo* doctrine in his final speculation. Just because Teilhard verbally disavows a preexisting substratum, one cannot assimilate him to orthodoxy. One must ask: In what terms, with what line of reasoning does he do it, and is he justified in his disavowal? De Lubac informs us: "Returning, then, to the problem of creation, Teilhard will point out that while the creative act can be conceived as an act of union, this is only subject to an express condition: if it is to be so conceived, 'we must reject the time-honoured evidence of common sense concerning the real distinction between the mobile and the movement and cease to imagine that the act of union cannot operate except upon a pre-existing substratum.' "[62]

Obviously, since every act of union in the history of the cosmos requires an antecedent multiple that already exists, Teilhard feels that the primal act of union, conceived by him as God's creative act, is in need of strong support by reason if it is to do away with an already existing antecedent multiple. He finds common sense against him, but he urges that common sense can be mistaken — as when it draws a distinction between the "mobile" and the "movement." What he means by this cryptic example is a situation in modern physics. I shall try to explain that situation and consider whether it can be of help to his difficulty. But first I shall take a look at de Lubac's attitude.

Does he find Teilhard convincing? Although he is happy with Teilhard's rejection of a preexisting substratum and says that it "should completely reassure theologians. . .on the essential point,"[63] his estimate of the Teilhardian argument is hardly reassuring: "We may, indeed, if we wish, hold that he is wrong here in 'rejecting the evidence of common sense' or in assimilating the case of the 'mobile-movement' couple to that of the 'unified-multiple' couple."[64] Well, if de Lubac grants that Teilhard could be, and most probably is, wrong in the grounds that he adduces, what value is there in simply agreeing with orthodoxy's formula in a broad and general connotation? De Lubac the logician is forced to make a wry face, while the priest in him smiles complacently. I am concerned with the logician, and if a fellow Jesuit is not convinced by Teilhard's last effort to prove his case, I need go no further in branding it as specious sophistry.

However, a glance may be cast at the "mobile-movement" couple. It alludes to the observation of increase in a body's mass when that body moves at an increasing speed of great rapidity. Teilhard's understanding of this phenomenon is expressed in a footnote to his essay "The Contingence of the Universe and Man's Zest for Survival."[65] He refers to "what happens in physics, where, as we now know, acceleration creates mass: which means that the moving object is posterior to motion." Translated to the case of God's creative act, the situation in physics would analogically imply that the elements unified are not required to be anterior to the unifying act: they can be taken as posterior, so that unification could occur without there being anything already existing to be unified and could be regarded as creating the unified elements.

Teilhard's argument is rather farfetched. First of all, he can put forth only an abstract possibility. He does not demonstrate that the example from physics necessarily holds for God's creative act, setting it quite apart from all the acts of union falling within the purview of science. The analogy can only be described as desperately wishful. Second, the example from physics is misrepresented as being an utterly exceptional occurrence in the phenomenal field. Teilhard himself has used it as just the opposite of exceptional in his argument for the universal existence of consciousness in nature, no matter how imperceptible it may be: "Consciousness (like such phenomena as the variation of mass according to speed, or radiation as a function of temperature) is a universal property common to all the corpuscles constituting the universe, but varying in proportion to the complexity of any particular molecule."[66] Acceleration is here understood — and rightly so — as increasing mass at all times and in every case of moving bodies, though the increase grows perceptible only at certain speeds — namely, those approaching the velocity of light. The "mobile-movement" couple should be valid, if at all, for each act of union and can have no precise application, from the side of physics, to God's creative act. But if that is so, it does not help to set the latter apart as requiring no preexisting substratum. It logically leaves room for such a substratum there as everywhere else.

Third, not in logic alone but in actuality, the increase of mass with acceleration, whether one takes it as universal or as effected only at certain high speeds, never does away with some preexisting substratum. The increase of mass happens to an existent body whose speed gets accelerated; there is no warrant in physics to conclude an utter lack of preexisting substratum.

Fourth, it is questionable whether in science one can speak of the moving object as being posterior to the motion or created by it. The situation is thus put by an authoritative writer on physics, J. W. N. Sullivan:

> We have already said that a moving body has a greater mass than is possessed by the same body at rest. Now the moving body, in virtue of its motion, has acquired a certain amount of energy—kinetic energy, as it is called. According to Einstein this energy has mass. Indeed, the extra mass of the moving body is due to the mass of its kinetic energy. And what is true of kinetic energy is true of any other form of energy. All forms of energy have mass. Since mass is the cardinal property of matter, this fact suggests that energy and matter are convertible terms.[67]

What one can gather from Sullivan's words is that energy is a species of matter or matter is a species of energy, but either way there is a physical reality possessing mass. The extra mass that Teilhard identifies with "the object that moves" belongs, properly speaking, to the energy of motion, and there is no point in considering it posterior or created, for it is simultaneous with and inseparable from *motion*.

Fifth, even if Teilhard's interpretation were unobjectionable, the manner in which he looks upon *motion* would not strike a philosophical reader as harmonious with Teilhardism itself. Discussing the two modes of energy that he postulates—"tangential" and "radial"—and that he basically ascribes to a single "psychic" energy, Emile Rideau, another fellow Jesuit, writes that Teilhard wants them to be "conceived not as things but as an 'action.' "[68] Then, for all his sympathy with Teilhard, Rideau, relying on the same footnote that I have quoted, remarks: "Here Teilhard seems to adopt the view that movement comes before the thing that moves. . . .In fact, the close connexion between structure and energy is so essential in Teilhard that there can be no question of his conceiving an energy that lacked support, however mysterious the support might be."[69] This connotes that, to Rideau's mind, Teilhard would be inconsistent with himself in employing an analogy that presented movement as an "action" without a "thing" acting. Although Rideau here does not directly touch the creation problem with which I am dealing, his criticism in general is enough to invest Teilhard's line of thought with an air of falsity and illegitimacy.

Finally, Teilhard himself has on two occasions pressed into the service of an almost reverse proposition the fact of mass increase with accelerated speed. The footnote I have quoted comes in an essay in which he is concerned to combat the emphasis of orthodoxy "on God's complete self-sufficiency and, in consequence, on the complete contingence of creation."[70] Teilhard declares that "it not only. . .humiliates the man in me, but also, and equally. . . offends the Christian in me"[71] that God should be posited, as in Scholastic philosophy, as *Ens a se*, Being by itself, "exhaustively and repletively, and instantaneously, at the ontological origin of all things" and that "all the rest (i.e. 'the world') appears in turn only as an entirely gratuitous supplement or addition: the guests at the divine banquet."[72] According to Teilhard, true Christianity emphasizes "the pleroma and pleromization,"[73] the ultimate synthesis of the universe and the Divine: do we not find in "the most authentic and concrete expressions of Christian revelation and mysticism. . .the affirmation and the expression of a strictly bilateral and complementary relationship between the world and God"?[74] Teilhard wants to replace Scholasticism's metaphysics of *Being* by a metaphysics of *Union*.[75] Just as, in his view, motion produces the moving object, so too Union produces Being. And by *Being* Teilhard means both God and the world.[76] For he says: "Treated in this genetic form, the problem of the co-existence and the complementarity of the created and the uncreated is undoubtedly solved in part: in so far, that is, as the two terms that are brought together, each in its own way, have an equal need both to exist in themselves and to be combined with each other, so that the absolute maximum of possible union may be effected *in natura rerum*."[77]

One may mark the phrase "the two terms. . .exist in themselves." This would really dispense with considering "the created" as the result of a production out of nothing. And indeed, Teilhard has a suggestive footnote on what Christian theology terms *participated being*—that is, the world, which exists not "by itself" but "by another." The footnote runs: "Thus participated being would be defined not so much by its opposition to non-being as by its positive relation to God, its power of entering into communion."[78] Although "non-being" as the source of the world is not denied in open language, it is fairly played down lest it should tend radically to divide from the greater reality the lesser, which is yet equally indispensable.

A parallel playing down of it is found in the other place in which Teilhard touches on the new physics "that is succeeding in abolishing any real distinction, for our reason, between extension and motion, between particles and waves, between matter and light, between space and time."[79] "Under the pressure and contagious influence of these revolutionary re-appraisals," Teilhard wishes to have "world and God combined in a general synthetic function. . .: God completely other in nature than the world and yet unable to dispense with it."[80] A footnote explains: "What I have in mind here is a synthetic re-definition of being, which, taken in its most general form would include, *both simultaneously*, an absolute term and a participated term. What makes the God-world antinomy insoluble is that we first split up a natural pair and then persist in considering the two terms *in succession*."[81]

Teilhard has not abandoned the idea of *creatio ex nihilo*, but if God is unable to dispense with the world and if God and the world are a natural pair that can be posed simultaneously, it is difficult to make God completely different in nature, an absolute term utterly against a participated one. A secret affinity, a subtle identity, appears to be in order as the implication of a synthetic redefinition of being. Teilhard, too, feels the affinity, the identity: that is why he soon declares that "participated being must. . .possess, *in its own way*, something that is absolute and non-contingent,"[82] and that is also why he proposes to "posit and define the real as a system" in which "it would seem to be possible *to deduce* the existence of the cosmic, peripheral, multiple on the same ground as the fontal and focal triune unity of God."[83]

Even when the point is not explicit, Teilhard's thought, probed deeply, is found to show the "cosmic stuff," for all its internal dissociation, to be not dissociated from God. The very first form of his speculation on the problem, to which Zaehner has referred (p. 56), closely connects the two: "In the beginning there were, at the two poles of existence, God and pure multiplicity (*la Multitude*). Even so, God was all alone. . .For all eternity God saw the shadow of his unity in a diffused state of disarray (*éparpillé*) beneath his feet; and this shadow was not another God."[84] The overall suggestion is that the same existence has two aspects and that this existence is basically God, and what is nonbasic is the shadow of the basic so that God's own substance of unity is in a shadowy form the multiplicity at the opposite pole.

A brand of monism or pantheism peeps out, though Teilhard does not accord it any recognition. What he ostensibly is concerned with, by means of his "nothing," is to avoid Manichaeanism, the view that God and chaos are two coeternal realities independent of each other—a pair of Gods, as it were—and that one God, in order to make this world, has to grapple with the other, who exists in his own right.

Only once was Teilhard bold enough to face the issue squarely instead of resorting to a kind of doublespeak. Straightforwardly he asserted:

> We would without doubt present a very incomplete idea of the Godhead if we described it exclusively by *personal* attributes: some aspects of the supreme Being can be interpreted only in terms that I might call material and cosmic. It is the same with the creative act. If we try to make it too free or operating too much *in vacuity*, we may well make it unintelligible. Is there any reason why we should not admit that the necessary existence of absolute unity entails, as a secondary consequence, *ad extra* —rather as though it were its antithesis or shadow—the appearance, at the opposite pole from being, of an infinite multiplicity? To do so, I believe, would not be in any way to belittle the Maker or his work.[85]

To "infinite multiplicity" Teilhard gave a footnote: "Thus there would somehow be two divine creative acts: the first *quasi-organic*, concluding in the appearance of pure Multiple (= the effect in conflict with the divine oneness); the second, *quasi-efficient*, unifying the Multiple (= creation properly so called)."

Here the pure Multiple is not merely true, physical, creatable nothing: it is the "material and cosmic" aspect of God. And the act of unifying the pure Multiple does not proceed in nothingness, "in vacuity." "The stuff of things," "the cosmic stuff," is explicitly recognized as "a pre-existing substratum," however diffuse. Now there is openly a brand of monism or pantheism: there is a sole existence, God, but with two attributes—absolute unity and infinite multiplicity, the one superior and the other inferior, the former a person and the latter a cosmic matter, the person really divine, substantially causative, and the cosmic matter a mere secondary antipodes, a shadowy effect.

Nor is this pantheism bound up necessarily with a peculiar definition of *nothingness*. For, that definition itself can be shown to be deceptive as soon as one probes it to its root. What exactly would be meant by plurality's getting completely realized, the multiple being pure or the stuff of things becoming infinitely loose-textured, infinitely dissociated? To be sure, it cannot be the same as interminable divisibleness. The matter that science analyzes is susceptible to division without end, as one sees more and more with the quarks beyond the so-called elementary particles, just as those particles were beyond the atom. By this susceptibility, it does not dissolve into nothingness. One arrives only at an increasingly refined state of infinitesimals. But, according to science as Teilhard himself understands it, the infinitesimals, like any other state of matter, cannot be taken as existing piecemeal: everywhere the entire universe en bloc ultimately swims into the scientific ken. "All around us," says Teilhard, "until it is lost to sight, radiates the net of spatial and temporal series, endless and untearable, so closely woven in one piece that there is not one single knot in it that does not depend upon the whole fabric."[86] Again, more to the point, one reads: "At the beginning of the perceptible world what existed was the Multiple; and that Multiple was already rising up, like one indissociable whole."[87] So what is logically conceivable as preceding the indissociable oneness and wholeness of the material cosmos is the existence of the infinitesimals, each in isolation and with no interconnectedness. Infinitesimals thus existing are Teilhard's pure multiple. They are far indeed from pure nothingness. But now comes the essential trickiness of the concept.

For, Teilhard, when visualizing the pure Multiple as the antipodal shadow of God's unity, has the threefold expression (as quoted by Zaehner): "In itself, it did not exist, nor had it ever existed, nor could it ever have existed" (p. 56). On the one hand, this expression would lead toward equating the pure Multiple with "true, physical nothingness," but, on the other hand, it would imply that the infinitesimals can never be thought of as lacking some kind of interconnectedness and as existing except as "one indissociable whole" of whatever kind. Then Teilhard's proposition would boil down to: "*If* there were, or ever had been, or ever could have been a multiplicity of infinitesimals, we should have true, physical nothingness." The proposition is merely conditional: it points to no realized state of affairs. In other words, not only pure nothingness but even the Teilhardian nothingness is, by Teilhard's own drift of thought, "a pseudo-idea," failing, as it does, to correspond to any actual possibility.

What then is one to conclude? The nonexistence of the pure Multiple means the existence always of the impure Multiple in one state or another of condensation, concentration, organization, unification. That is the trickiness of the Teilhardian concept. And the sole creative act possible is to increase the elementarily condensed, concentrated, organized, united state of a preexisting substratum. And the substratum preexisting in such a state can only be a certain aspect of God himself, the Being who, as Zaehner quotes Teilhard as saying, is "Unity" and "all alone" (p. 56). Adopting the *ex-nihilo* framework, one may conclude that God freely creates the world out of nothing except His own single yet multiformative reality.

This is how Teilhard's internal conflicts and contradictions could have been resolved if he had moved definitely beyond pantheism and Catholic Christianity alike.

In that direction, and not in any other, does he, "on some important points," need "to be completed" and there alone does he "open up a vast field of inquiry for theologians."

iv

Teilhard's innate urge toward accepting both pantheism and Catholicism in their essence and going past them to a greater synthesis, may be discerned even in the set piece "Pantheism and Christianity," which he wrote in 1923 apparently to avert all suspicion of heresy from his religion of the whole, his mysticism of a living cosmic unity. He wanted to show that he denounced pantheism in its generally understood connotation and was therefore faithful to Christian orthodoxy, while yet asking his Church to follow his pantheistlike turn toward the universal All — a drive that he took to be central to enlightened modernism and that he deemed indispensable to the Church if the latter were not to become obsolete and untrue.

As a Churchman, he was concerned to deprecate the submergence of the human elements in an impersonal cosmic Whole and to enforce the existence of a personal and transcendent God. But he persistently asserted that a cosmic Whole of a nonimpersonal kind enfolding yet not submerging the human elements is a vital necessity of religious experience just as much as a transcendent person. He expressed his basic aim to combine pantheism and Christianity instead of harping on the usual gap between them: "My approach. . .will be. . .to narrow that gap. . . by bringing out what one might call the Christian soul of pantheism or the pantheist aspect of Christianity."[88]

The pantheism that he sought to avoid was that which he dubbed "Spinozism, Hegelianism, theosophy, monism"[89] —especially the first-named, which all Catholics consider the arch-heresy. But when he came to describe the pantheistic trend that he saw as an unavoidable ingredient of human religious thought and emotion and most markedly of the modern spirit that stands perennially in front of a universe evolving as a single bloc, he employed terms no Spinozist would have rejected:

> What we reach out to grasp in our aspirations is something which is diffused throughout, which permeates everything. Fundamentally we have but one passion: to become one with the world which envelops us without our ever being able to distinguish either its face or its heart. . . .When we read the evidence of certain Christian and pagan mystics or even simply what many perfectly ordinary people may tell us in confidence, we cannot but quite seriously question whether there may not be a sort of cosmic consciousness in our soul, more diffuse than our personal consciousness, more intermittent, but perfectly well defined — a sort of feeling of the presence of all beings at the same time, so that they are not perceived as multiple and separate but as forming part of one and the same unit.[90]

To ward off the charge of Spinozism, Teilhard takes care to use the word *sort* when speaking of cosmic consciousness and adds after *unit* at the close of his definition the phrase, "at least in the future." With this phrase he brings in a gratuitous and ridiculous reservation. No mystic, Christian or pagan, talks merely of the future. Teilhard is trying to twist the pantheistic experience or the realization of the cosmic consciousness into just an inkling of the pleroma of Christ, the ultimate mystical body, the consummated creation that is his magnificent obsession — an event of universal spiritual union he expects to occur "some millions of years" hence.[91] However, one may note two things: first, the mention of "certain Christian mystics" and, second, the words he uses elsewhere in the same essay when, naming one Christian mystic of eminence, he focuses on a particular interpretation of the pleromatic union.

He leads up to those words through a general discussion of the pleroma. With his pantheistic tendency he inveighs against the current conception of the pleroma as an association like a family or a social group. Family or society is simply an aggregation formed by moral or juridical relationships and not by physical or organic ties. It is such ties that Teilhard wants. He regrets that even the theologians who think of the pleroma as holding together not by characteristics external to the soul but by a new and higher inner life, a superanimation from within, make "the very common mistake of regarding the spiritual as an attenuation of the material whereas it is in fact the material carried beyond itself: it is super-material."[92] Hence the so-called ties they want are of an "infra-physical nature." "Thus what they make. . .of the Pleroma is primarily a vast association, a family on a very large scale, in which the individuals are held together principally by bonds of common agreement and affection."[93] Even the most advanced Christianity, failing to go further than an "infra-physical" organicity, stands condemned in Teilhard's eyes. He appeals beyond it and still more beyond "the language of the Gospels, which are. . .inclined to announce and describe the kingdom of God in terms of the family or of society";[94] he appeals to some expressions in the Pauline and Johannine Scripture to support his own pantheistically slanted view. An association, having not the least sign of an aggregation, is for him the import of this Scripture.

"St. Paul," says Teilhard, "gives us to understand that the happiness of the elect should not be understood as a solitary, self-centred enjoyment of God. On the contrary, heaven will consist in the close association of all the elect, gathered into one single body under the influence of their head, Jesus Christ. However individual our salvation may be from many points of view, it is in consequence accomplished only in a collective fulfilment. The heavenly

Jerusalem, the Apocalypse tells us, knows but one medium of knowledge and action: the illuminating and unifying radiance emanating from the God-man. . .We shall be saved, and we shall see God only in so far as we are one in Christ Jesus."[95] There, Teilhard believes, the supernatural organism of the pleroma is hinted to have "a structure at least as consistent as that which we see in the tangible realities of the natural cosmos."[96]

In this structure, nevertheless, he finds no submergence of the individual soul. Not wanting to sacrifice either pantheism or Christianity, he writes: "We Christians can (and, what is more, we must) understand the mystical union of the elect in Christ as combining the warm flexibility of social relationships with the imperative rigour and irreversibility of the physical and biological laws or attractive forces operating in the present universe."[97] It is here that he introduces the name of one eminent Christian mystic and, in order to clarify his own view of the pleromatic Mystical Body, cautions the reader against this mystic's vision and yet comes out with a statement full of implications germane to the point I am seeking to make about Teilhard's ineradicable penchant for pantheism. He says:

> When we try to understand and express in physical terms the way in which the mystical body (pleroma) is held together, there is, of course, one extreme we must avoid if we are not to "founder in our faith." We should not do what could be read into the language censured in some mystics (Eckhart, for example) and try to make of the consummated Christ a being so unique that his subsistence, his person, his "I," takes the place of the subsistence, the personality, of all the elements incorporated in his mystical body. This concept of a hypostatic union extended to the whole universe (which, incidentally, is simply Spinoza's pantheism) is not in itself either contradictory or absurd; but it conflicts with the whole Christian view of individual freedom and personal salvation.[98]

What, first of all, is most surprising, as well as revealing here, is the joining up of Spinoza's pantheism with the consummated Christ visioned as a state in which all souls are absorbed into his supreme personal selfhood. Spinozism becomes the doctrine of a divine person whose incarnation is the entire universe. The "hypostatic union" of God and matter, which constitutes, in the eyes of the Church, the unique phenomenon of the Incarnate Word in the historical Jesus is seen to apply on a cosmically extended scale. So the pantheism of Spinoza remains no longer the arch-heresy of an impersonal whole of undifferentiated all-submerging unity: it figures an infinite "I" with whom human elements get identified in their final fulfillment. Spinozism is made equivalent to a conception à la Eckhart of Christ's Mystical Body. Teilhard's ostensible repudiation of pantheism in its generally understood connotation is thus undermined by himself and a "Christian soul" of pantheism found without further need of converting the idea of a monistic Whole with which all human elements are substantially one in their ultimate nature.

In the second place, there is the explicit judgment that Spinozism is neither contradictory nor absurd in itself. Teilhard is shown to be intellectually quite ready to embrace pantheism. Only his adherence to the Christian view that unless the human elements are distinct in substance from God they cannot either exercise free will or experience salvation from their sins holds him back. But when he sees Spinozist pantheism as a cosmicized Eckhart-visioned Christianity, the suggestion cannot be helped that the souls before they are absorbed in the consummated Christ could, in spite of their substantial oneness with God, know and feel themselves as Christianity conceives them. Surely, Eckhart, for all his implications of a "hypostatic union extended to the whole universe" — his Spinozist pantheism, in short — so regarded the souls.

Teilhard's sense of a conflict between the Eckhartian Christ-consummation and "the whole Christian view of individual freedom and personal salvation" is itself reduced to a vanishing point when he comes to consider the true meaning of the Christian rite of mass and communion. He asks us to realize "the full depth and universality of their mystery":

> We now understand that when Christ descends sacramentally into each one of his faithful it is not simply in order to commune with him: it is in order to join him, physically, a little more closely to himself and to all the rest of the faithful in the growing unity of the world. When, through the priest, Christ says, "*Hoc est corpus meum*," "This is my body," the words reach out infinitely far beyond the morsel of bread over which they are pronounced: they bring the entire mystical body into being. The priestly act extends beyond the transubstantiated Host to the cosmos itself, which, century after century, is gradually being transformed by the incarnation, itself never complete. From age

to age, there is but one single mass in the world: the true Host, the total Host, is the universe which is continually being more intimately penetrated and vivified by Christ. From the most distant origin of things until their unforeseeable consummation, through the countless convulsions of boundless space, the whole of nature is slowly and irresistibly undergoing the supreme consecration. Fundamentally—since all time and forever—but one single thing is being made in creation: the body of Christ.[99]

Reflecting on his own words, Teilhard rejoices that by thus translating "the mysteries and the practical application of our faith. . .into terms of organic and physical realities," and understanding "the universal function exercised by the incarnate God," the Christian "has. . .stolen the pantheist's fire, the fire with which he threatened to set the earth ablaze with an incandescence that would not have been Christ's."[100] And how exactly is the fire stolen? The Christian, says Teilhard, "is more successful in his 'unitarian' attempt" because he "knows that in the powerful embrace of the omnipresent Christ, souls do not lose their personality, but win it," whereas the pantheist, "while claiming to unify beings, merges them in an undifferentiated whole; which means, in fact, that his monism annihilates the mystery and joy of union."[101]

There is here the general suggestion that the Christian differs from the pantheist only insofar as souls preserve the experience of uniting in the midst of the union instead of losing it. Of course, Teilhard misconceives the loss as a disappearance of consciousness: what really happens is the all-effacing realization, by the parts, of their own ultimate whole self. But Teilhard's Christian does not directly emphasize that the parts are not the same in substance as the whole. Nor is there any stress on the Christ-Whole being altogether separate from the cosmos. The Teilhardian Whole has two sides: Christ eternally complete in himself and Christ becoming complete in his universal body of nature evolving through the ages into spirit. As regards this second side, there is, on the one hand, a divine process going on from "the most distant origin of things" and on the other hand, a diviner process from the time of Christ's birth. In both cases there is the presence of the Supreme Being in the substance of the world—a vari-aspected and vari-phased incarnation. Now and then Teilhard wishes not to commit himself to a worldwide "hypostatic union," but, by and large, his attitude appears to be that there is such a union without its implying necessarily a merger of the parts in the totality that has put forth partial self-expressions.

How else is one to interpret a passage written a few months earlier than "Pantheism and Christianity" dealing with an article on pantheism by Teilhard's friend Père Auguste Valensin, who had contributed it to the *Dictionnaire apologétique de la foi catholique*? In a letter of 17 December 1922 Teilhard criticizes Valensin:

> You leave the reader with the impression that Spinoza's position, for example, is *simpliciter mala, falsa*. How is it that you have not suggested that between Spinoza's "Incarnation," in which the whole is hypostatically divine, and the "Incarnation" of the over-cautious, extrinsicist theologians, in which the pleroma is no more than a social aggregate, there is room for an Incarnation that culminates in the building up of an organic whole, in which physical union with God is at different levels? You contrast Christian morality with the morality of Spinoza by saying that the former tells us only that we must become "like unto God." I don't accept the distinction. For the Christian, to be *summorphos Christo* is to participate, under a similarity of behaviour, in a common being; it is really "to become Christ," "to become God."[102]

That the position of Spinoza is not "simply evil, false," but only needs a little modification to be acceptable — such also would be the inference from Teilhard's insistence on the universe being "the true Host, the total Host." One may recall his letter of 1916 to Père Victor Fontoynont in which he speaks of "the Earth becoming like a great Host in which God would be contained for us."[103] All description of the cosmos as a Christ-containing host must mean, as in the rite of the consecrated and transubstantiated bread, that the universe is the body of Christ and that with each act of mass the increase of the cosmos's "Christification" — the increase that took place with the birth of Jesus — is reinforced and extended. With such a Host concept, Christianity is bound to shade off into pantheism, no matter how Christ-charged the latter may be.

Olivier Rabut leaves no doubt on this point. Commenting on certain phrases in Teilhard's *Divine Milieu* that also carry his crypto-pantheism, Rabut warns:

> We must be careful not to imagine that there is such a thing as a "pan-Christism," in which everything contains a fragment of Christ. Christ is *linked* with the cosmos, but the universe is

not, and never will be, a vaster Incarnation of him. It is better, then, not to speak of "a silently accruing presence of Christ in things." Earth is not (even if we add "beyond itself") "the body of him who is and him who is coming." There is no such thing as a cosmic Host; the phrase has only a metaphorical meaning, and is too misleading to be retained. The universe is an extension of the body of Christ; this concept, which is very profound, is well worth elaboration; but we must be careful to distinguish the body of Christ from its adjuncts. And the insistence on the physical or biological reality of the Mystical Body is also misleading; the vital (and real) bonds which unite are all supernatural.[104]

As against Rabut, Teilhard has the conviction:

It is Christ who in a real and unmetaphorical sense of the word holds up the universe. So incredible a cosmic function may well be too much for our imagination, but I do not see how we could possibly avoid attributing it to the Son of Mary. The Incarnate Word could not be the supernatural (hyper-physical) centre of the universe if he did not function *first* as its physical, natural, centre. Christ cannot sublimate creation in God without progressively raising it up by his influence through successive circles of matter and spirit. That is why, in order to bring all things back to his Father, he had to make himself one with all—he had to enter into contact with every one of the zones of the creation from the lowest and most earthly to the zone that is closest to heaven. . . .Even, therefore, in that aspect of its evolution which is regarded as the most "natural," it is towards Christ that the universe, since all time, has been moving as one integral whole. "*Omnis creatura usque adhuc ingemiscit et parturit.*" Has any evolutionist pantheism, in fact, ever spoken more magnificently of the Whole than St. Paul did in the words he addressed to the first Christians?[105]

Teilhard, as usual, formulates himself apparently in as Christian a way as possible, but the difference from Rabut cannot be missed. Rabut is anxious to make one understand things metaphorically; Teilhard is all for an unmetaphorical sense. The former takes supernatural bonds to be the vital and real ones; the latter gives primarily a physical and natural function to the Christ-Center of the cosmos and even labels the supernatural bonds "hyper-physical" (equivalent to "super-material"). The very quotation from Saint Paul conjures up a world picture to which Rabut could never subscribe. The footnote to the Latin words, by the editor of

Teilhard's book, runs: "After Romans 8:22: 'The whole creation has been groaning in travail together until now.' " If the universe can act like this, it must be basically a living universe, one single whole with consciousness in various modes of manifestation everywhere. To see the universe thus is to see it under a certain aspect of pantheism—the aspect that one may designate *panpsychism*. C. C. Martindale, a friend of Teilhard's and a fellow Jesuit, realizes such an aspect when in an article on Teilhard he refers to the same quotation and, apropos of the pleroma, says: "Since the Consummation is not yet reached, Saint Paul can say (Romans 8:22) that *all* creation is *still* 'groaning and suffering birth-pangs *along with us* and joins in our yearning' for the ransom of our humanity. We agree that a certain timidity has been felt about this apparent equipping *all* creation with a sort of consciousness: even the late Monsignor Ronald Knox said that if Saint Paul was referring to the whole of creation, he must be speaking with 'something of a poetic outlook.' "[106] In the same context of the world being not "yet complete," Martindale has also the remark: "When speaking of such matters it is hard not to sound pantheist, at least at times."[107]

Teilhard has two other phrases from Saint Paul. They come at the close of his "Pantheism and Christianity." The entire concluding passage may be quoted:

> Christ is clothed in the earth: let this earth, then, grow ever greater that Christ's raiment may be ever more magnificent! Christ guides from within the universal progress of the world: may our consciousness, then, of the bond that runs through all things, of their constant movement in being, grow ever more keen, and so make the impact of Christ upon us ever greater.
>
> Already, at this very moment, by everything we do, we all share in all, through and in him whom we might think distant from us, but in whom, quite literally, "*vivimus, movemur et sumus.*"† A little while yet—what hope could be grander?—creation, totally dominated by Christ, will be lost in him and through him within the final and permanent unity, where (in St. Paul's very words, the most clear-cut assertion we have of Christian "pantheism") "*estai o theòs pánta èn pãsin.*"††[105]

---

† "We live and move and have our being," after Acts 17:28, from p. 75 n. 7 of *Christianity and Evolution.*

†† "God will be all in all," after 1 Cor. 15:28, from p. 75 n. 8 of *Christianity and Evolution. Evolution.*

On the Greek quotation, which serves for a *leitmotiv* to many of Teilhard's works, I shall have a number of things to say at a later stage. Suffice it here to note that Teilhard himself suggests its pantheistic bearing, even if Christianized, and that it belongs to the same philosophical and mystical background against which Saint Paul's apostleship was carried out and from which it drew expressions at the same time connected with the pagan world and sliding into the Christian. The phrase in Latin is part of Saint Paul's speech "in the midst of Mars' hill" to the "men of Athens." Immediately after this famous turn, meaning in its full form "In him we live, and move, and have our being," one reads: "As certain also of your own poets have said, for we are also his offspring."[109] Albert Schweitzer says of the famous turn that its "God-mysticism. . .is Stoic" and adds about the succeeding one that it "is from Aratus (*Phaenomena*, 5), who like Paul was a native of Cilicia."[110] Schweitzer continues: "That which is expressed is the Stoic pantheistic Mysticism. It implies a way of looking at life in which the conception of the divine is immanent. God is conceived as the essence of all the forces at work in nature. Accordingly all that is 'is in God.' In man as capable of thought this fact becomes an object of consciousness."[111] If, unlike several Bible scholars, one accepts as authentic the words put into Paul's mouth by the author of the Acts, one should have to wonder whether the apostle was not harmonizing with his doctrine of the transcendent God the immanence of divine substance visioned by Stoic pantheism, rather than merely using for his own ends the ideas and language familiar to the Athenians. Such harmonization would be "Christian pantheism" in the most significant sense — the sense that so often, in spite of disclaimers, seems apt to Teilhard's pantheism-haunted Christianity. The aptness appears to be confirmed by Teilhard's own pen when he goes out of his way to assert that we live and move and have our being in the Divine "quite literally."

The utter literalness has indeed to be there once one talks of Christ's guiding the universal progress of the world from within and once this guidance of all the universe is seen to be an activity inward "even in that aspect of its evolution which is regarded as the most 'natural'." Teilhard is introducing a new formula of God's immanence. That formula runs through the entire mass of his writings and is always pantheistic in temper and tone. Nothing short of this characteristic faces one when he speaks of "the transparency of the world" to the eye of faith and explains that if one is to set God "as a focus at the summit of the universe" (Omega Point, pleroma) one must find God "simultaneously impregnating with his presence even the most insignificant evolutionary movement." What Teilhard thus expounded in *Human Energy* (1937) is equally obvious in *The Divine Milieu* (1926-27): "The Creator and, more specifically, the Redeemer have steeped themselves in all things and penetrated all things to such a degree that, as Blessed Angela of Foligno said, 'the world is full of God.' "[112]

Teilhard's "immanence" is surely not identical with "immanentism," which denies God's transcendence, yet neither can it be identified with the old Christian term that accompanied the concept of transcendence. While always defending divine transcendence, he had to make a special effort to reconcile it with "an immanence which. . .must be given progressively a more important and more explicit place in our philosophy and religion."[113] This immanence is not given greater weight merely because of world values as such: it is what it is because of "the new properties of a universe in process of cosmogenesis."[114] It is an immanence organic to the world: it carries on cosmic evolution by being united with it and by being internal to it and not just by an omnipresence such as Christianity conceives — namely, a power that is external to the cosmos and separate from it and that is everywhere only by its causative action supporting the existence of the cosmos and serving as the ground for the universe's dynamic continuance but never functioning as the inner soul of the world, as the Cosmic Christ, who is the all-evolver and all-consummator. Teilhard brings a crucial metamorphosing touch to the traditional omnipresence. While thereby wishing to save modern mankind from the traditional pantheism to which it feels drawn through the new properties of a universe in process of cosmogenesis, Teilhard still recognizes a core of vital truth pressing him to make Christianity pantheistic. And his metamorphosing touch, no less than his saving wish, is clear in those words in which his coreligionist editors summarize his stand: "It is faith in the divine Omnipresence, completed by the doctrine of the Universal Christ, that will provide the antidote to the temptation of pantheism."[115]

The doctrine of the Universal Christ — the Creator who, in Pantheism and Christianity," functions as the universe's "physical, natural center," "the bond" running "through all things," and makes himself "one with all" and enters "into contact with every one of the zones of the creation" and wears the earth as a "raiment," which is a living tissue secretly "groaning," charged with "travail" for a supreme goal and meant from the beginning to be increasingly the Creator's "Mystical Body," and growing, ever since his incarnation in a human form, more and more swiftly and extensively "Christified," and turned into a sacramental "Host" by means of "the universal function of the incarnate God"—it is this doctrine that is behind Teilhard's taking Paul's great declaration from Mars' Hill "quite literally." And the complete literalness cannot but push Teilhard beyond Roman Catholic orthodoxy, while his ubiquitous affirmation of God's transcendence as the originating background of the inwardly animated phenomenon of cosmogenesis must break through the usual limits of pantheism.

I may repeat what I have said earlier, that the double movement never found definitive articulation in Teilhard, but it is the central drive in him and the cause of all the ambiguities and ambivalences that his coreligionist commentators regret in his writings and attempt to gloss over.

v

The Universal or Cosmic Christ stands at the hub of the Teilhardian revolution of the Christian religion. It will be helpful to look at him a little more intimately with the assistance of some writings other than "Pantheism and Christianity."

In a preceding chapter I discussed Teilhard's view of Creation. By the action of "creative union" God organizes into ever higher levels of "complexity-consciousness" the pure Multiple that constitutes the shadow-antipodes of his supreme unity. The pure Multiple is what Teilhard means by the "nothingness" from which, according to Christian orthodoxy, God creates the world. Teilhard distinguishes his nothingness, which is "physical" or "creatable," a "positive non-being," from the sheer undefined *nihil* of orthodoxy, the concept of which he stigmatizes as "a pseudoidea." God himself, the Sole Being, under the aspect of an infinitely divided "cosmic stuff" is here for all intelligible purposes. One may now add that the power exercising creative union in this stuff is God as Christ, a divine-human Superperson, one whose humanity no less than his divinity is a mystical fact of all eternity, Saint Paul's Christ who is "theandric" (God-Man) even before the historical incarnation one knows as Jesus. This Superperson at the same time exceeds the cosmic process, includes it in himself, and is included in it as the animating force, the evolutive energy. A world in evolution, a universe in the making, a cosmos moving toward greater unification, is quite different from the full-blown creation that traditional Christianity, prior to the advent of the modern scientific age, postulated. Teilhard's vision is not of a cosmos as such but of a cosmogenesis, and to his mind the universal movement converges toward a future of completely unified mankind, a final totalization or universalization of consciousness that he labels *Omega Point*. Cosmogenesis requires a creative Christ functioning differently from the traditional Son of God empowered to create the world. Claude Cuénot phrases well the change the comes over God's face with cosmogenesis replacing cosmos:

The God of cosmos is the worker who acts efficaciously, whose deeds are extrinsic, so that the effects are produced outside himself and have nothing of their author but a distant imprint. On the other hand, if we look for the conditions of a God of convergent cosmogenesis, we find that the creator is bound to act as an internal animating principle, by a force of animation. He acts not so much as a workman, but as a force of evolution. A ready-made world (static or cyclical) *ipso facto* detaches itself from its creator. A world in the making, that is to say in the process of unification, on the contrary is no more able than an unborn child to detach itself from its creator, from the evolutionary and unifying principle which is giving it birth.

Thus, God must, in a certain fashion, enter into cosmogenesis. He will thus find himself partly immersed, incorporated in a system in the process of evolution and therefore suffering, since there is no evolution without suffering. The God of cosmogenesis therefore has an element of the incarnate and of the redeemer, and therefore of the fellow sufferer. Cosmogenesis seems to incline us towards a God who fairly closely resembles the Christian God, since the centre of convergence must be 'within' and cosmogenesis invites us to Christify the God appropriate to it. It therefore seems to call upon the Christian God. But by a return shock, it will act upon our religious representations in such a way that the Christian God is bound to be enormously enlarged, and Christ constrained to be formidably extended since he can only supernaturalize the world by completing it. To complete it in him, he must first complete it in itself since Christ is, at the same

time, the principle of supernaturalization, and the ultra-humanizing principle of evolution. In short, cosmogenesis compels us to
Christify the rational God and cosmify the traditional Christ.[116]

Cuénot also remarks:

> In cosmos, in a static vision of the universe the element behaves
> like a small piece in a mosaic, where juxtaposition reigns. The
> idea of a creation exclusively *ex nihilo*, however obscure it may
> be, is in harmony with this vision in cosmos. On the other hand in
> a vision in cosmogenesis we see a world which is groping, which
> is striving to unite, to arrive at constantly higher syntheses from
> the megamolecule to man, from man to planetized mankind.
> Now, union, like the dough which cannot rise without ferment,
> requires a binding force, an internal factor of unification.[117]

From Cuénot's exposition along Teilhardian lines one can see that
the change in God's face may be summed up, briefly, in Cuénot's
own words: "God is Christifying himself and becoming more
immanent."[118] But the increase in immanence, coinciding with
God's "Christification," cannot be equated merely to the cosmo-
genetic revision that Cuénot approvingly quotes from Pastor
Georges Créspy: "Things are no longer at all the same if the world is
in movement. . . .God, in this perspective, can no longer be
regarded as the necessary Being, the external cause of reality, and
we must make up our minds to look upon Him as the *direction* of
reality, *in proportion as reality deploys itself. If the world is
movement, then God is history,* or at least God can be no longer
thought of as immobile, eternally frozen in his Being, but must be
regarded as linked in some manner with the movement of the
world."[119] Just to have a link with the world in some manner does
not adequately characterize the more immanent God of
cosmogenesis. The true traits of God are indicated in such expressions of Cuénot's as "partly immersed, incorporated in a system
in the process of evolution," and "has an element of the incarnate
and of the redeemer." The central term is *incarnate.* Teilhard
regards the acknowledged and traditional Incarnation that is Jesus
Christ, the crucified God-Man, as "the visible aspect" of Creation
itself.[120] He says: "The first act of the Incarnation, the first
appearance of the Cross, is marked by the plunging of the divine
unity into the ultimate depths of the Multiple. . . .The Redeemer
could penetrate the stuff of the cosmos, could pour himself into the

life-blood of the universe, only by first dissolving himself in matter, later to be reborn from it."[121] Teilhard continues:

> The endless aeons that preceded the first Christmas are not empty of Christ, but impregnated by his potent influx. It is the ferment of his conception that sets the cosmic masses in motion and controls the first currents of the biosphere. It is the preparation for his birth that accelerates the progress of instinct and the full development of thought on earth. We should not, in our stupidity, be horrified because the Messiah has made us wait so interminably for his coming. It called for all the fearsome, anonymous toil of primitive man, for the long drawn-out beauty of Egypt, for Israel's anxious expectation, the slowly distilled fragrance of eastern mysticism, and the endlessly refined wisdom of the Greeks — it called for all these before the flower could bloom on the stock of Jesse and mankind. All these preparations were cosmically, biologically, necessary if Christ was to gain a footing on the human scene. And all this work was set in motion by the active and creative awakening of his soul, in as much as that human soul of his was chosen to animate the universe. When Christ appeared in the arms of Mary, what he had just done was to raise up the world.[122]

No wonder Teilhard frames the unforgettable formula: "the Redeeming Incarnation" was "a prodigious biological operation."[123]

Keeping this in mind, one should guard also against the suggestion that the Teilhardian Christ is only a modernized version of the Christ whom Duns Scotus, as opposed to Thomas Aquinas, pictured in medieval theology. Aquinas held that Christ would not have been born if Adam had not sinned and all mankind had not thereby been tainted and corrupted. Thus, the historical Incarnation was not an integral part of God's original world plan. Scotus said that Christ would have been born in any case: the Incarnation had been intended as the master event of history, an integral element in creation. Christ's role as a savior from sin was an additional one that arose from the circumstance of Adam's Fall: his essential role was that of the crowning piece of the world order. "Thus this interpretation," the Jesuit theologian N. M. Wildiers tells us,

> ascribes to Christ a central function in the cosmos — a function, that is, not to be understood in purely moral or juridical terms. In its very existence the world is centred on Christ — and not *vice versa*, as the first interpretation avers. In the beginning it

was oriented upon him, so that we are indeed right to say that he is the beginning and the end, the Alpha and Omega of all things. Christ's place in the cosmos is an organic function: that is, the world is centred on Christ in respect of its intrinsic structure, in its actual mode of being, so that—to use St. Paul's expression—he "is in all things preeminent."[124]

Wildiers's description portrays the Christ of Scotus as completely Teilhardian, except that Teilhard has to indicate the place of Christ not in such a world as "forms the background to mediaeval theology," but "in a creation with an evolving convergent character."[125]

Wildiers informs us that the Scotist interpretation no less than the Thomist has a right to exist in Catholic theology and is entirely consistent with the fundamental tenets of Christianity.[126] Hence, if all that Teilhard did was to give Scotism the background of an evolutionary world picture, he can be deemed perfectly orthodox in the basic sense. By calling the Scotist Christ "organic" to the world, Wildiers has made orthodox the question he imagines Teilhard as asking himself: "Is there any link between the God-man and this evolving world; and if there is, is it to be construed as a merely external juridical connection, or ought we to think of it rather as a close, organic relatedness?"[127]

The fallacy in Wildiers's presentation can easily be exposed. Scotism, like Thomism, pivots wholly on the issue of Adam's Fall. Is that Fall fundamentally responsible for Christ's appearance? Scotism's reply of no has nothing to do with whether the universe is static or evolutionary. Evolution, for Scotism, would be purely a view about the way universal history is constituted; it would not affect the way that Christ appeared. And indeed, Scotism is concerned only with the original plan of the universe, not with the mechanics and dynamics of the actual world existence. In an evolutionary world the Scotist Christ, organically connected with the world plan and bound to appear in the course of history irrespective of a possible event like Adam's Fall, would still not himself be evolutionary at all. He would incarnate himself simply when he judged that humanity was ripe for his birth—just as much from outside as the Thomist Christ. The fact of evolution would not render his birth per se a prodigious operation of biological forces, an incarnation from inside even though the Being incarnated may have his own transcendent aspect as well. God would do nothing more than intend to insert him into the evolving world at one sole historical point: Christ would not be inserted from the beginning into evolution so that when he emerged from it at a single point as a human-divine figure he would be merely the visible sign of what all creation according to Teilhard is—namely, a secret universal act of Divine Incarnation. It is in this view that the essence of the Teilhardian Christ lies. To have "a close, organic relatedness" to a world in evolution is for the Teilhardian Christ to be himself evolutionary: his historical advent has the whole past process of the universe as a history of his own hidden universal incarnation from the beginning of creation. Is there anything medieval modernized in this Christ? Wildiers has employed for the Scotist Christ the words *organic function* with no bearing in the least on the question Teilhard had to ask. There is a radical change of conception with regard to organicity. The Christ of Scotus has no relevance to that of Teilhard. To think otherwise is to adulterate the Universal or Cosmic Christ of Teilhardism.

I may add that those who equate Scotus with Teilhard merely because Scotus differed from Aquinas about Christ's meaning in the world plan forget one vital point in the rest of Scotism. Scotus was uncompromisingly hostile to any doctrine of nature as the seat of God's indwelling: nature to him was only the work of God's hands. Interested as he was in conserving the freedom and independence of the human will, he opposed every philosophical attempt to establish what he conceived as jeopardizing them. His position here is most un-Teilhardian: "Reacting against the determinism of Augustine, he pushed God out of the universe altogether and gave the latter a wholly external relation to its creator."[128] What rapport can such a position have with Teilhardism's Universal Christ?

On studying how Christ is universalized by Teilhard, one recognizes more clearly the lack of rapport with Scotus, as well as the adulteration of the Teilhardian view by expositors like Wildiers. Teilhard argues: "It is philosophically sound to ask of each element of the world whether its roots do not extend into the furthest limits of the past. We have much better reason to accord to Christ this mysterious pre-existence."[129] And in what form exactly shall one conceive of the preexistence of Christ? One may proceed from Teilhard's vision of the historical Christ's stance vis-à-vis the universe in which he appeared. As it would be in the case of time, so would it be in that of space. Teilhard speaks of each element of the world. In this instance he concentrates on each human element: "*Each and everyone of us*, if we are to observe it, is enveloped — is *haloed* — by an extension of his being as vast as the universe. We are conscious of only the core of our selves. Nevertheless, the interplay of the monads would be unintelligible if an *aura* did not extend from one to another: something, that is, which is peculiar to each one of them and at the same time common to all."[130] What is true of "each and everyone of us" must be supereminently true of the historical Jesus. One has to see "a magnification, a transformation, realised in the humanity of Christ, of the aura that surrounds every human monad."[131] But the magnification and transformation imply a master role of the Christ-aura:

> Just as one sees in a living organism elements, originally indistinguishable from the others, suddenly emerge as *leaders* so that they are seen to be centres of attraction or points at which a formative activity is concentrated:
> So (on an incomparably larger scale) the man, the Son of Mary, was *chosen* so that his *aura*, instead of serving simply as the medium in which interaction with other men might be effected *ex aequo,* might dominate them and draw them all into the network of its influence.

More vividly Teilhard writes of the aura of Christ and its cosmic function: "Around the radiant sun of love that has risen to light up the world, there extends into infinity a 'corona' that is seldom seen and that is, nevertheless, the seat of the encompassing and unifying activity of the Incarnate Word."[132] And, again, he says of "this universal physical element in Christ": "We must admit that there is in *natura Christi*, besides the specifically individual element of Man — and in virtue of God's choice — some *universal physical reality*, a certain cosmic extension of this Body and Soul."[133] The word *Body* is important. And a more direct sense of the physicality, however subtle, of the Cosmic Christ is evident in Teilhard's testimony before his Lord:

> In a light that consistently grows brighter, you show me ever more clearly your Body — your personal sacramental Body — enveloped

in a "corona" or living dust, as vast as the world. . .

I see your flesh extend throughout the entire universe, there to be mingled with it and so extract from it all the elements that can be made to serve your purpose.[134]

This is the Cosmic Christ after the historical Incarnation took place and the Eucharistic ritual started, the ritual by which Christ physically enters into the bread consecrated by the priest and from that center, which is the technical Host, spreads out to form "another, infinitely larger Host, which is nothing less than the universe itself—the universe gradually being absorbed by the universal element."[135] But "the Incarnation is an act co-extensive with the duration of the world."[136] "Even before the Incarnation became a fact the whole history of the universe (in virtue of a true notion of the humanity of Christ, mysterious but yet known to us through revelation) is the history of the progressive information of the universe by Christ."[137] Hence from all past, from the very act of world creation there is a Christ-Incarnation in the universe. In the Body of Christ there are various stages and states. The historical Jesus is the individualized direct manifestation of this primordial incarnation. That is why Teilhard designates the latter "a prodigious biological operation"—a natural emergence of the supernatural and the superhuman, which are also from the beginning a natural process one with the evolution. Here one has the hypostatic union extended to the universe in a more diffused sense than the historical Incarnation. But the diffusiveness does not diminish the reality of it. And in natural evolutionary emergence, just as in history, one has a Christ-self ruling the incarnative phenomenon. The individual body of Christ was ruled by a distinct person: so too the universal body is ruled by a distinct self. And what is the relation between the universal body and the universe? The universal body is the divine unity at work; the universe is the pure Multiple getting unified. Both are God; they are, respectively, his aspects of positive being and positive nonbeing. The slow leavening of the latter is the cosmogenesis that is simultaneously "Christogenesis," the biological operation that comes to a head in the historical Jesus. At that stage the leavening becomes crucial Christ's historical existence is "a vast hand to hand struggle between the supreme unity and the Multiple it was engaged in unifying."[138] But "the Resurrection is a tremendous cosmic event. It marks Christ's effective assumption of his function as the universal centre. Until that time he is present in all things as a soul that is painfully gathering together its embryonic elements. Now he radiates over the universe as a consciousness and activity fully in control of themselves."[139]

Yes, to Teilhard the life of the historical Jesus signifies a momentous turning point in evolution. Still, as he says, Creation, Incarnation, and Redemption are one continuous process. The historical Incarnation is, let me repeat, only the visible sign of what invisibly was the very identical fact as soon as Creation took place. And where there is incarnation in the true sense there must be the hypostatic union. But I showed in the preceding chapter how Teilhard himself recognizes a universal hypostatic union to be Spinozism; that is to say, pantheism.[140] The sole difference between Spinozist pantheism and the Teilhardian concept is that the Cosmic Christ is more than the Soul of the universe, he has a transcendent reality too; but as the Soul of the universe he certainly is Pantheos, and the universe is the gross form of his being. More precisely, the universe is his gross physicality, upon which his subtle physicality, his cosmic Christ-Body, has been at work from the start of creation.

The subtle body, constituting the Universal Christ, most active after the birth, death, and resurrection of Jesus, but basically active throughout the past history of the universe, is the Mystical Milieu, the Divine Milieu, which Teilhard has made famous — the milieu that cannot be equated with the old "omnipresence" or "immanence" of God but is something superadded to it, a new development of essential pantheism, as well as a new development of essential Christianity. Teilhard claims that it is exclusively the latter. But when one pierces through his effort to assimilate pantheism into Christianity's essence, one discovers that he is equally assimilating Christianity into the essence of pantheism. Added to the term *positive nonbeing* for the *nihil* converted by God's creative act into the universe, the term *Incarnation* for God's creative act itself leaves one with no alternative.

Teilhard's Cosmic Christ, involving a universal incarnation for all time, along with a historical appearance of God in human flesh and blood to concentrate and render triumphant the gradual action of "divinizing" the physical world — Teilhard's fusion of Christianity with pantheism sends one back to ancient India's vision of God and his way with the world emanating from him. One difference, of course, is that India believed not in a single and final Incarnation in mankind's midst but in a succession of avatars down the ages. In every other respect Teilhardism is more the many-sided Vedanta than the restricted Christianity within which Teilhard strove to express himself. Sri Aurobindo has well characterized the former vis-à-vis the Christian attitude to God's incarnational activity:

> India has from ancient times held strongly a belief in the reality of the Avatar, the descent into form, the revelation of the Godhead in humanity. In the West this belief has never really stamped itself upon the mind because it has been presented through exoteric Christianity as a theological dogma without any roots in the reason and general consciousness and attitude towards life. But in India it has grown up and persisted as a logical outcome of the Vedantic view of life and taken firm root in the consciousness of the race. All existence is a manifestation of God because He is the only existence and nothing can be except as either a real figuring or else a figment of that one reality. Therefore every conscious being is in part or in some way a descent of the Infinite into the apparent finiteness of name and form. But it is a veiled manifestation and there is a gradation between the supreme being of the Divine and the consciousness shrouded partly or wholly by ignorance of self in the finite. The conscious embodied soul is the spark of the divine Fire and that soul in man opens out to self-knowledge as it develops out of ignorance of self into self-being. The Divine also, pouring itself into the forms of the cosmic existence, is revealed ordinarily in an efflorescence of its powers, in energies and magnitudes of its knowledge, love, joy, developed force of being, in degrees and faces of its divinity. But when the divine Consciousness and Power, taking upon itself the human form and the human mode of action, possesses it not only by powers and magnitudes, by degrees and outward faces of itself but out of its eternal self-knowledge, when the Unborn knows itself and acts in the frame of the mental being and the appearance of birth, that is the height of the conditioned manifestation; it is the full and conscious descent of the Godhead, it is the Avatar.[141]

One Divine Reality, the universe its restricted self-manifestation, human beings its veiled expressions, and the Incarnation proper the direct revealing figure of the general descent of the Transcendent into name and form that all cosmos is—here in the Vedantic philosophy of incarnation, which combines transcendentalism and pantheism, one has the real visionary of the Cosmic Christ, the true Teilhard, who was constantly coming up yet who was repeatedly pushed down by himself.

vi

Better to drive to its mark my point that Teilhard fused the genuinely pantheistic with the genuinely Christian, I may revert to a topic already touched upon in an earlier chapter: de Lubac's claim that the Cosmic Christ of Teilhard is essentially present not only in Saint Paul but also in several commentators and interpreters of the apostle. The sole difference stressed is that Teilhard fitted this Christ into an evolutionary framework, thereby modernizing Christianity. Very cleverly de Lubac takes care to quote from Teilhard's own contemporary coreligionists, as if to show that the Church of his time was not at all blind to what may be termed Teilhardian truths.

The most important among the experts he begins with is Père Férnand Prat, author of the "classic work, *The Theology of St. Paul.*"[142] Prat writes: "without Christ all creatures would be scattered, would be fragmented, and, in mutual conflict, would sink back again into nothingness. It is Christ who preserves for them, with existence, cohesion and harmony. . . .He is the all-mastering centre of creation. . . .Even, then, in so far as he is man, Jesus Christ has a cosmic role."[143]

Next comes Père Joseph Huby "in his classic *Commentary on the Epistles of the Captivity.*"[144] Huby writes on Christ: "In him all was created as in the supreme centre of unity, harmony, and cohesion, which gives the world its meaning and its value, and so its reality: or, to put it another way, as in the 'foyer' (*the meeting point* — Light-foot) at which all the threads, all the generating forces of the Universe, are woven together and coordinated. . . .He is the dominating centre, the keystone of the Universe: 'In him all subsist'. . . .Of the created world he made an ordered cosmos, giving it a meaning, a value, and relating it to an end. . . . Creation is oriented towards him as to the perfection of its fulfilment."[145]

Then there is Père Pierre Benoit, O.P.:

> The person of Christ and his work are looked at from a *cosmic* point of view. Christian salvation takes on the dimensions of the universe. . . .To designate the whole, Paul uses the word Pleroma. . . .
> The central theme that strikes one immediately is that of the *cosmic supremacy* of Christ [Paul asserts] that the *plenitude* of

the cosmos lies in Christ. . . .Christ, God and man by virtue of the Incarnation crowned by the Resurrection, embraces in this plenitude not only God who saves, not only men who are saved, but the whole setting of humanity, that is to say, the cosmos, including the angelic powers. . . .From these views the Epistle to the Colossians acquires the *cosmic, celestial horizon* that characterises it.[146]

De Lubac exclaims: "The cosmic Christ! The cosmic function of Christ — 'not only moral but physical'! This we see is not simply something that Teilhard invented."[147] But de Lubac never offers an explanation of one glaring fact. The fact springs into relief from his own choosing of writers with a view to aligning Teilhardism with the contemporary Church. Actually, his choice cuts the ground from under his feet. Prat's authoritative work in French dates to 1926; its English translation appeared in 1945.[148] Huby's famous study, in *Verbum Salutis 8,* was published in 1935.[149] Benoit's *Les Épitres de Saint Paul aux Philippiens* saw the light in 1949.[150] And all these books carried the Catholic Church's *nihil obstat* and *imprimatur.* The censors found absolutely nothing objectionable in their Cosmic Christ. Yet in the same period they clamped down uncompromisingly on Teilhard's. If "the cosmic function of Christ," which he spoke of, was not "simply something that Teilhard invented," why was his concurrence with his fellow ecclesiastics so ruthlessly suppressed? They too lived in the modern milieu and not in one where "the world, the 'whole' (with all the organic definitions that these words imply for us), were still non-existent for human consciousness."[151] They too were aware that evolution as a world view had come to stay. So why the inequality of treatment by the Church? One may determine the answer from de Lubac himself. Those ecclesiastics never underwent the conversion of thought that de Lubac describes in Teilhard's case without properly understanding it: "It became increasingly more evident to Teilhard that, if Christ was to remain himself, without diminution, at the centre of our faith, then — if the world is an evolution — the cosmic Christ, the Beginning, the Bond and the Term of all creation, must now offer himself for our adoration as the 'evolutive' Christ."[152]

It is this " 'evolutive' Christ" that is the rub. But to fit Christ into an evolutionary framework does not automatically set up the evolutive Christ or, as another phrase of Teilhard goes, "Christ the Evolver."[153] The crucial step lies in passing from the "moral" to the "physical" or, to put it otherwise, from the "juridical" to the "organic." One can stick to the former category in either pair even in an evolutionary framework, and then there is really no modernization of Christianity. Teilhard is very precise in this matter and permits no loose thinking. Apropos of "the mystery in which Christianity is summed up, the mystery of the Incarnation," he writes:

> So long as it is described and treated in juridical terms, the Incarnation appears a simple phenomenon—one that can be superimposed upon any type of world. Whether the universe be large or small, static or evolutionary, it is equally simple for God to *give* it to his Son: for all that is involved, to put it briefly, is a declaration. A very different situation comes to light if we look at it from an organic point of view, which is basically the point of view of all true knowledge of the real. The Christian's (or rather, to be more precise, the Catholic's) dearest belief is that Christ envelops him in his grace and makes him participate in his divine life. When we go on to ask by what physical possibility this mysterious process is effected, we are told "by the divine power." Very well—but this is no more an answer than is the Negro's who explains an aircraft by saying "white man's magic." How exactly is the divine power to put the universe together in such a way that it may be possible for an incarnation to be biologically effected in it?. . .If we Christians wish to *retain* in Christ the very qualities on which his power and our worship are based, we have no better way—no other way, even—of doing so than fully to accept the most modern concepts of evolution.[154]

So we see that Christ has to be born in the world biologically, evolutively. To posit such a birth and not merely to adopt an evolutionary framework is what is meant by modernizing Christianity. And an even more direct gloss on the modernization is available when Teilhard discusses the phenomenon of revelation. "God," he tells us, "never reveals himself to us from outside, by intrusion, but *from within*, by stimulation, elevation and enrichment of the human psychic current."[155] Teilhard gives a footnote to the words *from within*. The footnote runs: "I.e. *Evolutively*. Correctly speaking, the basic principle that in all domains (creation, redemption, revelation, sanctification) God never acts except evolutively seems to me necessary, and all that is necessary, for modernizing Christianity." Thus, if Christianity is to be modernized and Christ to be evolutive, one must think of him as revealing himself in history not from outside but from within the world by a stimulation, elevation, and enrichment of, in the immediate instance, the general human psychic current and, in the intermediate instance, all the biological currents of the earth and, in the remote initial instance, the currents of the whole universe studied by physics.

Teilhard succinctly puts this view of Christ's historical incarnation and of whatever future results follow from it: "Christogenesis. . .is none other than the 'soul' of cosmogenesis."[156] Conversely, one may affirm that, to Teilhard, cosmogenesis is the process of bringing out the Christ who dwells as a soul in the evolving body that is the whole cosmos. This would make Christ "incarnate" himself from the beginning in the universe and proceed through all evolution to become the historic Incarnation proper. The basic identity of primal Creation and later Incarnation is the very quick of Christianity's modernization. This identity is implied in a phrase such as "the *axis* of Incarnation, that is to say, of Creation."[157] To Teilhard, creation consists in the "progressive unification of the multiple,"[158] — "pure multiplicity" that is God's " 'antipodial' aureole" (or shadow).[159] When "creation is presented essentially in terms of evolution. . .*the same* fundamental process can be called creation, incarnation, or redemption according to what aspect of it is considered;" thus creation can be called incarnation, for "the Divine 'I,' as a direct result of its own operation, cannot but 'immerse' itself in its work" — just as creation can be called redemption, for, "at whatever point *during* the process of unification the created is considered, it represents a portion of residual non-organization or disorganization (actual or potential) which is the determining factor in all forms of evil. . .evil which has to be atoned for and overcome."[160] Teilhard also writes of "Creation (*because* it is unifying) entailing a certain immersion of the Creator in his work, and at the same time (*because* it is necessarily productive of evil as a secondary statistical effect) entailing a certain redemptive compensation."[161]

The basic equating of Creation with Incarnation stands out again when Teilhard appreciates the traditional concept of God as Triune, a trinity in unity, three persons in one. He says: "If God were not 'triune' (if, that is, he contained no inner self-distinction). . .we could not conceive the possibility of his creating (and in consequence being incarnate) without totally immersing himself in the world he brings into being."[162] This is tantamount to saying that creation is a (progressive) universal incarnation that yet leaves God "transcendent"—subsisting free, independent, self-fulfilled.

Does de Lubac or any other Catholic commentator understand Teilhard's universal incarnationism? And which of the Pauline expositors who were Teilhard's contemporaries could have subscribed to it? Unless this incarnationism is granted, Christ's "cosmic function" cannot truly go beyond being moral and juridical to being physical and organic. The cosmicality that these ecclesiastics, Saint Paul's followers, attribute to Christ is easily seen for what it is through some passages in Prat. Prat has other Teilhardian phrases that de Lubac does not quote—such as that Christ makes all things "converge towards him, as to their common centre." Still, he is leagues away from Teilhard. After expounding Saint Paul's formula that in all things Christ holds the primacy (Col. 1:18) as fundamentally meaning the same as "he is before all things" (Col. 1:17), Prat goes on to deal with some outstanding cosmic suggestions in the Apostle:

> The absolute primacy of the Son is expressed by this other formula "All things are in him, all things are by him, all things are for him." All things are *in* him because, being the perfect image of God, he comprises the ideal and the model of all things possible and is thus the exemplary cause of all contingent beings. All things are *by* him, as the efficient cause, God, in his outward operations, acting by the Son in the Holy Spirit in accordance with the order and harmony of his inmost life. All things are *for* him by a double right, both because the creation is his work and because God, embracing at a glance the whole multitude of his counsels, connected with his Son, in advance and by a special bond of finality, the world of nature and the world of grace. For these two relations of Christ as God and as man, as the author of nature and as the author of grace, are hardly ever separated, but, whether he be considered as God or as man, his transcendent dignity comes originally from his primacy.[163]

This kind of cosmicality, based on the so-called cosmic passage of Col. 1:15-20, is what one would ascribe to all divinity acting with the power of creative and controlling consciousness. It is just to be expected in one who is the Second Person of the Holy Trinity, the Word that was in the beginning no less than the Word that became flesh. And de Lubac has little difficulty in displaying various exegeses almost right from the earliest centuries of Christianity, proclaiming Christ's universal presence and domination in vivid concept and concrete imagery.[164] These texts can never smack of heresy, no matter how closely they may seem to anticipate Teilhardian formulas. De Lubac is wrong in labelling as Teilhard's "spiritual ancestry" either "a disciple of St. Hippolytus" or Origen, Saint Gregory of Nyssa or Saint Maximus the Confessor, Rabanus Maurus or, in less olden times, Cardinal de Bérulle. Nowhere does de Lubac's evidence have any precise relation to the "physical" cosmicality of Teilhard's Christ. Teilhard would scarcely have been stifled for teaching, however vividly in concept and concretely in imagery, the general cosmicality of God.

Starting with this cosmicality, he brings out an entirely new shade of theological vision. From Saint Paul's paean to the Christ in whom all was created, he *in quo omnia constant* ("in whom all things hold together" — Col. 1:17) and who consummates everything, Teilhard conjured up an aspect quite original. That is why, despite the cosmicality in the general sense that had always been admitted, he could urge the need for "the rise in Christian consciousness of what we might call the *Universal-Christ*," and write with urgent emphasis:

> Hitherto, the thought of the faithful could hardly be said explicitly to distinguish in practice more than two aspects of Christ: the Man-Jesus and the Word-God. Yet it is clear that a third aspect of the theandric complex was left in the background. By that I mean the mysterious super-human person constantly underlying the Church's most fundamental institutions and most solemn dogmatic affirmations. . . .Until today, I repeat, this third aspect of the *incarnate* Word has been insufficiently distinguished from the other two — for lack, apparently, of a concrete, "phenomenal" substratum which could be materialized in Christian thought and piety. But consider that is happening today. Under the combined influence of men's thoughts and aspirations, the universe around us is seen to be knit together and convulsed by a vast movement of convergence. Not only theoretically, but experientially, our modern Cosmogony is taking the form of a cosmogenesis (or rather a psycho-or noo-genesis) at the term of which we can distinguish a supreme focus of personalizing personality [Omega Point]. Who can fail to see the purport, the reinforcement, the stimulus which this discovery of the physical pole of universal synthesis contributes to our view of revelation? Just suppose that we *identify* (at least in his "natural" aspect) the cosmic Christ of faith with the Omega Point of sci-

ence: then everything in our outlook is clarified and broadened and falls into harmony. First, the term of the world's physical-biological evolution no longer appears indeterminate to our reason: it has been given a concrete peak, a heart, a face. And secondly there is the effect on our faith. The exaggerated properties attributed to the incarnate Word by tradition lose their metaphysical and juridical character; they take their place smoothly and realistically among and at the head of the most fundamental of the currents now recognized in the universe by science. Christ is indeed, we must admit, in a fantastic position; but, just because it is fantastic, it fits the true scale of things. The fact is, that the keystone of the arch to be built is there in our hands. If we are to effect the synthesis between faith in God and faith in the world, for which our generation is waiting, there is nothing better we can do than dogmatically to bring out in the person of Christ the cosmic aspect and function which make him organically the prime mover and controller, the "soul," of evolution.[165]

Thus adjusting Christ into a new position, Teilhard says: "Projected, then, on the screen of evolution Christ in an exact, physical, unvarnished sense is seen to possess those most awesome properties which St. Paul lavishly attributes to him."[166]

Surely, no one can take Teilhard's universalization of the Pauline Christ for granted. By contrast, how expected and commonplace the general cosmicality of God could be to a non-Teilhardian exegete of Saint Paul is illustrated by the greatest of Pauline authorities tapped by de Lubac. Prat never speaks of Christ's "cosmic role" in this connection. It is a specific phase of Christ's work that elicits the term from Prat. The term comes in only when Christ, from being the Lord of the universe in a general sense, grows in Saint Paul's prophetic eyes to being the Dispenser of harmony to all existence at the end of human history, as well as the Deliverer of the entire universe at that time. Also, the term in question or any equivalent of it appears in Prat as applying to situations that are rare in Saint Paul and that do not constitute the apostle's usual "soteriology," his prevalent conception of Christ's savior mission. If one follows Prat, one is not entitled to make too much capital, for Paul's "cosmicism," out of a few nontypical verses. Prat is worth hearing on these points.

He commences: "In general, the redeeming plan has our earth for its horizon and comprises only the human race. Sometimes, however, the prospect widens out and the divine plan comprehends the universality of being, making the whole of creation converge towards Christ." Then Prat quotes Col. 1:19-20, in which Christ, who has complete primacy and in whom all fullness dwells, is ordained by God to reconcile among themselves all things on earth and in heaven. Prat stresses the particle *re* in the verb *reconcile*, suggesting "a return to a previous state of concord before the appearance of sin." Next, he comments on a similar text, Eph. 1:9-10, in which God has willed ultimately to "re-establish all things in Christ, that are in heaven and on earth." Prat writes:

> In the parallel passage the field of vision remains as wide, but the union of beings under the sceptre of the incarnate Word is marked in it by a still more definite characteristic. . . .
>
> In both there is indicated — or insinuated — the return to a primitive state of harmony and concord; finally, in both the cosmic role of Christ serves as a prelude to the reconciliation of the pagans with God and to the reunion of the Jews and Gentiles in one and the same mystical body.
>
> Even as man, therefore, Jesus Christ has a cosmic role; he is the head of the angels and has dominion over all creation. If we think of the disorder produced by sin in the entire work of God and of the harmony which the presence of Christ restores to it, we see that this cosmic role is in some way closely related to soteriology. It is a sort of cosmical reaction of the incarnation and a sudden enlargement of the horizon contemplated by the Apostle, whose gaze does not usually go beyond the salvation of man.[167]

To the term *soteriology* Prat has the footnote: "All creatures participate *to a certain degree* in the blessings of redemption. The glorification of man sheds its influence morally over the whole universe. For this idea see Roms. viii 20, 21."

Apropos of the text here referred to, Prat remarks:

> When man has once arrived at the term of his destinies, what will become of his former dwelling-place? Only one text of the Apostle authorizes us to make some rather uncertain inferences on the subject. It represents the material creation as awaiting with anxiety and impatience the glorification of the elect, in which God has promised to make it participate.
>
> Without laying undue stress on this poetical word-picture it is evident that the material creation — for it is of this that the Apostle speaks in contrast to rational things — was associated in some measure with the fall of man and that it will to some degree participate in his glorification.[168]

Then Prat asks whether the earth actually "lost its natural fertility" or whether the situation was merely such as to make "man lose the providential aid which protected him from the hard law of toil." The question also involves asking what kind of redemption there will be. Prat deals with the pertinent points thus: "This isolated text does not allow us to reply to this question with certainty. The curse pronounced by God upon the earth punished man directly, but affected the earth only by reaction. . . .We should ask Paul, less than anyone, to describe to us the destinies of the material creation. All his interest is concentrated on the history of humanity. Even this history, in proportion as it progresses, becomes bounded within an ever-narrowing horizon; first the human race, then the Church militant, then the elect associated with the triumph of Christ, and finally, God all in all."

These frank, judicious, and cautionary expressions are an excellent antidote to the infection common today of Pauline Christology by the cosmic outlook. And they are more than sufficient to cure one of identifying with the out-and-out cosmicality of the Teilhardian Christ this Christology, as well as the Christology of Paul's exegetes in Teilhard's day. No ground is essentially shared by Teilhard and his fellow religionists of the first half of the twentieth century. The venture to prove the Roman Catholic Church not a purblind tyrant toward Teilhard and to suggest a basic affinity between it and him in spite of every contrary appearance is disingenuous and unconvincing.

In all likelihood, Teilhard was acquainted with the Pauline exegesis current in his lifetime. He must have found it totally inadequate and felt that it did not do justice either to the apostle's vision or to his own sympathetic modern version of it. In his understanding of Paul, he was, as Prat's treatment of the Colossians passage as well as of other verses leads one to think, quite in error, notwithstanding Rom. 8:19-22 and the text in Acts 17:28, in which Paul is credited with the strikingly pantheistic phrase, "In him we live, and move, and have our being." The cosmicality read in Paul by Teilhard's ecclesiastical contemporaries and fully approved by Rome was to his mind no more than "moral." About the Christ who would possess it without possessing "physical" cosmicality he had a very poor opinion, as one may recognize from his assertion that "we must unhesitatingly attribute to the Incarnate Word," whom Saint Paul (Phil. 3:21) invests with the power to subject everything to himself, an organic cosmicality of evolutive energy "if we are not to allow a world to assume greater dimensions, to overflow its limits, around the figure of Christ—a world that would be more beautiful, more majestic, more organic and more worthy of adoration than Christ."[169] This clearly shows that—once again to use Teilhard's turns of speech—unless one holds that "the universe is physically impregnated to the very core of its matter by the influence of [Christ's] supernatural nature" and that "the presence of the Incarnate Word penetrates everything, as a universal element,"[170] Christianity, in Teilhard's eyes, lamentably falls short. The traditional Christ, whatever the cosmicality accorded him by the orthodox representatives of the twentieth-century Roman Church, is not Teilhard's Christ: he lacks the latter's universal incarnationism.

This incarnationism was misunderstood by that Church as being, in the words of Dom Georges Frénaud, "contradictory of the personal God"; but the Church was right to think that, once more in Frénaud's phrase, "the 'Cosmic Christ' [in Teilhard] is necessarily an expression tainted with pantheism."[171] Of course, the participle *tainted* draws its condemnatory life from the mistake in believing that a personal God has to be sacrificed if pantheism is affirmed. But the essentially pantheistic component of Teilhardism emerges with definitive clarity from the very attempt de Lubac makes to deny it by citing Catholic interpreters of what Père Irénée Hausherr designates Paul's "obsession with totality" and with Christ's "universalism."[172]

The same component gains emphasis from some quotations by de Lubac from orthodox predecessors of Teilhard, meant to prove that pantheistlike expressions are not really anathema to the Church. Thus, Saint Ignatius Loyola, the founder of Teilhard's order, taught his followers to "contemplate God as existing in every one of the creatures."[173] Saint Teresa believed that God is present in all beings, and Saint Thomas Aquinas said: "God must be present in all things, and that in an intimate manner."[174] There is also a contemporary of Teilhard's, the Thomist theologian Pierre-Thomas Dehau, O.P. "whose only concern is to state the most fully traditional teaching" and who wrote:

Our habitual concepts tell us only about personalities exterior to and therefore foreign or strange to our own. When we are concerned with God, we must realize that we are concerned with a being who is certainly distinct from us, but who is at the same time the reason for our own being. . . .If I take myself, suppressing all my imperfections and magnifying to infinity my own poor perfections, even those most personal and peculiar to myself, the most incommunicable, then I have God. That is why theologians can say, "God is not another, he is virtually and eminently myself, he is an infinite myself, pure act." . . .It is thus that, while completely rejecting pantheism, we retain anything legitimate that may be contained in its tendencies.[175]

The end of this statement, appearing in 1942, strikes a note very much like Teilhard's sentence: "The 'universalised' Christ takes over, correcting and completing them, the energies that undoubtedly lie hidden in modern forms of pantheism."[176] And yet Teilhard's sentence could not be published during his lifetime. Even now de Lubac, although considering Dehau's expression bolder than any of Teilhard's, has to be at considerable pains to defend Teilhard from those who are inclined to accuse him of worshipping nature. This is because there are directly pantheistic overtones in a doctrine that figures the Christ of orthodoxy as less divine than the infinite evolving universe of modern science, if that Christ is not "universalized" in a form "which is more organic and takes more account of physics."[177] "A Christ who is no longer master of the world solely because he has been *proclaimed* to be such, but because he animates the whole range of things from top to bottom; a Christ who dominates the history of heaven and earth not solely because these have been *given* to him, but because his gestation, his birth and gradual consummation constitute *physically* the only definitive reality in which the evolution of the world is expressed; there we have the only God whom we can henceforth worship sincerely. And that is precisely the God suggested to us by the new aspect the universe has assumed."[178]

One may attend to the point that cosmic evolution is equated with the gestation, birth, and gradual consummation of Christ. Christ and universal history are identified in the sense that the former underlies the latter and the latter unfolds the former. A divine incarnation coextensive with all time and space progressively manifested is implied. To return to a theme already mentioned, Creation, Incarnation, and Redemption are now, as they are not in orthodox Christianity, the continuity of a single event in three focuses, each of which discloses more emphatically one or other perspective of the same movement. As Teilhard has put it: "To create is, for God, to unite himself to his work, that is to say in one way or another to involve himself in the world by incarnation. And is not 'to be incarnate' *ipso facto* to share in the suffering and evils inherent in the painfully concentrating multiple?"[179] After the participation in the world travail there comes at long last the fulfillment or pleroma, in which the world will be openly filled with the presence of the Cosmic Christ and become directly his vast Mystical Body.

In a more fervent and personal manner, Teilhard expresses his cosmic Christian credo thus:

> Lord of Consistence and Union, You whose distinguishing mark and essence are that You can grow indefinitely, without distortion or break in time with the mysterious Matter at whose heart You lie and of all whose movements You are the final controller — Lord of my childhood and of my end — God, fulfilled for himself, and yet for us, God whose birth has no end — God who, since You offer Yourself for our adoration as "evolver and evolutive," are now the only God who can bring us satisfaction — tear away at last all the clouds that still veil You — and tear away the clouds too of hostile prejudices and false beliefs.[180]

De Lubac, in order to remove the fear of some readers that "Teilhard did not believe sufficiently in the eternal present-ness of God or in the initial divinity of Jesus of Nazareth," comments: "The passage. . .contains expressions that remove the double ambiguity: the God to whose birth for us there is no end is the God 'fulfilled for himself,' and the 'evolutive' Christ is first, in himself, Christ 'the evolver.' " De Lubac is right in assuring one that the traditional divinity of Christ is not negated, but he hardly realizes the full implications of Teilhard's credo. I may sum them up best by harking back, at the start, to his expression that the universe as newly seen by science shows itself as worthy of adoration. If it draws one to adore it, Teilhard takes it to be a divine entity in its essential being. And his Cosmic Christ cannot be interpreted in any way to undivinize it. This Christ provides the true reason for its adorableness, the real ground of its divinity. He is the perfect soul, of which it is the evolving body. Nor is this all. There is not only Christ the Evolver by whom the universe evolves; there is also the evolutive Christ, the Christ who himself evolves in what appears to be a universe evolving. A God is being engendered in the cosmos at the same time that a complete and fulfilled God already exists both in himself and as the directing cosmic principle of evolution. They are the same God—one who is transcendent even while being a perfect Pantheos and one who while being this perfect Pantheos is also progressively emergent in matter and life and mind and, beyond individual minds, a collective superconsciousness.

vii

In tune with de Lubac's enlistment of the early Greek fathers as part of Teilhard's spiritual ancestry, a whole book has been written by a Jesuit admirer of both Teilhard and de Lubac.

George A. Maloney's "purpose is to present a vision of Christ in his relation to the world shared across the ages by many Christian theologians for whom Jesus Christ was encountered in and through the material cosmos."[181] Architects of this tradition include not only Saint Paul and Saint John but also the entire school of religions exegetes belonging to the Eastern Church, from Irenaeus down to Maximus the Confessor. After dealing with them, Maloney treats of "Teilhard de Chardin's christological contribution and the development of contemporary Christian secularity." Here one is told about Teilhard: "He has succeeded in recapturing the same vision of the cosmic Christ so dear to earlier Christians."[182]

The book unrolls a fascinating panorama of religious ideas and aspirations. But its linking of the early Greek Fathers with Teilhard is open to serious question. Maloney is too much carried away by general resemblances and verbal similarities to serve as a reliable guide in comparison. His unreliability is brought into focus at the threshold of his comparative scrutiny, when he sums up his admirable survey of antiquity before launching on the cosmic Christology of Teilhard. He tells us:

> The work of the Greek Fathers of the first seven centuries of Christian existence was well done. The Church has need of thinkers of the twentieth century who can complete the teaching of the Fathers in terms that are intelligible to us today. We turn to one such modern teacher, Teilhard de Chardin, as representative of a modern school of Fathers eager to explore the cosmic dimensions of the christology formulated by the Greek Fathers, in ways, at times, so strikingly presaging Teilhardian thought, as when Maximus speaks across twelve centuries of "Christ. . .as a centre upon which all lines converge."[183]

On reading this conclusion, one may recall from the preceding chapter that, in interpreting Saint Paul, Férnand Prat, another Jesuit, has almost exactly the same words as Maximus. Does not Prat speak of Christ's making all things "converge towards him, as to their common centre"? And yet can Prat's Paulinism be given a Teilhardian meaning? The fact that his book received Rome's *nihil obstat* and *imprimatur* in 1927 for the French edition and in 1945 for the English, is itself a suggestion of its non-Teilhardism. Besides, I have shown positive reasons why it cannot be regarded as Teilhardian. Such words as Prat and Maximus use arise naturally from a study of Paul's Epistles but need have no bearing on the content of Teilhardian phraseology.

How can they have any bearing when, like every other utterance of the Greek fathers, they have behind them a non-Teilhardian vision of "the presence and activity of Christ in the cosmos,"[184] or, as Maloney puts it elsewhere, "the immanence of Christ in the material world"?[185] All the fathers were at one with Athanasius, who called God the world's "Artificer,"[186] with Gregory of Nyssa, who wrote of "the instant and simultaneous" making of all things,[187] and with Maximus, who described God as "the universal cause who made creatures distinct from one another in the beginning."[188] Christ's immanence, therefore, must have meant to the Greek Fathers such presence and activity in the universe as would be consonant with the being of a God extrinsic to nature, a Creator of her *ab extra* by an instantaneous act. This immanence is in contrast with the Teilhardian sort. The latter is tied up with Teilhard's view of world creation as evolutive and with Christ's physical and organic involvement in the universe from the dawn of creation up to the highest evolutive stage possible. The contrast with it should have struck Maloney the moment he was led to admit: "With their level of scientific knowledge, the Fathers were in no position to see the interrelationships of all material creatures and their mutual dependence."[189] He appears to believe that here is no basic cleavage and that Teilhard had only to carry "the total, unified vision" of the ancient patristic epoch further in modern scientific terms. A capital mistake, this—as will be seen in an exposition of Teilhard by himself.

He begins by mentioning "our generation's gradual wakening to consciousness of a movement which is cosmic in breadth and organicity: a movement which, whether we welcome it or not, is drawing us, through the relentless building up in our minds of a common *Weltanschauung*, towards some 'ultra-human' lying ahead in time." Behind this *Weltanschauung* Teilhard traces this age's scientific perception that "nothing exists. . .except as a function of a vast and single combined process" of forming complex unified structures, "in the course of which can be distinguished the phases of a gradual and irreversible 'interiorization' (development of consciousness) of what we call (without knowing what it is) matter." First there are simple particles of apparently unconscious "Pre-life." Next, "with the emergence of life. . .we have beings that are simply conscious." And now human beings are not only "reflective" but are growing "co-reflective" by an increasing association, until there shall be one "planetized" consciousness. One can discern in the future the infallible appearance "of a peak of unification at the higher term of cosmic ferment."[190] This peak is, of course, Teilhard's famous Omega Point, on which the cosmos converges in its evolution. From the scientific sense of Omega "arises the general maladjustment one sees on all sides in the old moulds in which either morality or religion is contained."[191]

Then Teilhard comes out with his crucial statement:

> We still hear it said that the fact that we now see the universe not as a cosmos but henceforth as a cosmogenesis in no way affects the idea we used to be able to form of the Author of all things. "As though it makes any difference to God," is a common objection, "whether he creates *instantaneously* or *evolutively*."
> I shall not try to discuss the notion (or pseudo-notion) of "instantaneous creation," nor dwell on the reasons which make me suspect the presence of an ontological contradiction latent in this association of the two words.
> On the other hand I must emphasize with all the power at my command the following cardinal point:
> While, in the case of a static world, the creator (the efficient cause) is still, on any theory, *structurally* independent of his work, and in consequence, without any definable basis to his immanence — in the case of a world which is by nature evolutive, the contrary is true: God is not conceivable (either structurally or organically) except in so far as he coincides with (as a sort of "formal" cause), but without being lost in, the centre of convergence of cosmogenesis. I say, advisedly, either structurally or organically: because if God did not appear to us now at this supreme and exact point at which we see that nature is finally held together, our capacity to love would inevitably gravitate not towards him but (a situation we could not possibly accept) towards some other "God."

Ever since Aristotle there have been almost continual attempts to construct "models" of God on the lines of an outside Prime Mover, acting *a retro*.* Since the emergence in our consciousness of the "sense of evolution" it has become physically impossible for us to conceive or worship anything but an organic Prime-Mover God, *ab ante*.**

In future only a God who is functionally and totally "Omega" can satisfy us. . . .

Where, then, shall we find such a God? And who will at last give evolution *its own* God?. . .

As a result. . .of life's very recent passing through a new critical point in the course of its development, no older religious form or formulation can any longer (either factually or logically) satisfy to the full our need and capacity for worship. . . .So true is this that a religion of the future (definable as a "religion of evolution") cannot fail to appear before long: a new mysticism of evolution, the germ of which (as happens when anything is born) must be recognizable somewhere in our environment, *here and now*. . . .

Christ has never ceased since his first coming to reemerge from every crisis of history with more immediacy, more urgency and greater penetrative power than ever before.

If then he is to be able to offer himself once again to our new world as the 'new God' for whom we are looking, what does he still lack?

Two things, to my mind, and two only.

The first is this: that in a universe in which we can no longer seriously entertain the idea that thought is an exclusively terrestrial phenomenon, Christ must no longer be constitutionally restricted in his operation to a mere "redemption" of our planet.

And the second: that in a universe in which we can now see that everything is co-reflective along a single axis, Christ must no longer be offered to our worship (in consequence of a subtle and pernicious confusion between "super-natural" and "extra-natural") as a peak distinct from and a rival to that to which the biologically continued slope of anthropogenesis is leading us.[192]

Finally, Teilhard speaks of the "fundamental identity" of "the two Omegas. . ., the Omegas of experience and of faith.."[193]

Clearly, one can mark the incompatibility between the old immanence and the new. The old, because God created a static

* "Starting from the beginning."

** "Drawing us ahead."

cosmos from the outside as its Artificer or efficient cause, was something without a proper basis, something vague that was not organically linked either to the Creation or to the Creator. The new coincides with the evolutive process and will find its full evolutive expression in the ultrahuman totalization of mankind in a vast unanimity toward which life seems to be heading. The Christ who is thus immanent is certainly not "lost" in the cosmogenesis: he is never completely immersed in the creation but has his independent, free, self-fulfilled aspect as the transcendent Divine. But he is, with equal certainty, no mere presence and activity in the world: he is the world's all-permeating indweller or soul, the cosmic Self of selves, such as pantheism has visioned and worshipped. In Teilhard's own phrase, this Christ, the Omega of faith, is fundamentally identical with the physical-biological Omega of experience. The genuine essence of pantheism is thus synthesized with the genuine essence of Christianity. Not just a furthering of the patristic Christology in new terms is achieved. This is a concept different toto coelo, and, being poles apart from the cosmic Christology of the Greek fathers, it is also at basic variance even with Saint Paul's.

What obscures this fact is, ironically enough, Teilhard's own eagerness to find common points between his notions and theirs. In one place he proposes to pass beyond the Latin fathers, who "overdeveloped the rabbinical and legalistic side of St. Paul." He considers the Church of his time as "unmindful of a nobler tradition" and speaks of the modern scientific pressure obliging us "to return to a form of Christianity which is more organic and takes more account of physics."[194] One can guess that he has persuaded himself that the original Pauline doctrine, as well as the expression of it by the Greek fathers, had a side conformable to a physics-founded religion of evolution. In the very context that I have quoted from him to pit him against the stand of the Greek fathers on God and the created world, he recalls Saint Paul: "For Christ would not still be the Consummator so passionately described by St. Paul if he did not take on precisely the attributes of the astonishing cosmic pole already potentially (if not as yet explicitly) demanded by our new knowledge of the world: the pole at whose peak the progress of evolution must finally converge."[195] But a parity between the Pauline Christ and the Teilhardian is impossible so long as Saint Paul believed, as Teilhard says he did, "in one week of creation and a past of 4,000 years."[196] Teilhard has himself noted in the apostle "the ideas of a first-century Jew," "those outdated formulations."[197] Again, "For St. Paul, we must remember, the world was only a week old when Adam sinned."[198] Unquestionably, Teilhard believed that Saint Paul's background had been a static nonevolutive cosmos instantaneously created. Hence, whatever immanence either the apostle or his early Eastern commentators might imply for Christ could never be—for all the "dynamic" or "existential" color of their mysticism—the kind of cosmicality that Teilhard would designate *physical and organic*. His self-obscuration sprang from his fervent wish to have a legitimate place in the Catholic Church whose minister he was, and even more from his deep devotion to the historical Jesus as pictured by Saint Paul and Saint John, with a stress on Christ's being he in whom and by whom and for whom all things had been created. Seized by that great formula of Col. 1:15, he let himself slur over the fact that the cosmicality for which both the Pauline-Johannine Scripture and the writing of the Greek fathers showed such zest was yet no more than the general cosmicality inseparable from any being taken to be supremely divine and posited as a transcendent creator and preserver of the cosmos.

For what indeed does that Pauline formula signify? Prat explains: "The Son is the efficient cause, the exemplary cause, and the final cause of all beings." Prat observes that the Greek grammatical tense —the perfect—used by Saint Paul in saying of the Son what is translated as "all things are by him" subsumes under the category of Christ's creative activity—that is, his efficient causality—two concepts. The case is unlike that of John 1:3, in which the aorist tense is employed and the reference thereby is solely to "the first production of created beings." Saint Paul does not only indicate this first production: he "also designates the present relation of creatures to the Son as to their Creator. They have been created by him, and 'they consist in him' [Col. 1:17]. . . .He it is who preserves their existence, cohesion and harmony."[199] Readers of Teilhard will at once notice that Prat has pressed into service a phrase repeatedly at the tip of Teilhard's pen—"*In quo omnia constant*," which is rendered in his context as "In whom all things hold together." Thus the holding together of things, on which Teilhard, overlooking the distinction between the aorist and the perfect, would found part of the physical and organic relationship of Christ to the cosmos, is, in

Paul, a part of Christ's role as efficient cause. And, as the efficient cause, the Pauline Christ can be no more than the extrinsic Artificer of the world—a world of continuing existence as an artifact. Teilhard could never impose such a limitation upon his Christ, who is the God of evolution, an intrinsic divine principle.

As the exemplary cause, the Christ of Saint Paul, in spite of the preposition *in* of the phrase "he in whom," does not contain the world literally. Prat is quite explicit here and he rests his interpretation on the Greek patristic tradition itself as to how the world was created in Christ: "Many of the Fathers, following St. Hippolytus and Origen, suppose that it is in his quality as a divine exemplar, as the home of ideas and universal archetype." Although one must carefully avoid ascribing to the Pauline concept of Christ "Platonian and Philonian speculations in the *intelligible world*," the cosmos "was in him and could be in him only in an intelligible way, as in its model or exemplar."[200] Such an exclusive gloss would hardly be acceptable to Teilhard: his Christ is not confined to being "a home of ideas." Besides constituting the "universal archtype," he is one with the movement of evolution.

This additional mode of relationship to the world lends a new nuance to Christ in the role of "final cause"; for the Omega Point as the world's finality makes Christ in that role identical not only with the supracosmic Son of God and with his historical Incarnation, but also with the physical-biological force that culminates in Omega Point. And this identification, in turn, brings in the issue of a fourth kind of cause, which has been mentioned by Teilhard in the passage about the old immanence, which was "without any definable basis," and the new, which is based on God's coinciding, structurally and organically, with the center of convergence of cosmogenesis.

Here Teilhard uses the expression "as a sort of 'formal' cause." Prat too speaks of this cause but only in the phrase "exemplary or formal cause."[201] The two usages have entirely different senses. Prat's sense is somewhat analogous to that of Plato's "forms" existing in the ideal realm beyond the universe, whereas Teilhard's refers to the universe where God is "functionally and totally 'Omega.' " The whole Teilhardian situation and the need to introduce a formal cause along with the final is well brought out by Donald B. Gray in discussing Teilhard's attitude to God as the efficient cause in the traditional connotation. Gray offers a quotation from Teilhard on how the universal Christ functions: "The characteristic attribute of the Universal Element, as it appears to us realized in the figure of Christ, is to be not a quasi-matter, a plastic element, an agent of absorption, but a quasi-Soul, a plasmatic element, a determining force."[202] Then Gray writes:

> The cosmic Christ is the soul, the physical or organic centre of the evolutionary movement *in toto*, but most particularly of humanity in process of socialization. Because evolution for Teilhard is primarily a movement of unification, and unification is a work which belongs properly to the soul or spirit, it follows logically that in attempting to determine the relationship which obtains between God and the world, Teilhard quite naturally thinks of this relationship in terms of formal, or rather quasi-formal, causality (the causality appropriate to the soul) rather than in terms of efficient causality. A causal relationship of a quasi-formal kind establishes an organic relationship between God in Christ and the world, whereas a causal relationship of an efficient kind seems to Teilhard to establish a relationship which is altogether too extrinsic and hence inadequate to describe the organic kind of unity which Teilhard envisions as being the goal of mankind's thrust towards socialization. Furthermore, inasmuch as evolution for Teilhard is the form assumed for us by God's creative activity, God's creative activity is understood in terms of quasi-formal rather than efficient causality. From being the artisan of a static universe, God becomes in the framework of Teilhard's system the soul of creation as an ongoing process of unification. Or, to put the matter more accurately, *Christ* becomes in the framework of Teilhard's system the soul of creation, the quasi-formal cause of unity. . . .
>
> In an essay written in 1918 ["Forma Christi," *Writings in Time of War*, p. 265], Teilhard expresses in a particularly clear way his animus against the category of efficient causality:
>
> "The term *efficient causality* when applied to *creation* quite accurately affirms the distinction which separates the Creator from his work (i.e. it serves to deny pantheism); however it tells us virtually nothing about the nature of the process which links *participated being to uncreated* Being; — on the contrary, it introduces between the two an *exteriority* which is surely exaggerated."
>
> If the notion of efficient causality adequately safeguards the contingency of the universe and the transcendence of God and accurately describes God's creative action considered as an isolated act in the remote past establishing a fundamentally static universe, it is incapable of giving expression to God's involvement and immanence in a creation conceived of as an ongoing process.

If the notion of final causality adequately underlines the fact that God is the goal and hence magnetic pole of the movement of creation, it also fails to illuminate satisfactorily the actual modality of God's creative activity within the ongoing process. What is needed is a notion which goes beyond creative action (linked as it is to efficient causality). What is needed is a notion like creative union, for God creates by uniting, not extrinsically but immanently. The proper mode of God's creative action is quasi-formal, for he is the soul (or quasi-soul) of evolution, since the essential function of the soul is to unite.

The reason why Teilhard insists on the fact that God acts upon the creation in a *quasi*-formal mode of causality, as a *sort* of soul, is not difficult to discern, for if he did not, his position would fall into pantheism. The term "quasi" is used by Teilhard, then, to safeguard the transcendence of God vis-à-vis his creation; but it is also used to safeguard the integrity of the creation itself as well. To underline this latter fact Teilhard coined the expression "l'union différencie," which in its broadest acceptation may be translated as "union differentiates," but which is more aptly translated as "union personalizes" in the context of its more usual reference to the relationship between God and mankind. God's quasi-formal relationship to mankind not only does not destroy personhood, but actually enhances it and brings it to fulfilment. Such is the intent of the formula "l'union différencie."[203]

Some issues of capital moment get clarified in Gray's account. I shall leave for a later occasion a probe into the true drive of "l'union différencie" in connection with pantheism. At present I shall consider only the various causalities in that connection. Teilhard draws away from efficient causality because it makes pantheism of whatever shade impossible. Whether some type of such causality, which would not be exclusive, is part of Teilhardism is not clear. But inasmuch as Teilhard posits God's transcendence, it may be counted as a part. Perhaps that is the drift of a note by Gray: "De Solages. . . argues that efficient causality does play a role in Teilhard's thought, thus assuring that his Omega functions also as an Alpha." But Teilhard's Alpha can never allow, between God and the world in the act of creation, "an exteriority which is. . .exaggerated." And, because an entire exclusion of pantheist interiority goes against Teilhard's insight of the world process, he accepts formal causality as the central truth. However, he believes that an out-and-out pantheism would jeopardize divine transcendence on the one hand and human personality on the other. Thus, his favored causality is qualified as quasi-formal. The qualification renders him at the same time a pantheist and a Christian. But if in one respect there is, as I have noted more than once, an identity between the Cosmic Christ and the peak of cosmogenesis, then cosmogenesis gradually unfolds the Cosmic Christ and is in essence Christogenesis. This proves that, for all the preservation of God's transcendence and man's personhood, an authentic pantheism is implicit in Teilhard's Christology. It is idle to run away from its presence, even if the shape of its presence is rather unusual by being open-ended, so to speak, and even though Teilhard's Roman Catholicism leads him again and again to hedge. To put Teilhard, in spite of his authentic pantheism, in a straight line with Saint Paul and the Greek fathers is a profound error.

Maloney is very valuable on the early Christian tradition, but he fails to come to grips with the true Teilhard.

The main cause of Maloney's failure to see that Teilhardism is not truly descended from Saint Paul, Saint John, and the Greek fathers lies in his misconstruing their mysticism.

This mysticism is rooted in the vision that Maloney states: "Christ is not to be separated from material reality. All reality is already christologically structured by the incarnation whereby God inserted himself into his creation."[204] The inner movement set up by such a vision was a powerful one: God's presence and activity everywhere through Christ were vividly figured and felt. Christ was the Logos, the Divine Word, that bore an image of the unseen transcendence and brought it into direct relationship with a material universe whose center was man. Man's intellect and man's will fitted him to be God's immediate instrument: they constituted the seeds of his likeness to God and of his claim to be a son of God, a coheir with Christ. But the rest of creation too had a claim to transformation. The whole cosmos has its source in the Logos that holds the exemplary idea, the supreme end or finality of all things. All things were created for a divine consummation, and this purpose constitutes their Logos, the reason for each thing's particular existence. But the sin of Adam, the first man, spoiled the original design, and disorder entered the universe. The Incarnation of Christ is God's gesture to save man and, with his salvation, to restore harmony in the cosmos. Assuming a body like that of all humanity, Christ linked divinity to earth and established forever God's communication with and infusion of the world. He is the second Adam come to undo the sin of the first Adam. "Faith shows us Christ immanently working to transform and complete God's creation. Instead of fleeing the material world we are to encounter Christ there."[205]

Thus, to encounter Christ and restore God's original design by self-discipline and love and the proper approach to the earthly environment was the mysticism of the Greek fathers trying to follow the trail blazed by Saint Paul. "Saint Paul," continues Maloney, "more than any other early sacred writer beheld Christ immersed in and energizing the created, material world."[206]

The Pauline mysticism of the Greek fathers may be called that of realizing the Cosmic Christ in the sense that a universal harmony was the aim through a moral-religious development of the individual Christian. But basically it is a mysticism of the transcendent Christ. There was no inherent divinity perceived in material existence. Maloney himself points this out when, before throwing into relief the characteristics of the new religion, he contrasts with Christianity the attitude of the pagans among whom it first arose:

> For the pagan Greeks, the world was inhabited by numinous beings. Because God was not conceived by the Greeks as transcendent, he became the immanent director of the entire cosmos. The world of God and the world of men became one. God became many gods with a small *g*, while man became Man with a capital *M*. Judaeo-Christianity, aware of its true mission, exalted the other-ness of God, his absolute transcendence. Creatures are absolutely worldly because in no sense are they God. For this reason early Christians were considered by the pagan Greeks as atheists *(atheoi)* because they denied the existence of immanent Gods. . . The God of the Old and New Testaments. . .was utterly distinct from creatures, as Being is distinct from Becoming, as Allness is distinct from Nothingness.
>
> Still, early Christian thinkers did not despise the world but recognized it ontologically for what it truly is. It is not God. It possesses by its nature nothing of God's inner life. . . . In the historical person of Jesus Christ, God and human beings communicate in a relationship hitherto unknown. . . .Through Christ, he communicates his being to something other than himself. . . . God has given himself to us through other finite creatures by giving extrinsically of his perfections in a finite, imperfect, participated mode of existence. But the incarnation reveals God's *intrinsic* giving of himself, the gift of his very inner life to mankind in a visible, human form, an autonomous human consciousness, that can never be reversed or extinguished. . . .
>
> Not only is [Christ] the exemplar, the Divine Logos according to whom, as St. John tells us in his Prologue, God created all things and in whom all things have their being, but also he is this

Body-Person who has become the working agent to effect the fulfillment of God's plan of creation. The [Greek] Fathers' vision reveals the structure of cosmic Christology: Christ, the God-man, is the redeeming and fulfilling centre of the total created universe. . . .

It is necessary to establish an intimate relationship between ourselves and Christ, first, in order to bring about within us the "new creation" . . .and secondly, to effect the transformation of the total cosmos under Christ's actual dominion. . . .

Man has the power through his free will to use, rule, dominate and direct the entire universe; but this power has been given so that through the proper exercise of it he can subordinate his will to that of the Supreme Ruler. This is what many of the Eastern Fathers, such as St. Cyril of Alexandria and St. John Damascene, affirmed:it is in the fact that God has bestowed on man power and dominion over the non-human comsos that we see in man the "image and likeness" of God. As co-creator with the immanent divine Logos present in the cosmos, man is to achieve the fullness of his being.[207]

What is one to make of the term *immanence* as used by Maloney? The "divine Logos" of the Eastern fathers is not immanent in the Greek sense of directing the universe from within it. This is the first point. The next insists that only after Christ's Incarnation is the Logos irreversibly present in the universe as a force restorative of all things through man. Before Christ, it can be said to be immanent just in so far as there is implicit in all things the divine destiny envisaged for them in the exemplary idea, the end or finality of them, conceived by the transcendent Logos. What can be defined as *immanence,* therefore, is the potency that the transcendent Logos, as the extrinsic creator of a world other than God, has put in all things to follow its guiding plan. This potency, this implicit destiny in all things is their Logoi, their varied raisons d'être. But they have no living divine dweller within them, any more than the fitting parts of a machine, each meant for a certain cooperative function, have any indweller. The parts represent a purpose operating from outside them. So, before Christ's life in the world, the Logos, with its Logoi, has its workings here in an extrinsic manner. These workings may be termed its immanent functions, but the extrinsic manner renders the alleged immanence indirect. After Christ, there is a dynamic presence and activity of God commingled with the stuff of the universe. This may be more validly described as "Christ immanently working" or "the immanent divine Logos present in the cosmos." Yet, even after Christ's coming, it is the transcendent Logos with whom the universe's stuff is commingled. The Christic Logos is the transcendent Second Person of the Trinity, the extrinsic "Son of God," in two states: one utterly separate from the world though having the world's destiny in its operative vision, and the other inseparabaly associated with the world and acting as a power of achieving the world's destiny. In between is the transcendent Logos giving itself not intrinsically as in Christ but extrinsically in imperfect instruments, none of whom is its incarnation. Here there is an association with the world, but no question of any immanence arises.

Can one really compare with the Teilhardian kind of immanence whatever immanent presence and activity the early Pauline school of mysticism offers one? Maloney, surveying both the ancient and the modern interpreters of Paul, singles out Teilhard as the greatest among the latter in reviving earlier Christianity's vision of the Cosmic Christ. With reference to all the moderns and to him in particular, Maloney writes:

> The "immanence" thinkers, although they recognize a clear distinction between the natural and the supernatural orders, the secular and the sacred, the world and the Church, do not seek to separate them in their concrete reality but to unite them through the finality of God's continuous creative act that is vitally related to God's redemptive and sanctifying activity.
>
> In his unpublished work, Comment je vois (1948), Teilhard de Chardin speaks the mind of these thinkers in complaining of the various distinct acts in the drama of human salvation conceived as independent of each other. He rather binds them together by his vision of the creative union. For Teilhard there is no creation without an incarnation and no incarnation without redemption. These fundamental mysteries of Christianity are but three "faces" of the one great mystery, the divine process of pleromization, the fulfillment of perfecting through the unifying reduction of the multiple.[208]

What Maloney appears to suggest here is as follows: pleromization, the final gathering-together and divinizing of the cosmos in Christ at the end of history, is the cardinal truth of existence. All history organically serves this cosmic "Christification" so that one must take Creation, Incarnation, and Redemption to be one indivisible process. Each of the three "acts" necessarily involves the other two. And all of them are successive phases of what Teilhard often calls Christogenesis, one ever-increasing formation of, in

Maloney's phrase, "a Christ-in-the-cosmos," rather than of a Christ realization bearing us moment by moment away from cosmic realtiy into another world. Maloney's suggestion, on the strength of Teilhard's vision, is valid, but it does not do full justice to the specific quality of the vision.

By this vision Teilhard is not merely expressing in a modern style what was "articulated by the leading theologians of the ancient Church"—namely, "Christ's dynamic presence and activity in this world."[209] Teilhard goes much further, and Maloney misses the heart of Teilhardism by not realizing the meaning of the term he employs in writing of the key phenomenon discerned by Teilhard—*creative union,* with its "unifying reduction of the multiple." *Creative union* is the way in which Teilhard conceives the creative act of God. This act, which in traditional theology produces the universe from nothingness, is to Teilhard God's totally unified Trinity brought into intimate relation with a totally dissociated multiplicity. To unify that pure multiple, one aspect of God's Triune being joins itself to it, and thus creation begins. But creation does not complete by an instantaneous act the unification of multiplicity. It is a continuous movement resulting in more and more amount of creative union until the pleroma is achieved. For the world that is created is "evolutive." And to be evolutive does not mean simply that there is progressive unification; it means also that the world is a single whole extending unbroken in all directions of time and space so that one and the same process is always and everywhere going on in a greater and greater degree. The creative act thus is continuous in the most literal sense. What happened at the start is in one form or another what has been happening ever since. That is why Incarnation and Redemption are Creation itself appearing in different shades. Conversely, the creative act that took place at the start is Incarnation and Redemption themselves in an initial modality. And such a way of seeing things brings out clearly the significance of the Teilhardian truth that at creation God, without being drawn out in his entirety, joins himself to the Multiple. By creation God in some measure incarnates in the universe. The uniquely spotlighted Christian Incarnation is only a visible crystallized sign of God's immersion in the cosmos, of God's direct omnipresent immanence in the universe from the very commencement of space-time reality.

In the two preceding chapters I have culled several texts from Teilhard about this theme. To clinch my contention that Maloney gives a watered-down version of it, I shall briefly refer to them again and add one more as an introduction. Teilhard writes: "[Christianity's] three fundamental personalist mysteries are in reality the three aspects of one and the same process (Christogenesis) considered either in its motive principle (creation), or in its unifying mechanism (incarnation), or in its ascensional work (redemption)." Elsewhere Teilhard takes up the "unifying-mechanism" idea, which involves the operation of the divine Unity upon the absolute multiplicty, which is for Teilhard the sole form of nothingness from which God can create. He tells us: "To create is for God to unite himself to his work, that is to say in one way or another to involve himself in the world by incarnation. And is not 'to be incarnate' *ipso facto* to share in the sufferings and evils inherent in the painfully concentrating multiple?"[211] Teilhard also speaks of "creation (*because* it is unifying) entailing a certain immersion of the creator in his work and at the same time (*because* it is necessarily productive of evil as a secondary statistical effect) entailing a certain redemptive compensation."[212] A summing-up in the most straightforward fashion, employing "shock tactics," as it were, is in Teilhard's statement: "The first act of the Incarnation, the first appearance of the Cross [Redemption] is marked by the plunging of the divine Unity into the Ultimate depths of the Multiple."[213]

An incarnation on a universal scale, effectuating an immanence of God with a concrete, physical, organic, "definable basis," is, for Teilhard, the starting point of the evolutive universe. Maloney hardly provides for such an incarnation, and yet this is precisely the Cosmic Christ of Teilhard. The cosmicality that Christ assumes after his historical birth, death, and resurrection is just the intensified or glorified play of an immanent divine cosmicality that was there before the appearance of God's Son upon earth. And this immanent cosmicality of Christ in a pantheistic sense is something thatChristianity, whether of the Greek fathers or of a later day, can never accept, no matter if Teilhard himself asks with optimistic wishful thinking: "Is there anything in what I have said that is not both extremely Christian and extremely consistent?"[214] What he has said does have extreme consistency, but it drives an uncompromising wedge between his Cosmic Christ and the one acceptable to orthodoxy.

The feature that Teilhard has in common with his predecessors is that God, for him, remains transcendent in the Christian sense even while being cosmic in the pantheistic sense. Inasmuch as God does so, Teilhard cannot be called a sheer pantheist, but inasmuch as his Christ is universally immanent in a direct manner Teilhard cannot be labeled a sheer Christian. His point of resemblance to the Greek fathers and to their successors can scarcely be brought home by saying that his Christology, like theirs, is dynamic, this-worldly, and, in consequence, that their Christology, like his, is cosmic. The dynamism that he shares with them has an entirely different background and basis of theology. Theologically, the transcendent Christ and not the Cosmic Christ is what runs from their outlook to his. The Cosmic Christ proper to him is founded on a Christ-colored Vedanta, for Vedanta alone combines transcendence and Pantheos.

How Vedantic Teilhard is can be judged perhaps most comprehensively from a very succinct passage of his, as late as 1945, about the two phases of what he designates *theogenesis*. *Theogenesis* means God-origination, God-formation, God's self-making. Teilhard pictures Christianity's Holy Trinity as God positing his own Trinitarian structure by reflecting himself on his own being and achieving a "trinitization"—the eternal union of three persons as one. In his Trinitarian structure he has a self-sufficient existence. Trinitization is the primary phase of theogenesis. The secondary phase concerns not his self-sufficient existence, where his activity is turned inward, but what Christian theology dubs *participated being*, where his activity is turned outward. Participated being does not exist in its own right: it is real by means of Another, it exists by participation in God's existence, God's reality. Here Teilhard has the words: "He envelops himself in participated being, by evolutive unification of pure multiple ('positive non-being') born (in a state of absolute potency) by antithesis to preposited trinitarian unity: *Creation*."[215] Here two points stand out.

One is God's envelopment in the universe created by him—that is to say his universal incarnation. The other is that the *nihil*, the non-being from which God creates, is not only defined as multiple, and characterized as positive, but also described as an antithesis to God's Triune being. Surely a shadowy existence is posited as necessarily counterpointing the trinity in unity. Even if it is in a state of absolute potency, such an existence, born as an opposite balance to God's plenary actuality, is God's antipodal reflection of himself. Therefore, God makes his own reality on the one hand by an eternally perfect self-vision and on the other by an evolutive self-vision by which he is incarnated in his antipodal self and gradually grows perfect in space-time. Thus Teilhard, in however veiled a fashion, conjures up Pantheos no less than transcendence.

It is in the light, caught from various directions, of a Christ-colored Vedanta that one has to look at the Logos of the Greek fathers and the Logos of Teilhard. The Logos of the Greek fathers does not suffice for the Teilhardian stance in Christology. The Teilhardian stance demands a new one. Christianity is asked not simply to adapt the ancient Logos to a novel purpose but to add a new dimension to its Logos vision. In the same essay that contains the succinct passage I discussed above, Teilhard writes:

> In the first century of the Church, Christianity made its definitive entry into human thought by boldly identifying the Christ of the gospel with the Alexandrian Logos. The logical culmination of the same tactics and the prelude to the same success must be found in the instinct which is now urging the faithful, after two thousand years, to return to the same policy; but this time it must not be with the ordinating principle of the stable Greek kosmos but with the part of neo-Logos of modern philosophy—the evolutive principle of a universe in movement.[216]

Here Teilhard is trying to persuade orthodox Christianity to modernize itself; thus he employs expressions like "the logical culmination of the same tactics" and "to return to the same policy." But actually what he is urging is a revolutionizing of the concept of *immanence*. And in this revolutionizing, what is desired is that Christianity should rectify the error it committed in the course of assimilating the Alexandrian Logos—the error of dropping out the pantheistic immanence of "the ordinating principle of the stable Greek kosmos." Now not only is the stable character of the or-dinated universe to be revised and movement introduced, but the mode of ordination also has to be revised. For when the ordinating principle was Christianized, its true Greek spirit underwent a change. How it did so may be gathered from Glen R. Morrow's account of the Logos doctrine in early times. After defining the term *Logos* in its philosophical sense as "a cosmic reason which gives order and intelligibility to the world," and after touching on its first appearance in Heraclitus, he comes to the period when Christianity was in its infancy. He goes on to explain:

> The conception is developed more fully by the Stoics who con-ceive of the world as a unity, perfect in the adaptation of its parts to one another and to the world and animated by an immanent

and purposive reason. As the creative source of this cosmic unity and perfection, the world-reason is called the seminal reason (logos spermatikos) and is conceived as containing within itself a multitude of logoi spermatikoi, or intelligible and purposive forms operating in the world. As regulating all things, the Logos is identified with Fate (heimarmene); as directing all things toward the good, with Providence (pronoia), and as the ordered course of events, with Nature (physis). In Philo of Alexandria, in whom Hebrew modes of thought mingled with Greek concepts, the Logos becomes the immaterial instrument, and even at times the personal agency, through which the creative activity of the transcendent God is exerted upon the world. In Christian philosophy the Logos becomes the second person of the Trinity and its functions are identified with the creative, illuminating and redemptive work of Jesus Christ.[219]

One can see that the Christian Logos, in consonance with the Christian God's continuity with the Judaic Jehovah, was adapted from the Alexandrian school of mystic Judaism, which had already lost the essential pantheistic element of the Stoic Logos. Teilhard's "Christified" neo-Logos of evolution, while retaining the transcendent element received by Christianity from the Philonian version, involves a rturn of the Stoic immanence with Teilhard's "generalization of Christ-the-Redeemer in a true Christ-the-Evolver (he who, with the sins, bears the whole weight of the world in progress)."[218] The return is inevitable in "this elevation of the historic Christ to a universal physical function," "this final identification of cosmogenesis with a Christogenesis."[219] The inevitability strikes one all the more forcibly when Teilhard discusses the new mystical orientation to which his suggestions for a new theology gives rise. He paints the cosmic picture that would serve as the background of that orientation:

> Supposing. . .the universal-Christ assumes the place and fulfills the function of Omega-point: we shall then find that a warm light spreads from top to bottom and over the whole cross-section of the cosmic layers, rising up from the nethermost depths of things. With cosmogenesis being transformed. . .into Christogenesis, it is the stuff, the main stream, the very being of the world which is now *being personalized. Someone,* and no longer something, is in gestation in the universe.[220]

The Universal or Cosmic Christ is evidently at the same time an already existent fullness and a fullness in the making, "in gestation." In his evolving aspect he is "the stuff, the main stream, the very being of the world." Hence, Teilhard has spoken not only of Christ the Evolver but also of the Evolutive Christ, and it is both in unison that constitute the Cosmic Christ. The Christ already "full" is the transcendent acting as the immanent, as the cosmically immersed and incarnate, the divine Unity plunged into the multiple. The Christ in the process of fullness is the multiple getting more and more reduced to divine Unity, the incarnate and the immersed and the immanent growing one on a cosmic scale with the transcendent to make the pleroma. On the long road to pleromization the universal incarnation attains an individual incarnation in which the transcendent acting as the immanent shows forth, concentratedly uplifting "the whole weight of a world in progress." Subsequent to the "epiphany," the Cosmic Christ has an increased "diaphany," an intensified shining through universal matter in order to divinize all things into the Mystical Body whose completion or total manifestation will be the pleroma.

Such is Teilhard's vision of the Cosmic Christ. It has no real parallel in any of the Greek fathers expounded by Maloney. And Teilhard himself points to the nonparallelism when he writes of the new orientation of mysticism that results from Christianity's acceptance of the neo-Logos, the principle of evolution:

> To believe and to serve was not enough: we now find that it is becoming not only possible but also *imperative* literally to love evolution.
>
> Analysed from the Christian point of view, as spontaneously and necessarily born from contact between faith in Christ and faith in the world, love of evolution is not a mere extension of love of God to one further object. It corresponds to a radical reinterpretation (one might almost say it emerges from a recasting) of the notion of charity. "Thou shalt love God." "Thou shalt love thy neighbour for the love of God." In its new form, "Thou shalt love God in and through the genesis of the universe and of mankind," this twofold gospel commandment is synthesized into a single meaningful act, with an as yet unparalleled field of application and power to make new. Indeed, as a result of this transposition (still only made *possible* today by a decisive advance in human reflection) Christian charity is forthwith both dynamized, universalized and (if I may be allowed the word, taken in its most legitimate meaning), "pantheized."
>
> a. *Dynamized:* no longer merely to ease the suffering, to bind up the wounds, to succour the weakness, of mankind; but, through every form of effort and discovery, to urge its powers, by love, right up to the higher term.

b. *Universalized:* no longer merely to concentrate our attention and our concern on souls adrift in a neutral or hostile universe; but, with passionate drive, to accept and urge on the complete and total operation of the cosmic forces in which the universal-Christ is born and fulfilled in each one of us.

c. *"Pantheized":* no longer to adhere vitally to God through some central and specially favoured point of our being; but to communicate, to "super-communicate," with him (without fusion or confusion—for as love unites its terms, so it differentiates and personalizes them) through all the height, the breadth, the depth and the multiplicity of the organic powers of space and time.[221]

It should be obvious that if the mystical orientation from the Teilhardian vision of the Cosmic Christ has "a radical reinterpretation," almost "a recasting," and not "a mere extension" of teh idea of Godward love, the vision itself must be worlds away from that of the Greek fathers and the moderns who walk in their footsteps.

I may well end on the word *pantheized*. Teilhard tries to guard against its essential sense by qualifying his usage with the phrase "taken in its most legitimate meaning." The illegitimate meaning, to his mind, would involve an exclusion of divine transcendence and of persistent individual "souls." But the language in which he couches "love of evolution" demands that somehow—along lines like those of the original Vedanta—he should reconcile pantheism with transcendentalism, and identity of divine substance with diversity or differentiation of souls. When he asks us "to love God in and through the genesis of the universe and of mankind" or when he afterwards frames the formula: "Love God in and through the universe in evolution,"[222] one cannot help but get the impression that he takes the cosmos—where the multiple is being unified—to be fundamentally an antithetical projection of God in an evolving form whose consummation will be an emerged Godhead, the divine "someone" whose gestation in space-time is cosmogenesis. Teilhard, through all his struggles to keep within orthodox Christianity, comes out at the end with a Christianity genuinely "pantheized" no less than with a pantheism genuinely Christianized.

Notes

1. Pierre Teilhard de Chardin, *Writings in Time of War* (London: Collins; New York: Harper & Row, 1973), p. 270.

2. Pierre Teilhard de Chardin, *Hymn of the Universe*, trans. Simon Bartholomew (Harper & Row, New York, 1965), p. 68.

3. Teilhard de Chardin, *Hymn of the Universe*, p. 65.

4. Pierre Teilhard de Chardin to Victor Fontoynont, 1916, in Henri de Lubac, *The Religion of Teilhard de Chardin* (London: Collins; New York: Desclee, 1967), p. 244.

5. Ibid., p. 245.

6. Pierre Teilhard de Chardin, *Science and Christ* (London: Collins; New York: Harper & Row, 1968), p. 41.

7. Pierre Teilhard de Chardin, *Letters to Léontine Zanta* (London: Collins, 1969), p. 50.

8. Pierre Teilhard de Chardin, *Christianity and Evolution*, trans. René Hague (London: Collins; New York: Harcourt Brace Jovanovich, 1971), p. 72.

9. Teilhard de Chardin, *Science and Christ*, p. 59.

10. Ibid., p. 53.

11. Ibid., p. 85. The same passage occurs in Pierre Teilhard de Chardin, *The Future of Man*, trans. Norman Denny (London: Collins, Fontana Books; New York: Harper & Row, 1965), p. 305. Zaehner, *Evolution in Religion*, p. 86, has it in a translation of his own that rather surprisingly cuts down the final sentence to: "The dream of every type of mysticism will have found its full, legitimate satisfaction."

12. Pierre Teilhard de Chardin, *Activation of Energy* (London: Collins, 1970; New York: Harcourt Brace Jovanovich, 1972), p. 219.

13. Teilhard de Chardin, *Writings in Time of War*, p. 213.

14. Ibid., p. 148.

15. Ibid., p. 70.

16. Pierre Teilhard de Chardin, *The Phenomenon of Man* (London: Collings; New York: Harper & Row, 1960), p. 262.

17. Pierre Teilhard de Chardin, *Human Energy*, trans. J. M. Cohen (London: Collins, 1969; New York: Harcourt Brace Jovanovich, 1971), p. 83.

18. Ibid., p. 103.

19. de Lubac, *Religion of Teilhard de Chardin*, p. 158. Quoted words are from Marcel Méry, "Les deux dialectiques de Blondel," *Annales de la Faculté de Lettres d'Aix* (1961), p. 15.

20. Teilhard de Chardin, *Science and Christ*, p. 124.

21. Ibid.

22. Ibid.

23. Ibid.

24. de Lubac, *Religion of Teilhard de Chardin*, p. 139.

25. Ibid., p. 353 n. 22.

26. Teilhard de Chardin, *Writings in Time of War*, pp. 51-52.

27. Ibid., p. 60.

28. Ibid., p. 108.

29. Teilhard de Chardin, *Human Energy*, p. 31.

30. *Études*, May 1946, p. 116.

31. Teilhard de Chardin, *Hymn of the Universe*, pp. 53-54.

32. Teilhard de Chardin, *Human Energy*, p. 91.

33. Teilhard de Chardin, "Mon Univers" as quoted in de Lubac, *Religion of Teilhard de Chardin*, p. 155.

34. Ibid.

35. O. Rabut, *Dialogue with Teilhard de Chardin* (London and New York: Sheed & Ward, Stagbooks, 1961), p. 142.

36. Ibid.

37. de Lubac, *Religion of Teilhard de Chardin*, p. 203.

38. Christopher Mooney, *Teilhard de Chardin and the Mystery of Christ* (London: Collins; New York: Harper & Row, 1966), p. 199.

39. Pierre Teilhard de Chardin to Auguste Valensin, 21 August 1925, in ibid., p. 193.

40. Ibid., p. 201.

41. Teilhard de Chardin, *Human Energy*, p. 67.

42. Mooney, *Teilhard de Chardin*, p. 201.

43. Ibid.

44. Ibid., p. 202.

45. Ibid., pp. 203-4.

46. Ibid., p. 262.

47. Ibid., p. 207.

48. Ibid., pp. 207-8.

49. Ibid., pp. 208-9.

50. de Lubac, *Religion of Teilhard de Chardin*, p. 200.

51. Teilhard de Chardin, *Writings in Time of War*, p. 94.

52. Ibid., p. 95.

53. Ibid., n. 4.

54. Teilhard de Chardin, *Writings in Time of War*, p. 163.

55. Ibid.

56. Ibid.

57. Ibid., p. 164.

58. Ibid., n. 9.

59. de Lubac, *Religion of Teilhard de Chardin*, p. 197. The references given on p. 351 n. 7 are: "L'Union Créatrice" (1917-18) and "La Centrologie" n. 27a. For the latter, see Teilhard de Chardin, *Activation of Energy*, p. 116.

60. de Lubac, *Religion of Teilhard de Chardin*, p. 197.

61. Pierre Teilhard de Chardin, "Comment je vois," as quoted in Emile Rideau, *Teilhard de Chardin: A Guide to His Thought*, trans. René Hague (London: Collins, New York: Harper & Row, 1967), p. 541.

62. de Lubac, *Religion of Teilhard de Chardin*, pp. 199-200.

63. Ibid., p. 200.

64. Ibid.

65. Teilhard de Chardin, *Christianity and Evolution*, p. 227 n. 7.

66. Pierre Teilhard de Chardin, "The Planetization of Mankind" (1945), in idem *The Future of Man*, p. 135.

67. J. W. N. Sullivan, "The Physical Nature of the Universe," in *An Outline of Modern Knowledge*, ed. William Rose (London: Victor Gollanez, 1934), p. 102.

68. Rideau, *Teilhard de Chardin*, p. 79.

69. Ibid., p. 396 n. 42.

70. Teilhard de Chardin, *Christianity and Evolution*, p. 224.

71. Ibid., p. 226.

72. Ibid., p. 224.

73. Ibid., p. 227.

74. Ibid., p. 226.

75. Ibid., p. 227.

76. Ibid.

77. Ibid.

78. Ibid., n. 9.

79. Teilhard de Chardin, "Action and Activation," in idem, *Science and Christ*, p. 182.

80. Ibid.

81. Ibid., n. 3.
82. Ibid., p. 185.
83. Ibid., p. 186 n. 6.
84. Teilhard de Chardin, *Writings in Time of War*, p. 95.
85. Ibid., p. 164.
86. Teilhard de Chardin, *Science and Christ*, p. 79.
87. Ibid.
88. Teilhard de Chardin, *Christianity and Evolution*, p. 56.
89. Ibid.
90. Ibid., p. 58.
91. Pierre Teilhard de Chardin, *Man's Place in Nature* (London: Collins; New York: Harper & Row, 1966), p. 112.
92. Teilhard de Chardin, *Christianity and Evolution*, p. 68.
93. Ibid.
94. Ibid.
95. Ibid., pp. 66-7.
96. Ibid., p. 69.
97. Ibid.
98. Ibid.
99. Ibid., pp. 73-4.
100. Ibid., p. 74.
101. Ibid.
102. Pierre Teilhard de Chardin to Auguste Valensin, 17 December 1922, in Rideau, *Teilhard de Chardin, p. 528.*
103. Pierre Teilhard de Chardin to Victor Fontoynont, 1916, in de Lubac, *Religion of Teilhard de Chardin*, p. 244.
104. Rabut, *Dialogue with Teilhard de Chardin*, pp. 189-90.
105. Teilhard de Chardin, *Christianity and Evolution*, pp. 71-2.
106. C. C. Martindale, "Thy Labour Under the Sun," in *Teilhard de Chardin: Pilgrim of the Future*, ed. Neville Braybrooke (London: Darton, Longman & Todd, Libra Books, 1966), p. 94.
107. Ibid., p. 93.
108. Teilhard de Chardin, *Christianity and Evolution*, p. 75.
109. Acts 17:28, New Testament (Cambridge, 1899).
110. Albert Schweitzer, *The Mysticism of Paul the Apostle*, trans. William Montgomery, B.D. (London: A. & C. Black, 1931), p. 7.
111. Ibid., p. 8.
112. Pierre Teilhard de Chardin, *The Divine Milieu*, trans. Bernard Wall (New York: Harper & Brothers, 1960), p. 94.
113. Pierre Teilhard de Chardin to Père André Ravier, 3 August 1952, in Pierre Teilhard de Chardin, *Lettres Intimes* 1919-1955, Introduction et notes par Henri de Lubac (Paris: Aubier Montaigne, 1974), p. 410. The English translation is mine.
114. Ibid.
115. Teilhard de Chardin, *Writings in Time of War*, p. 121 n. 10.
116. Claude Cuénot, *Science and Faith in Teilhard de Chardin*, trans. Noël Lindsay (London: Garnstone Press, 1967), pp. 88-89.
117. Ibid., p. 65.
118. Ibid.
119. Georges Créspy, *De la Science à la Théologie: Essai sur Teilhard de Chardin* (Neuchâtel: Delachaux et Niestle, 1965), p. 22, as quoted in ibid.
120. Teilhard de Chardin, *Science and Christ*, p. 64.
121. Ibid., p. 60.

122. Ibid., p. 61.
123. Teilhard de Chardin, *The Phenomenon of Man*, p. 293.
124. N. M. Wildiers, *An Introduction to Teilhard de Chardin*, trans. Hubert Hoskins (London: Collins, Fontana Books, 1968), p. 132.
125. Ibid., p. 133.
126. Ibid., p. 132.
127. Ibid., p. 130.
128. James Hasting, ed., *Encyclopaedia of Religion and Ethics*, 12 vols. (Edinburgh T. & T. Clark, 1946), 7:169.
129. Teilhard de Chardin, *Science and Christ*, p. 61.
130. Teilhard de Chardin, *Writings in Time of War*, p. 25.
131. Ibid.
132. Ibid.
133. Ibid., p. 252.
134. Ibid., pp. 218-19.
135. Teilhard de Chardin, *Science and Christ*, p. 65.
136. Ibid., p. 64.
137. Teilhard de Chardin, *Writings in Time of War*, pp. 253-54.
138. Teilhard de Chardin, *Science and Christ*, p. 62.
139. Ibid., p. 63.
140. Teilhard de Chardin, *Christianity and Evolution*, p. 69.
141. Sri Aurobindo, *Essays on the Gita* (New York: Sri Aurobindo Library, 1950), pp. 12-13.
142. Henri de Lubac, *Teilhard de Chardin: The Man and His Meaning*, trans. René Hague (New York: New American Library, Mentor Omega Book, 1967), p. 40.
143. Ibid.
144. Ibid., pp. 40-41.
145. Ibid., p. 41.
146. Ibid.
147. Ibid., pp. 41-42.
148. Férnand Prat, *The Theology of Saint Paul*, trans. John L. Stodd, 2 vols. (London and Dublin: Brown, Oates and Washbourne, 1945).
149. de Lubac, *Teilhard de Chardin*, p. 41 n. 18.
150. Ibid., n. 19.
151. Ibid., pp. 43-4.
152. Ibid., p. 43.
153. Teilhard de Chardin, *Christianity and Evolution*, p. 138.
154. Ibid., pp. 126-27.
155. Ibid., p. 160.
156. Ibid., p. 166.
157. Ibid.
158. Ibid., p. 83.
159. Ibid., p. 178.
160. Ibid., pp. 133-35.
161. Ibid., p. 198.
162. Ibid., pp. 157-58.
163. Prat, *Theology of Saint Paul*, 2:146-47.
164. de Lubac, *Teilhard de Chardin*, pp. 55-57.
165. Teilhard de Chardin, *Christianity and Evolution*, pp. 179-80.
166. Ibid., p. 88.
167. Prat, *Theology of Saint Paul*, 2:89-94.
168. Ibid., pp. 381-82.

169. Teilhard de Chardin, *Science and Christ*, p. 57.

170. Ibid.

171. de Lubac, *Teilhard de Chardin*, p. 42.

172. Ibid., p. 40.

173. Ibid., p. 31.

174. Ibid.

175. Ibid., p. 32.

176. Teilhard de Chardin, *Science and Christ*, p. 134.

177. Teilhard de Chardin, *Christianity and Evolution*, p. 89.

178. Ibid.

179. Ibid., pp. 182-83.

180. Pierre Teilhard de Chardin, "Le Coeur de la matière" as quoted in de Lubac, *Teilhard de Chardin*, p. 50.

181. George A. Maloney, *The Cosmic Christ: From Paul to Teilhard* (New York: Sheed and Ward, 1968), p. 14.

182. Ibid., pp. 14-15.

183. Ibid., p. 181.

184. Ibid., p. 178.

185. Ibid., p. 100.

186. Ibid., p. 263.

187. Ibid., p. 270.

188. Ibid., p. 277.

189. Ibid., p. 178.

190. Teilhard de Chardin, *Christianity and Evolution*, p. 238.

191. Ibid., p. 239.

192. Ibid., pp. 239-42.

193. Ibid., pp. 242-43.

194. Ibid., p. 89.

195. Ibid., p. 242.

196. Ibid., p. 33.

197. Ibid., p. 40.

198. Ibid., p. 81.

199. Prat, *Theology of Saint Paul*, 1:291.

200. Ibid., p. 292.

201. Ibid.

202. Teilhard de Chardin, *Writings in Time of War*, p. 299, as quoted in Donald B. Gray, *The One and the Many: Teilhard de Chardin's Vision of Unity* (London: Burns & Oates, 1969), p. 119.

203. Gray, *The One and the Many*, pp. 120-21.

204. Maloney, *The Cosmic Christ*, p. 8.

205. Ibid., p. 7.

206. Ibid.

207. Ibid., pp. 9-11, 15, 13, 12.

208. Ibid., p. 8.

209. Ibid.

210. Teilhard de Chardin, *Christianity and Evolution*, p. 155.

211. Ibid., pp. 182-83.

212. Ibid., p. 198.

213. Teilhard de Chardin, *Science and Christ*, p. 64.

214. Teilhard de Chardin, *Christianity and Evolution*, p. 183.

215. Ibid., p. 178.

216. Ibid., pp. 180-81.

217. Dagobert D. Runes, ed. *The Dictionary of Philosophy* (Bombay: Jaico Publishing House, 1957), pp. 183-84.

218. Teilhard de Chardin, *Christianity and Evolution*, p. 181.

219. Ibid.

220. Ibid., p. 184.

221. Ibid.

222. Ibid., p. 185.

6
Teilhard's Misunderstanding of Vedanta; Teilhard and Ecumenism; Teilhardian Christianity and the Gītā's Spiritual Vision

At this point in our inquiry of Teilhard, one cannot help being amazed that a pantheist born should frequently be so touchy about the pantheist realization. Troubled by his own instincts, he is, of course, likely to repeatedly reassure both himself and his colleagues of his good faith as a Christian and his freedom from pantheism of any reprehensible brand. But why should he often take the offensive, adopt a positively hostile attitude, and indulge in wholesale misrepresentation? The reason can only be surmised as an element of fanatical dogmatism that, as Zaehner tells us, has made its home in some sections of Christianity ever since the days of Saint Augustine and Emperor Constantine (pp. 89, 112). Not all Christians, not even all members of the large denomination to which those two zealots belonged, suffer from such obscuration and perversion; but, by a paradox, Teilhard, who was "irreducibly hyper-Catholic," did.

The folly to which he was led reaches its climax in his assessment of Vedanta. I have already cited some utterances bearing on it. I may quote two more in which he misrepresents this arch-example of what he dubs the various "sophisms" of the East. One utterance is thus translated by Zaehner:

> At first it would appear that in the eyes of the Hindu *everything comes to life;* but, in reality, *everything is materialized.* The luminous destiny of all things, the paradise of which souls dream,

are *confused with the dark source* from which they spring, the fundamental reservoir of homogeneous ether and latent life into which everything must return and be lost, there to find the destined beatitude, for it is from there it came forth. *Life is understood and experienced as a function of matter.*[1]

Elsewhere, Teilhard, describing the Hindu type of religion, writes:

> In order to become "spiritual" (that is, one with all beings) . . . why not . . . follow the road of suppression and negation and so try to wipe out everything that produces the "differences" between us and all the objects in the world?. . . Each infinitesimal centre expands, through release of its individual characteristics, to the dimensions of, and within, one and the same general substratum in which its dream is realized and in which it forms one with all the rest around it. And so, by entry into unconsciousness, we find a complete solution, it would seem, to the problem of perfection and happiness.[2]

Reading these and the earlier extracts, one may assuredly pronounce that in the whole history of modern religious comment one would look in vain for anything more inept and ridiculous. What the Upanishads term Infinite Existence-Consciousness-Bliss, the Mind of the mind, the Sense of the senses, the One who is ever awake even in things that sleep, the eternal World-Self, the God-Being who has become all existences while remaining more than their entire sum-total, the Brightness whose shadow is all that is bright, the supreme "He" (*Sa*) no less than the absolute "That" (*Tat*), the Lord for whose habitation is this whole universe — the vast and varied spirituality of ancient India, which is still practiced today, is for Teilhard a lapsing into some state of undifferentiated matter, a sinking into a general substratum of unconsciousness. As Zaehner has twice remarked, Teilhard appears to be utterly ignorant of Eastern mysticism, and yet he pontificates on it in season and out (pp. 7, 17). In view of this, one has to make a serious reservation in one's overall estimate of him.

Doubtless, his prime significance to the modern age rests in his interpretation of evolution and his brilliant deductions about the future development of man. Second, he is important for his endeavor, as priest-cum-paleontologist, to reorientate scientific thought by means of a Christ-inspired religious insight no less than to give Christianity a new start as a religion of cosmic evolution.

What he saw or failed to see in the religions of the East is really a marginal issue. But that a powerful and original thinker, who had the living sense of "One World" of the Spirit lying within all and inevitably emerging by an evolutionary drive, should still be unaware of the superconscious world-oneness that is the true object of ancient India's spirituality, and be quite dense in his general approach to the spiritual phenomenon when it occurs in the East — that such a thinker should remain so narrowly Christian as well as perversely anti-Vedantic should give one pause in two respects. First, when one hears his name mentions as herald to the Ecumenical Movement in Europe today, which seeks a dialogue not only of Roman Catholicism with Protestantism but also of Christianity with humanist Marxism, on the one hand, and with the religions of the East on the other. Next, when one faces his final conception of the spirituality of the future.

Zaehner himself is constrained to note Teilhard's unfitness to rank as the preparer of a dialogue of religions or as a satisfying pioneer of the coming age (p. 17):

> Indeed, had Teilhard read more widely, he . . . might have hesitated to write with so superb a self-confidence these not very ecumenical words:
> The time has certainly arrived when at last, at the opposite pole of a dated orientalism, a new mysticism can and must emerge which will be both fully human and fully Christian: the highway of the West — the highway of the world of tomorrow."*

Surely, the Roman Catholic Christianity that might be a vital component of the complex modern soul would not altogether be that of Teilhard but one that, along with the Teilhardian idea of a superhumanity achieved through evolution, would find in itself something of the wideness one perceives in the *New Catholic Encyclopedia* (published by the Catholic University of America, 1967). There Dom Bede Griffiths, at the end of a twenty-four-column article on Hinduism, writes: "To a Christian, Hinduism presents on the whole the most profound *preparatio Evangelica* the world has seen." Even in this there is a soupçon of patronage, but the attempt to understand and evaluate correctly is evident and the Christian bias is far indeed from being offensive. In fact, since the author is a

---

Oeuvres 7, p. 236. [Cf. English translation, Teilhard de Chardin, *Activation of Energy*, p. 227.]

Christian minister, it is perfectly natural; yet it does not vitiate in the least the genuine appreciation shown of the Indian vision.

Face to face with a host of declarations of his faith by Teilhard, one would expect their author to be preeminent in such appreciation as Griffiths's. Consider, for instance, this passage: "Precisely because there exists in all beings a common centre, scattered and separate though they are in appearance, they meet together at a deeper level. The more they perfect themselves naturally and sanctify themselves in grace, the more they come together and fuse into one, within the single, unifying Centre to which they aspire: and we may call this Centre equally well the *point* upon which they converge, or the *ambience* in which they float."[3] One is at once reminded of the words in the Chhāndogya Upanishad (3.14.4), which Zaehner quotes in a different connection. With the above passage from Teilhard in mind, we can press into our own service Zaehner when he says: "At last we can begin to understand what the Upanishad meant when it spoke of 'the Self within the heart, smaller than a grain of rice or a barley corn, or a mustard seed, or a grain of millet,' and of how this infinitesimal something is at the same time 'greater than the earth, greater than the atmosphere, greater than the sky, greater than all these worlds' " (pp. 51-2). The inner point of convergence for all being, the Center of centers, is also an illimitable ambience, the "Divine Milieu" or "Universal Element," as Teilhard often terms it, which is a cosmic Presence.

It may be argued that Teilhard has in mind the Cosmic Christ, the Mystical Christ-Body that is extended from the phenomenon of God's Incarnation as Jesus and of Jesus' glorified resurrection, or rather, that is intensified in its primordial cosmic existence by these phenomena. To Teilhard, the point and the ambience are a deific Person identical with a historical God-Man. Can Indian spirituality parallel such an aspect? Certainly it can. Does not Zaehner proffer the information that in the Gītā "God speaks in the first person" (p. 69) as an Incarnation, and does not this Incarnate God—Krishna, Son of Vāsudeva—declare at once that he is within all hearts and that everything in the universe is secretly he—*Vāsudevaḥ sarvam iti* (Bhagavad-Gītā 7.19), which can be translated "The son of Vasudeva is all" as well as "The omnipresent Godhead is all"? Further, do we not have even the Cosmic Krishna—the Mystical Krishna-Body, as it were—directly represented in one of its aspects, the aspect of *Kāla*, Universal Time as Destroyer? Zaehner's own translation of some verses on this Mystical Body is highly suggestive. In another book, he writes, beginning with Arjuna's plea to be allowed to see Krishna in his form of "Lord" and "All-Highest Person":

> Krishna grants his request and promises to show him "this whole universe. . .centred here in One, with all that it contains of moving and unmoving things; [behold it] in my body" [Bhagavad-Gītā 11.7]. Such a vision, however, cannot be seen with ordinary mortal eyes, so Krishna bestows on Arjuna a "celestial" eye, and:
>> So saying Hari, the great Lord of power and the skillful use of it, revealed to the son of Prithā his highest sovereign form. . . .
>> If in [bright] heaven together should arise the shining brilliance of a thousand suns, then would that perhaps resemble the brilliance of that [God] so great of Self. Then did the son of Pāndu see the whole [wide] universe in One converged, there in the body of the God of gods, yet divided out in multiplicity. [Bhagavad-Gītā 11.9-13].

The Gītā also copes and crowns the persistent tendency in Indian spirituality to combine the Within and Without, the absolute reality and this life of ours. Noting that tendency, Zaehner in one place translates the Isha Upanishad's beginning:

> This whole universe must be pervaded by a Lord, —
> Whatever moves in this moving [world].
> Abandon it, and then enjoy:
> Covet not the goods of any one at all.

He returns to the subject later:

> Teilhard is. . .quite wrong when he writes off Eastern mysticism as being "dated". . . .What he criticizes is only one tendency in Eastern mysticism, the tendency to renounce the world rather than to merge into it so as the better to dominate it.
> He is right when he says that "the incomparable greatness of the religions of the East lies in their having been second to none in vibrating with the passion for unity. . ."* But he is wrong when he adds that "the Hindu sages thought that if a man is to attain this unity he must renounce the earth, its passions and cares, and the efforts it demands." For did not the Isā Upanishad say: "Renounce, and then enjoy"? And this is the message, much

---

*Écrits du temps de la guerre, p. 442: E.T. in Hymn of the Universe, p. 65.

elaborated, it is true, not only of Aurobindo but also of Teilhard.

What Teilhard is attacking is Śankara's Illusionism and the world-denying austerity of Theravāda Buddishm; but this is less than half of Indian religion, and this too was the object of Aurobindo's scarcely less stringent criticism. (p. 23)

I may add that the Isha Upanishad next says (in Sri Aurobindo's translation): "Doing verily works in this world one should wish to live a hundred years. Thus it is in thee and not otherwise than this: action cleaves not to a man."[5] The theme of "free" action in a long life amidst men links what Zaehner has called "the full teaching of the Upanishads" with the Gītā's insistence on unattached action—action done against the background of an inwardly realized infinite Unity and offered up to the Supreme Lord so that ultimately his will alone may move the worker. The avatar, the God-Man, acts as an example par excellence of world work. Zaehner indicates a part of this example: "In the Gītā (4.8) Krishna, himself a God incarnate, says that the purpose of his becoming man was 'for the protection of the good, for the destruction of evil-doers, for the setting up of the law of righteousness.' " (p.75). Zaehner has omitted the further phrase in the same context: "I am born from age to age." And even in his transcendent status Krishna is still the worker: "I have no work that I need to do in all the three worlds [of Matter, Life, Mind], I have nothing that I have not gained and have yet to gain, and I abide verily in the paths of action [Bhagavad-Gītā 3.22]."[6] A very important side of this action is the repeated birth of the avatar at critical moments of history. The Gītā's doctrine of the Incarnation is thus significant not only of focusing in a human form God's super-personhood but also of God's charging the world with a more and more dynamic power of secret pantheistic presence. An ultra-Teilhardism is implied here: Teilhard's "Divine Milieu" building up Christ's Cosmic Body acquires an extra vibrancy and vitality.

So one may well generalize and enlarge a phrase that Zaehner employs in observing that the Gītā does not see "salvation solely in terms of spirit," matter being "that from whose bondage release must be sought. . . .The two cannot be brought together unless spirit enters deeply into matter and moulds it towards a higher and more unified form of existence. This is what the Gītā does, and in this it supplements and completes Christianity" (p. 70). One does not quite know what the last phrase implies. It would ordinarily mean that something that comes later in time is added but that this something, though valuable, is not anything really new: the addition, while giving fullness, yet continues by way of elaboration and explicitness what was already there in vital substance earlier. The true position, as between the Gītā and Christianity, is rather different.

The core of the Gītā—the Krishna-Cult, from which springs its doctrine of matter's infusion with spirit—may be traced to several centuries before Christ. Already in ca. 300 B.C. Megasthenes, the Greek ambassador of Seleucus Nicator to the Court of "Sandrocottus" (Chandragupta) at "Palibothra" (Pataliputra), testifies to the prevalence of the Krishna-Cult. Even earlier than Megasthenes was the Indian grammarian Panini (undoubtedly prior to 400 B.C. and perhaps as ancient as 700 B.C.) who referred to the worship of Krishna. And, according to all Indologists, even the Gītā is pre-Christian.[7] Therefore, instead of saying that it supplements and completes Christianity, we should make two points in the opposite direction. First, the Gītā contains many precious spiritual elements ranging farther than the Christian religion and rendering this Indian scripture much more eligible to be called a complete revelation. Second, the Gītā anticipates essential Christianity by one great element in it—an element that loses some of its integrity in the orthodox Christian doctrine because of the latter's cleavage between God and the universe, but whose wholeness glimmers out once more in Teilhard in spite of that doctrine through his innate, though consciously resisted, oriental bent.

Perhaps Zaehner himself, whatever the precise content he may have intended in his phrase in the book under review, would not in general be averse to this position. Briefly scanning the development of worship "in the course of the centuries that had elapsed between the time of the Rig-Veda and the compilation of the Great Epic and the Purānas," Zaehner, in another book, says:

> In fact, by the time the Epic came to be written—let us say in the third century B.C.,† though everyone agrees that there are strata of antiquity in it, the earliest of which may be separated from the latest by as much as six hundred years—two gods and two gods only had emerged whose devotees claimed for them the title of *Parabrahman* and *Paramātman*, the "highest Brahman"

and the "highest Self," thereby identifying them both with the God who "encompasses" all things in time and eternity and with the God in the human heart who is "no larger than the fine point of an awl" [Śvetāsvatara Upanishad 5:8]. These gods were Rudra Śiva, the God of the Śvetāsvatara Upanishad, and Vishnu, who in his incarnation as Krishna is the God of the Bhagavad-Gītā, a religious classic which is not only by far the best known and by far the most influential text within the Hindu tradition, but also, to my mind, ranks as the most significant sacred text in the whole history of religion.[8]

In view of this pronouncement, perhaps Zaehner would not disagree with the contention that, considered all around, Teilhardism is indeed best describable as the Gītā in the garb of an evolutionary world interpretation. Unlike Christianity, the Gītā's Vedenta admits a universal incarnationism that a religion based on the fact of evolution must imply. And it has at the same time all that Teilhard holds beyond what he understands by "pagan pantheism" or "pantheist humanism." An un-Christianizable Cósmic Godhead, unfolding himself in the very stuff of the universe even while being transcendent of it, an infinite All in which the universe has its oneness and that can yet be a Person of persons, a savior and conserver of souls and, when necessary, concentratedly manifest as an Incarnation—such a Godhead is the very substance of the Gītā's teaching. How Teilhardism is the Gītā itself in a new shape may be gathered most effectively from a brief summing-up of this culminating Vedantic scripture by Sri Aurobindo in the context of its past background of spiritual systems and schools from which it brings forth "something rich and strange" while synthesizing them:

> The thought of the Gita is not pure Monism although it sees in one unchanging, pure eternal Self the foundation of all cosmic existence, nor Mayavada [illusionism] although it speaks of the Maya of the three modes of Prakriti [nature-force] omnipresent in the created world; nor is it qualified Monism although it places in the One his eternal supreme Prakriti [Para-Prakriti or Supernature-force] manifested in the form of the Jiva [individual soul] and lays most stress on dwelling in God rather than dissolution as the supreme state of spiritual consciousness; nor is it Sankhya [a system of analysis of existence] although it explains the created world by the double principle of Purusha [soul as being] and Prakriti [nature as becoming]; nor is it Vaishnava Theism although it presents to us Krishna, who is the Avatar of Vishnu according to the Puranas, as the supreme Deity and

allows no essential difference nor any actual superiority of the status of the indefinable relationless Brahman over that of this Lord of beings who is the Master of the universe and the Friend of all creatures.[9]

Then Sri Aurobindo goes on to place the Gītā in the perspective of "other syntheses in the long history of Indian thought." He writes:

We start with the Vedic synthesis of the psychological being of man in its highest flights and widest rangings of divine knowledge, power, joy, life, and glory with the cosmic existence of the gods, pursued behind the symbols of the material universe into those superior planes which are hidden from the physical sense and the material mentality. The crown of this synthesis was in the experience of the Vedic Rishis something divine, transcendent and blissful in whose unity the increasing soul of man and the eternal divine fullness of the cosmic godheads meet perfectly and fulfill themselves. The Upanishads take up this crowning experience of the earlier seers and make it their starting-point for a high and profound synthesis of spiritual knowledge; they draw together into a great harmony all that had been seen and experienced by the inspired and liberated knowers of the Eternal throughout a great and fruitful period of spiritual seeking. The Gita starts from this Vedantic synthesis and upon the basis of its essential ideas builds another harmony of the three great means and powers, Love, Knowledge and Works, through which the soul of man can directly approach and cast itself into the Eternal. There is yet another, the Tantric,* which though less subtle and spiritually profound, is even more bold and forceful than the synthesis of the Gita, —for it seizes even upon the obstacles to the spiritual life and compels them to become the means for a richer spiritual conquest and enables us to embrace the whole of Life in our divine scope as the Lila [play, game] of the Divine, and in some directions it is more immediately rich and fruitful, for it brings forward into the foreground along with divine knowledge, divine works and an enriched devotion of divine Love, the secrets also of the Hatha and Raja Yogas, the use of the body and of mental askesis for the opening up of the divine life on all its planes, to which the Gita gives only a passing and perfunctory attention. Moreover it grasps at that idea of the divine perfectibility of man, possessed by the Vedic Rishis but thrown into the background by the intermediate ages, which is destined to fill so large a place in any future synthesis of human thought, experience and aspiration. [10]

*All the Puranic tradition, it must be remembered, draws the richness of its contents from the Tantra.

Sri Aurobino next looks forward while turning to the task of understanding and expounding the Gītā:

> We of the coming day stand at the head of a new age of development which must lead to such a new and larger synthesis. We are not called upon to be orthodox Vedantins of any of the three schools or Tantrics or to adhere to one of the theistic religions of the past or to entrench ourselves within the four corners of the teaching of the Gita. That would be to limit ourselves and to attempt to create our spiritual life out of the being, knowledge and nature of others, of the men of the past, instead of building it out of our own being and potentialities. We do not belong to the past dawns, but to the noons of the future. A mass of new material is flowing into us; we have not only to assimilate the influences of the great theistic religions of India and of the world and a recovered sense of the meaning of Buddhism, but to take full account of the potent though limited revelations of modern knowledge and seeking; and, beyond that, the remote and dateless past which seemed to be dead is returning upon us with an effulgence of many luminous secrets long lost to the consciousness of mankind but now breaking out again from behind the veil. All this points to a new, a very rich, a very vast synthesis; a fresh and widely embracing harmonisation of our gains is both an intellectual and a spiritual necessity of the future. But just as the past syntheses have taken those which preceded them for their starting-point, so also must that of the future, to be on firm ground, proceed from what the great bodies of realised spiritual thought and experience in the past have given. Among them the Gita takes a most important place."[11]

From the Gītā's vast ground one has to follow the Teilhardian development of spiritual thought into modern evolutionism and read the mystical heart of significance in the evolutionary theory. There one joins the world vision Sri Aurobindo conjures up from India's multitude of the past spiritual syntheses and infuses with his discovery of anew and hitherto unmanifested power of the Divine Consciousness. This power, from its supercosmos of ideal realities, projects at the end of a hierarchy of subtle planes a Divine Unconsciousness, as it were, a Light utterly concealed, a Truth abysmally involved, as a prelude to a many-grade evolution back into the Plenitude. But the regain Plenitude, at which the Aurobindonian Integral Yoga aims, has to be an embodied one—God's self-fulfillment on earth.

Notes

1. Pierre Teilhard de Chardin, *Writings in Time of War* (London: Collins, 1968; New York: Harper and Row, 1973), p. 29.

2. Pierre Teilhard de Chardin, *Activation of Energy* (London: Collins, 1970; New York: Harcourt Brace Jovanovich, 1972), pp. 220-21.

3. Teilhard de Chardin, *Writings in Time of War*, p. 171.

4. R. C. Zaehner, *Concordant Discord: The Interdependence of Faiths* (Oxford: Clarendon Press, 1970), p. 143.

5. Sri Aurobindo, *Eight Upanishad*, Pondicherry: Sri Aurobindo Ashram, 1953), pp. 3, 5.

6. Sri Aurobindo, *The Message of the Gita as Interpreted by Sri Aurobindo*, ed. Anilbaran Roy (London: George Allen & Unwin, 1946), p. 56.

7. According to S. Dasgupta, it is actually pre-Buddhist. See his *A History of Indian Philosophy*, 5 vols. (Cambridge: At the University Press, 1922-55), 2:551.

8. Zaehner, *Concordant Discord*, p. 117.

9. Sri Aurobindo, *Message of the Gita*, pp. xvi-xvii.

10. Ibid., pp. xvii-xviii.

11. Ibid., pp. xvii-xi.

7

Teilhard's "Moments of Truth"; His Commitment to Pantheism

In connection with Teilhard's oriental bent and yet his "rather condescending attitude towards Eastern mysticism, the less excusable perhaps in that he seems to have had no first-hand knowledge of it," Zaehner tells us:

> This is the greater pity since he might have found there insights akin to his own and used them to strengthen his position against the legalist postures of Rome. This he for a moment realized when he met a missionary in China who assured him that "there existed. . .the old Buddhist preoccupation to sound the rhythm of the world, to establish a perspective of its countless evolutions, to await the supreme Buddha who is to redeem all things. "Such assurances," he says, "confirmed me in my old hope that we could perhaps learn from the mystics of the Far East how to make our religion more 'Buddhist' instead of being over-absorbed by ethics . . .and at last discover a Christ who is not only a *model of good conduct* and of '*humanity,*' but the *super-human* Being who, for ever in formation in the heart of the world, possesses a being capable of bending all, and assimilasting all, by vital domination." (pp. 17–18)

Elsewhere Zaehner characterizes Teilhard as speaking here "in a moment of truth" (p. 24). Teilhard also has other moments of truth. A few that are particularly relevant may be noted. One not unrelated to the above is what he writes on first coming into contact with the people of the Far East and with their way of thinking:

177

When I look at this extraordinary variety and this vast mass, seeing it as it really is, I feel more strongly than ever that we must free our religion from everything it it that is specifically Mediterranean. . . .I do say that if you look at these forms, worn out though they may be, you will find such a proliferation of possibilities in human philosophy, mysticism and morals that you can hardly continue to see mankind entirely and finally shut up in the narrow network of precepts and dogmas in which some people imagine they have expressed the whole broad sweep of Christianity."[1]

No doubt, Christianity, for Teilhard, is still the summum bonum, yet varied and widened enormously, so that in its present version it is not itself the desired end but simply, as he goes on to say, "the axis along which the religion of the future is developing."

Another "moment of truth" is rather directly affined to the very first. Teilhard writes: "I was positively moved by the serenity and majesty of a Buddha in Peking: we have no finer representation of Divinity!"[2] His usual attitude to Buddhism is well ticked off by Zaehner after quoting his resolve not to try to extend himself throughout the universe of matter without discernment. Zaehner says: "This merging into the material All Teilhard gratuitously identifies with the Buddhist Nirvāna which he seems to think is synonymous with 'effortless enjoyment,' oblivious of the fact that one of the parts of the Noble Eightfold Path is 'right *effort*' and that Nirvāna, so far from being a merging into the infinite stream of matter, is, on the contrary, a total dissociation from all that is impermanent, that is, from matter itself" (p. 22).

The next moment is analogous. It comes in the wake of Teilhard's practice of labeling as antipodal ways "the road of the East" (Vedanta) and "the road of the West" (Christianity)—one leading to "dissolution of individuals in a diffuse immensity" where all "tension" is lost in mere "expansion," the other to "tension and centration" and personal completion in the Divine. Abbé Jules Monchanin pointed out that Teilhard was indulging in a certain pragmatist emphasis and a too exclusively Western presentation.[3] Teilhard, on hearing of Monchanin's criticism from de Lubac, replied to his friend that he was only outlining a schematic picture and that all he wished to do was "to distinguish two possible essential types of mysticism" without claiming that either was ever to be found "in the pure state."[4] But if the extreme claim is dropped, the whole polemic against Vedanta loses its point, and it becomes imperative to consider how the two mysticisms are Vedantically reconciled: the wedge that Teilhard's Christianity drives between them must grow suspect.

Again, in 1950, even while defining as "two converse forms" or "two isotopes" of Spirit the Vedantic "fusionism" and "the centric and centrifying character" of Christianity, Teilhard admits: "Mystically speaking, it is difficult not to be aware of considerable traces of fusionism in the appeals directed towards the inexpressible by an Eckhart or even a St. John of the Cross: as though, for those great contemplatives, the two isotopes of the spirit were appreciably confused."[5] The "moment of truth" constituted by this assertion signifies that, whatever theoretical or dogmatic distinctions one might draw, the actual *via mystica* at its height sets them at nought. Neither Eckhart nor Saint John of the Cross was making a confusion: in their experience the two so-called converse forms were merely variants of the same mysticism. One may observe that this moment is in glaring contrast to Teilhard's own statement in "Comment je vois" (no. 33). De Lubac reports: "He notes 'the extreme confusion' that runs together or identifies the Inexpressible of the Vedanta with that of St. John of the Cross."[6]

An earlier moment finds Teilhard demurring, in a letter, to his fellow Jesuit Auguste Valensin for having dismissed too summarily, in an article on pantheism, "living pantheism," the pantheism of the poets, which, according to Teilhard, was "the mysticism of which Spinoza and Hegel were the theologians."[7] Obviously, the explicit and systematized pantheism of the two philosophers, though not directly approved, is left uncondemned and even seen to have a background connection with the "living pantheism" that is not to be brushed aside. What the latter represents may be gathered from two other Teilhardian sources. The first is a letter in which he says that the pantheism of the poets is "a lived psychological force" and that it contains a part of "lived truth."[8] The second is a context in which he describes the urge from which he has escaped: "To be all, fuse myself with all." He writes: "This is the mystical act to which, following poets and Hindu mystics, I would logically have been drawn by an innate and imperative need to find my level."[9] Helped by this conjunction of "Hindu mystics" with the pantheistic "poets," one can reach, through his words in that letter to Valensin, the true sense of "the mystical act" that had intensely pulled him in youth and that had been resisted because of several factors but was repeatedly "black-washed" afterward. One may note that the pantheism of the poets is there considered "living" because it is

"mysticism" and that in the context referring to his youth comes
again a glance at mysticism — the "Hindu" or Vedantic. This makes
the Valensin letter imply an instinctive defense of "living" Vedanta
as being, to borrow the phrase of the other letter, a part of "lived
truth."

A still earlier moment is Teilhard's admission in "A Note on the
Universal Element" (December 1918): "In addition to *materialistic
pantheisms* (which look for the 'universal element' in a plastic or *informable principle of the world*) there is a whole category of
spiritual pantheisms (which believe that this element may be found
in a plasmatic or informing principle — vital or intellectual — of the
universe). One can, for example, conceive a theory in which universal Being could be seen in the form of a soul which is the Soul of the
World, in process of being formed from the sum of all individual
souls — these being particles of it."[10] Then Teilhard makes a most
important pronouncement: "This theory differs from the theory I
am adopting only in this respect: it regards the universal Centre of
the world as entirely immanent, and the monads that concentrate
around it are (or rather become) entirely divine as they join it." A
pronouncement equally important follows to the effect that what
the theory in question lacks is the seeing of the Universal Element as
"not only something that is everywhere present" but "also, and
primarily, something *Absolute*." The absolute character, according
to Teilhard, cannot be possessed by "a mere sum-total of contingen-
cies, which is what a World-Soul, purely immanent and in a real
process of becoming, must be." However, in Teilhard's view,
spiritual pantheism can admit something absolute into its universe
by the one single means possible — namely, by attributing to its informing principle "a certain transcendence (by making it emerge
from the stream of evolution)."

What is eye-opening in these statements are two points. First, the
possibility of a pantheism whose Soul of the World is both transcendent and immanent is suggested. Second, the implication is that
Teilhard's own theory is a pantheism of this order: the
transcendence possessed by its Soul of the World goes hand in hand
with the immanence ascribed to the World Soul in the pantheisms
that he finds one-sided and therefore criticizable: in other words, his
theory is pantheistic in the essential sense even while exceeding the
pantheistic formula familiar to him.

A complete confirmation of the second point comes when in a

subsequent and longer essay (February 1919) on the Universal Element he sums up the latter's properties after equating it to Christ: "We can see, then, that what characterizes the Universal Element as we find it realized in Christ, is not that it is a quasi-matter, a plastic or informable element, an agent of absorption, but a quasi-soul, a plasmatic or informing element, a force of determination."[11] Here, in spite of the partial haze spread by the two *quasi*s, we have quite conspicuously the same operative expressions as in Teilhard's definition of "spiritual pantheisms," and we are particularly led to the comparison between those pantheisms and his Cosmic Christ as the Universal Element by the footnote his Roman Catholic editors give to the passage. They observe: "The manuscript reads *plastique,* where the sense calls for *plasmatique,* which we find, moreover, in the 'Note on the Universal Element' (p. 273)."[12]

There can be no denying that, on one side of him, Teilhard's Cosmic Christ is Pantheos in the essential sense. What commonly covers up this truth and misleads one to cut this Christ off from pantheism is his other side: his transcendence of the cosmos and, by virtue of the transcendence, God's becoming describable as "essentially distinct from creation." But that distinctness makes no odds to the fact that, along with a recognition of it, the Christian "has a need that will take no denial to apprehend the divinity under the form of a universal element," by virtue of which "in every creature there exists . . . *something of Christ.*"[13]

The way in which there can be essential pantheism without the exclusion of transcendence is indicated equally in the first essay and in the second. The "plasmatic or informing element" of the latter possesses, as one of its capacities, the capacity "of dominating us, as a power that assimilates us" and yet completes us, and it is visioned as "a supreme 'cosmic' Reality, present in all things."[14] It is thus that it is distinguished from the merely "plastic or informable element." In the former essay the same indication of dominance and supremacy is evident from a footnote of Teilhard's, which says: "Instead of looking for the *universal element* in an *informable principle* of the world, we should recognize it in an *informing* supreme principle. If that principle is not operative, we immediately have multiplicity."[15] The term *supreme* is common. What is called "operative" in the later version is equivalent to the act of domination mentioned in the earlier, and the equivalence is driven home by a sentence on the very page where the footnote occurs. It is a sentence about the Universal Element itself: "The *more dominating its position in the monads, the more fully are they realized 'in unitate universi.'*" The two versions of the Teilhardian Universal Element do not differ at all, and thus this Element must have the same relation in both to "spiritual pantheisms": it subsumes them from a superior level.

Perhaps there will be a protest in the words of the Roman Catholic editors' own introductory comment on the earlier essay: "The whole of this note, attached to the manuscript of 'Forma Christi', has been crossed out in pencil. Père Teilhard was evidently dissatisfied with it; as would appear, too, from the existence of a new essay entitled 'The Universal Element' in which, only two months later, he treated the same subject."[16] But would this imply Teilhard's total rejection of the "Note"? Not in the least. One can easily understand why he must have been dissatisfied with it. For one thing, the treatment in the "Note" in about four pages was evidently insufficient: what he had in mind receives nearly thirteen pages later. For another, the second thoughts that the Note gives to pantheism, correcting the wholly materialistic interpretation by throwing a glance at "spiritual pantheisms" in a passage introduced by the sentence about the preceding formulation—"this paragraph is too cut and dried"—pinned Teilhard down to making the cosmos one in substance with God despite God's being transcendent no less than cosmic. They left him with no face to show his Church.

Actual rejection would mean a later contradiction of the second thoughts. But that *quasi*, repeated twice and connoting *seeming* or *almost*, is there merely to throw dust in our eyes. It can only amount to saying that to pantheism the Universal Element is as if it were matter, while to Christianity it is as if it were a soul. But in the same essay Teilhard writes that "from the pantheist point of view. . . either. . .the universe is born from an involution (deduction) of thought, or. . .it emerges from an evolution of matter."[17] This remark, bringing in thought as a possibsle world basis, grants en passant the existence of "spiritual pantheisms." A little further, apropos of "the multiple elements of the world" or "the various individual determinations," one reads that one of the ways in which pantheism views them is: "Their differentiation and the progress they make are used for building up a consciousness, a universal soul, in which every elementary consciousness is destined to be lost."[18] Here again appears a pantheism that is spiritual, and the actual word *soul* occurs—and that too with the qualifier, *universal*. The sense, therefore, that one is obliged to put into the term *quasi matter* is simply that, just as a reversal to a state of homogeneous matter would dissolve all particular entities, so also even in spiritual pantheism the particular consciousnesses disappear. *Quasi matter* does not and cannot exclude the type of pantheism envisaged in "A Note on the Universal Element": "a theory in which universal Being could be seen in the form of a soul which is the Soul of the World, in process of being formed from the sum of all individual souls—these being particles of it." On the other side, the term *quasi soul* has no power to exorcise from the Christian Universal Element, for all its transcendent aspect, the presence of the same world soul undergoing the identical process, for Teilhard, after speaking of the Universal Element as "ultimately Christ," goes on:

> Of the cosmic Christ, we may say both that he is and that he is entering into fuller being.
> He has already appeared in the world; but a long process of growth awaits him in this world, either in isolated individuals—or still more, perhaps, in a *certain human spiritual unity*, of which our present society is no more than an adumbration.[19]

Is there not here the picture of "the Soul of the World, in process of being formed from the sum of all individual souls"? The answer has to be an emphatic yes, especially in view of the footnote that Teilhard gives to the end of his passage: "It is possible in fact that side by side with our *supernatural unification* in Christ *a natural unification* of Spirit may be taking place in the world (= the work of natural human effort, the natural term of progress), the latter providing the *foundation* for the former. On that hypothesis, Christ would act vitally upon the universe by means of (by taking the place of) what would almost be a 'Soul of the World.' "[20]

Nothing could more clearly establish that Teilhardism's transcendent Christ does not shut out Christ as the world soul in a spiritually pantheistic connotation. That *almost* in regard to "a Soul of the World" is an echo of the *quasi* and appears to be inserted as a safeguard against the charge of pantheism, against the danger that despite the mention of a transcendent aspect his Cosmic Christ might be understood as Pantheos pure and simple. A Soul of the World is an inalienable part of Teilhardism, as is proved by the essay "The Soul of the World," written nearly a year and a quarter (December

1917) before "A Note on the Universal Element." The editors' introduction to that essay informs us, in Teilhard's own words, that originally "a natural cosmic entity (= the soul of the world), which is the natural form of the absolute in our universe" was conceived by Teilhard as "intermediate between the world and Christ."[21] The essay elaborates this theme and explains: "Christ and the soul of the world are not two opposed realities, independent of one another, . . .but one of those realities is the medium in which we are transformed into the other." Moreover, the World Soul "holds together only through the unifying action of a centre which we must assume to be transcendent" — namely, Christ; and "the soul of the world and Christ. . .carry their being further in the identity of one and the same Reality." It is thus that Teilhard gives "a satisfactory answer to the questions that modern minds, haunted by pantheism, are asking." He even considers his answer to be true to Christianity itself by arising in a pantheism-haunted atmosphere: "The current of 'pantheist' (cosmic) mysticism is no stranger to Christianity. . .But we Catholics. . .regard such types of spiritual attitude as inferior or questionable: we accordingly leave them out of account. . . .We can afford to wait no longer: we must *explicitly Christianize* the compulsion that leads us to divinize the world."

The pantheistic strain in the essay is unmistakable. And what Teilhard subsequently came to believe does not remove it one jot. The editors, exhibiting his final position, quote him as saying: "I want to show that the life of our Lord Jesus Christ flows through all things, the true Soul of the World."[23] The only difference now is that there is no longer an intermediary to serve as the world soul, for Christ himself is conceived as such and is called the Cosmic Christ, who is at once transcendent and what the spiritual pantheisms have posited to the exclusion of transcendence. All he has done is to transpose these pantheisms into Christian terms. We should be in gross error to follow the trail along which he often seems to lead us — to the effect that the pantheistic inner oneness of the world with God has been avoided. The very fact that in "The Soul of the World" he rejects "any religion that offers [men] a God. . .who appears completely other than the world"[25] testifies to the nonavoidance.

What precisely is avoided and what is not is demonstrated in the course of "A Note on the Universal Element." Teilhard seeks to define *"something* that corresponds" to the "special intuition," the "specifically characteristic psychic state" that he names "cosmic consciousness." This consciousness consists in "apprehending a *universal physical element* in the world, which establishes, at all times and in all things, a relationship between [men] and the Absolute—both in them and around them." It is the "impassioned vision of a supreme 'cosmic' Reality, present in all things." Teilhard has a further shade to add: cosmic consciousness "is, essentially, the need for, and joy in, *union* with *Another* (this Other being the universal element)."[25]

On the strength of this shade he discards "the *pantheist answer*" to his problem of discovering the source and ground of the world's unity. According to him, pantheism is characterized by "total immanence, absolute monism" and therefore in it "there can be no '*Other*' (and, even more certainly, no higher Other to whom one can give oneself)." Here he has taken a rather superficial view, in which "the Absolute is *integrally convertible* into its fragmentary elements, and *vice versa*," so that when the parts exist as parts there is no actual whole existing and when the whole as such exists no parts remain in existence.[26] Surely a pantheism is possible, where the whole is not a universal soul that has to be built up by the progress that the parts make but, rather, an already existing cosmic Being, of which they are phases or aspects progressively moving toward a realization of it, collective as well as individual. The pantheist then can recognize "Another"—a divine Whole, the universal All—with which or with whom he yearns to unite and so heal his own finitude and fragmentariness. Of course, this "Another" is ultimately his own cosmic Self—the single infinite and complete Self whose phenomenal expressions are the many limited selves—the numerous psychisms that are the subjective side of phenomena (the countless "withins" that Teilhard discerns behind all "withouts" from matter up to man). But, just because there is basic identity between part and whole, the part as it is cannot be put on an equality with the whole: the whole is "certainly" a "higher Other." And in the pantheism of an already existing Self of selves, there would be this Self's transcendence of the universal nature movement, though there would not be a transcendent Superperson with whom the parts could have a varied intimate relationship: only an impersonal higher consciousness basic and common to all would be there. A different order of pantheism—such as one discovers in the ancient Vedanta where there is the One who is both the cosmic Self and the supreme

Lord—would be required to allow that Superperson. And it is Teilhard's feeling of this lack in the pantheisms intelligible to him that compels him to look beyond them.

However, the so-called Christian solution that he offers has in fact nothing truly Christian about it. For he recounts three successive stages through which he passed before being able to make his "way to God in all the sincerity and fulness of a soul that is irrevocably 'cosmic'." Out of these stages only the first two are Christianly acceptable. They are "the *Will of God*, conceived as a special energy instilled into beings to animate them and order them towards their end," and "God's *creative action*. . .entering the sphere of external experience in which we move"—this second stage corresponding "more or less exactly to the views developed by St. Ignatius in his meditation *ad amorem*." But even the Ignatian stage, which should have sufficed for a member of the society founded by the saint, fell abysmally short. Teilhard confesses: "For all God's intermixture with my being through his almighty action, there still remained between him and me a hiatus, a void, an icy gap, representing the distance that separates necessary from participated being. I felt that I was *not united* to him but *juxtaposed.*" He could feel united only when he took as the principle of universal unity *"the cosmic influence of Christ."* His conclusion runs: "It is through the organic unity of the total Christ . . .that God's will and his creative action finally come through to us and make us one with him." By this unity "every being. . .has its own particular essence crowned by a certain quality, a certain *form* (common to all) which makes it an integral, rightly adapted, part of the single Whole with which it shares a natural harmony."[27]

Teilhard attempts to read in his Cosmic Christ traditional Christianity's "mystical Body of Christ. . .haloed by a *cosmic body*, that is to say by *all things* in as much as they are drawn by Christ to converge upon him and so reach their fulfilment in him, in the Pleroma."[28] But what he actually obtains by his "pan-Christism," by Christ as the Universal Element, is spiritual pantheisms' "Soul of the World" open instead of closed to a transcendent status of itself.

That such is the case can be further demonstrated from the essay "Forma Christi" to which "A Note on the Universal Element" was "attached as an appendix" and with which the later and longer article on the same theme must be taken as connected. In "Forma Christi" Christ is presented as "in a very real way the only concrete end awaiting the universe," but Teilhard immediately adds "that his Being operates through extensions of his aura in which his divinity is not always equally embodied, and therefore manifests itself to us through a *gradual* and *creative* attraction."[29] Explaining his additional remark, he writes:

> It would seem that through a first surface of himself that he presents to us (the most external and most "ambivalent") Christ acts upon our hearts as an ill-defined, impersonal, generic centre of universal union. When life in its lower stages is moving towards consciousness, when men are passionately striving for the complete freedom and unanimity of their spirit, when thinkers and poets thrill with excitement at the emergence of a "world-soul," it is in fact Christ whom they are all seeking — Christ who still keeps hidden his personal and divine being, but nevertheless Christ himself. . . .
>
> Under this *natural form* assumed by *his supernatural being in order* to enter into our universe* Christ arouses and claims for himself what we have agreed to call the natural demands of the heart of man. . . .
>
> The time comes, however, when God, speaking through the Prophets or his Son, allows his influence to be openly apparent. He manifests himself as living and personal. . . .
>
> Thus the felt attraction of Christ — which was almost without form, no more than a general summons to rise higher, in the pagan soul — gradually grows richer in power in the Christian. . . .
>
> It is, therefore, a mistake to distinguish in man two different attractions that influence him: one, towards a hypothetical natural end of the cosmos, and the other towards the supernatural end that awaits us in the presence of God. There is only *one single centre* in the universe; it is at once natural and supernatural: it impels the whole of creation along one and the same line, first toward the fullest development of consciousness, and later towards the highest degree of holiness:** in other words towards Christ Jesus, personal and cosmic.[30]

The thrilled "excitement" of "thinkers and poets" "at the emergence of a 'world-soul' " — the excitement that is considered "the felt attraction of Christ" from behind a veil hiding "his personal and divine being" and which is defined as "no more than a general sum-

---

* If the *supernatural* term of the world did not at the same time "round it off" *naturally*, it would leave the universe facing a void, and our hearts impervious to feeling.

** That is, first towards the fulfilment of the natural monads *in se*, and then towards their association *in Christo*.

mons to rise higher, in the pagan soul" — this response to "a first surface" of Christ serving "as an ill-defined, impersonal, generic centre
of universal union" and recognized by Teilhard to be Christ "cosmic"
rather than Christ "personal" is evidently identical with the perception one can ascribe to spiritual pantheisms with their "theory in
which universal Being could be seen in the form of a soul which is
the Soul of the World, in process of being formed from the sum of
all individual souls — these being particles of it."

And what would inevitably follow if the theory of spiritual pantheisms were absorbed into pan-Christism — namely, that "side by
side with our *supernatural unification* in Christ" there would be "a
natural unification of Spirit" — is here stated as a fact and not put
forward a little shyly, as in the later article on the Universal Element, a fact of evolution on the way to the Parousia. It is there the
necessary preparation for that supernatural event, the result of the
same all-fulfilling divine focus that is also a divine milieu, a cosmic
component complementing the personal component in the one
Christ.

Thus, "Forma Christ" aligns the two articles beyond all doubt.
And one returns to the "moment of truth" of the early "Note,"
which straightforwardly convicts Teilhard of being a pantheist in
the direction of the mode whose full flowering is in the Vedantic synthesis of the cosmic and the transcendent.

Notes

1. Pierre Teilhard de Chardin to Auguste Valensin, 27 May 1923, quoted in Emile Rideau
Teilhard de Chardin: A Guide to His Thought, trans. René Hague (London: Collins; New
York: Harper & Row, 1967), p. 525.

2. Pierre Teilhard de Chardin, *Letters to Léontine Zanta* (London: Collins, 1969), p. 53.

3. See L'Abbé Jules Monchanin, "Formes, vie, et pensée," in *L'Abbé Jules Monchanin*
(1960), pp. 162-175.

4. Pierre Teilhard de Chardin to L'Abbé Jules Monchanin, 29 April 1934, in Pierre
Teilhard de Chardin, *Lettres Intimes* 1919-1955 (Paris: Aubier Montaigne, 1974), pp.
273-74.

5. Pierre Teilhard de Chardin, *Activation of Energy* (London: Collins, 1970; New York:
Harcourt Brace Jovanovich, 1972), p. 225.

6. Henri de Lubac, *The Religion of Teilhard de Chardin* (London: Collins; New York:
Desclee, 1967), p. 332 n. 15.

7. Pierre Teilhard de Chardin to Auguste Valensin, 28 August 1919, quoted in ibid., p.
157.

8. Pierre Teilhard de Chardin to Auguste Valensin, 17 Decembr 1922, quoted in ibid., p.
333 n. 32.

9. Pierre Teilhard de Chardin, "Le Coeur de la matière," as quoted in ibid., p. 336 n. 56.
10. Pierre Teilhard de Chardin, *Writings in Time of War* (London: Collins, 1969; New York: Harper & Row, 1973), p. 273.
11. Ibid., p. 229.
12. Ibid.
13. Ibid., pp. 294, 297.
14. Ibid., pp. 299, 294.
15. Ibid., p. 275 n. 2.
16. Ibid., p. 271.
17. Ibid., p. 292.
18. Ibid., pp. 292-93.
19. Ibid., pp. 297-98.
20. Ibid., p. 298 n. 7.
21. Ibid., p. 178.
22. Ibid., pp. 185189.
23. Ibid., p. 177.
24. Ibid., p. 188.
25. Ibid., pp. 290-94.
26. Ibid., p. 293.
27. Ibid., pp. 294-97.
28. Ibid., p. 297.
29. Ibid., p. 254.
30. Ibid., pp. 254-56.

* That is, first towards the fulfillment of the natural monads *in se*, and then towards their association *in Christo*.

8

Teilhard's Attempt to Divide "God Is All" from "God All in All"; A Clue from Sri Aurobindo

With the universal Center of Teilhard revealed in a moment of truth as essentially, though not exclusively, pantheistic, the single problem remaining in connection with this Center is the nature and destiny of the "monads that concentrate around it." Here Teilhard's cynical contention is, as a later text has it, that in a pantheism like the Vedantic "the elementary egos" disappear, whereas in his own theory "they reinforce one another as they come together."[1] The reason for the differences lies, according to him, in the absence of love in the Vedantic consummation. Referring to Teilhard's differentiation between the Vedanta's "Inexpressible" and that of Saint John of the Cross, de Lubac further cites "Comment je vois" (no. 27) to say: "It is 'love that enables us to distinguish' those two inexpressibles."[2]

The theme of love, along with the question of destiny of the individual soul's loving God and being loved by him, keeps recurring in Teilhard. This theme and that question attain perhaps their most succinct expression when he sums up the supposed incompatibles, the "two converse forms" or "two isotopes" of Spirit—the Vedantic and the Christian pantheisms: "Pantheism of identification, at the opposite pole of love: 'God is all.' And pantheism of unification, beyond love: 'God all in all.' "[3] Zaehner also refers to the incompatibles in his own translation of the above phrase (p. 20). "God all in all" is a key refrain in Teilhard, and he interprets Saint Paul's words to involve a threefold truth: a persistence of the human person even in its final consummation in the Divine Being, a persistence due to a basic difference between soul and God as between creature and creator, and a persistence that renders possible by the virtue alone of such a difference that supreme relationship—love—between soul and God, since there can be no love if there is no "Other." In Teilhard's eyes pantheism is excluded as well as found wanting, by the Pauline "God in all."

An element significant to Teilhard in his argument is the way he construes Saint Paul's phrase. The Greek runs *theòs pánta èn pãsin.* The Latin is *deus omnia in omnibus.* Here *pãsin* and *omnibus* can be read either in the neuter gender or in the masculine: "all" can be equated to "everyone," "all persons" as well as to "everything," "all things." As Zaehner shows by his quotation from Teilhard, Teilhard translates *èn pãsin* and *in omnibus* not by "en tout" (neuter) but by "en tous" (masculine) (p. 15). De Lubac also makes a note of the point and lends Teilhard the support of an eminent Pauline exegete, Férnand Prat: "Teilhard habitually translates Paul's *èn pãsin* (*in omnibus*),. . . as Prat does by 'in all' (*en tous*) and not 'in all things.' His universe is a personal universe."[4] Thus, the separate existence of souls, rather than their pantheistic submergence, is sought to be emphasized. In one context Teilhard has: "everything to everyone."[5] This reading can be matched from the Revised Standard Version of the Bible as well as the Moffat translation, in contrast to the Jerusalem Bible and the New English Bible, which follow the older rendering "all in all." The unusual reading removes the Pauline phrase from the arena of controversy over pantheism. I shall come to the new universe of discourse later. At the moment I may add only that Zaehner, although he sticks to the Teilhardian metaphysical "slant," is himself not consistent. In one place he translates: "God, whole in all things"—thereby employing the neuter gender (p. 20).

Actually, the issue of genders involves hairsplitting. The distinction is not crucial so long as one keeps the formula within the scope of conflict between pantheism and nonpantheism. For, "all things," broadly speaking, can include persons no less than objects and may even be taken exclusively to mean them. Otherwise, N.M. Wildiers would not be able to write: "The return of Christ must be prepared for by the gradual building up of the Mystical Body, that is, the unification of all men around and in Christ—for the total Christ

consists of a Head *and* the members. All things are to be brought into unity under the one Head, Christ (*recapitulare omnia in Christo*:
Eph. I. 9-10), so that the whole world is made the 'pleroma'
(fullness, the completion of Christ)."[6] Wildiers quite legitimately
makes *omnia* cover the totality of human beings. And the role that
the word plays here, as in several other places in the Pauline
Epistles, is akin to the one called for in *pãsin* or *omnibus* if this locution is taken to mean the members collected in the pleromatic
Mystical Body by the Head. Such a role strongly pleads for the
neuter gender in this locution.

Be that as it may, can one really drive a division down to bedrock
between "God is all" and "God all in all"? The very logic of "allness,"
in whatever shape, should involve a basis of the One. If in all entities
God is the whole reality — and that is what is meant by His being
"all" in them — then, in spite of their continuing as themselves, God
must be their essential constituent. This would not be the case if he
were just something or the main thing or the most thing in them: he
is said to be everything. No ultimate room is left for any reality except him. Hence, essentially, none can be other than he, though ex-
istentially all may retain their individual characters as modes or
phases of the One. The pantheism of unification must have for its
ground the pantheism of identification.

Indeed, to read the latter as implicit in the Pauline formula
would seem the natural procedure even from the fact of linguistic
usage. The naiveté of making out of that formula a special case for
the preservation of personality in the Universal is perceived as soon
as one attends to H.D. Lewis's account of the non-Christian type of
mysticism, "which claims that, in the last analysis, the distinction
between us and God disappears." Lewis writes: "We become God or
are absorbed in the being of God, or we realize that, rightly
understood, the distinction between finite beings and God is an illusion. God is strictly all in all."[7] The Pauline formula really takes
away the stress from any ever-separate finite personality.

Naive thought in Christianizing pantheism on the strength of
Saint Paul's words can be linguistically exposed by looking at the
very definition of pantheism as originally given. "The term 'pantheist'," says the *Encyclopaedia Britannica*, "was introduced by John
Toland. . ., who also gives its essential tenets: 'All things in the world
are one. What's all in all things is God' (*Pantheisticon*, 1770, part
ii)."[8]

Saint Paul himself took his formula from a pantheistic context.

Teilhard refers in general to the latter when he observes how philosophers of all times have followed the poets by making intellectual constructions of their concern for the Whole: "There is no need for me to labour the point—you can see it in the powerful ventures into monism of the earliest Greek philosophers, and in the Alexandrians' subtle attempts to establish the existence of the Logos, and in the Stoics' contemplation of the soul of the world."[9] Msgr. Lucien Cerfaux, in a quotation from him by de Lubac, focuses attention on Saint Paul's source in the last-named of Teilhard's examples with the most relevant exactitude: "The ancient Stoic formulas, pantheist in tone, the identity of the one with the whole, God all in all, are Christianized."[10] The specific expressioin under debate may have been Christianized, but Teilhard's claim that it is totally at variance with "God is all" and can only involve a "Christian pantheism," in which the soul is persistently other than God, is false. It was, in Saint Paul's own time, vitally associated with pantheistic paganism and, whatever Cerfaux may say, it is doubtful whether the old content can quite be washed out of the form unless one takes the apostle to have used the expression in an entirely different manner that had no bearing on any issue between a pagan pantheism and a Christian one.

In order to save Saint Paul from all taint of the old content, the universe of discourse in which Teilhard has put his phrase will have to be changed. In relation to pantheism, the phrase can either introduce an emphasis on a particular shade of it or it can merely be an emphatic manner of saying the same thing. Cut off from it, one must take the ordinary dictionary meaning—namely, "of paramount or exclusive importance"[11] —and link it with the specific posture of the terms within the Pauline declaration. Zaehner has supplied the precise context: "Through Christ and his Church the human race is destined to grow together until 'everything is subjected to him [and] then the Son himself will be subject in his turn to the One who subjected all things to him, so that God may be all in all [Cor. 15:28]' " (p. 12). A striking impression is obviously given here of the Son's having been at one time of paramount or exclusive importance in connection with the whole Creation and of his being now withdrawn from that role, because he has fulfilled the end set up for it, and of his giving place to God the Father, who had accorded to him that primacy—with the result that now God has paramount or exclusive importance.

This understanding of the passage has actually been a widely ac-

cepted interpretation, among both Roman Catholics and Prot-
estants. Claude J. Peifer, O.S.B., has the gloss: "On the last day,
when Christ will have become master of all creation then he will also
subject himself to the Father. Then God himself will be in direct
contact with all of redeemed creation; there will no longer be any
need of a mediator."[12] The *Encyclopaedia of Religion and Ethics*
also makes the point that God's being all in all is in reference to the
coming to an end of Christ's "mediatorial kingdom."[13] The same
point is implicit in Matthew Henry's reading, which goes on to opine
that Christ's delivering up the kingdom to God will show that during
his administration as sovereign king he was a subject of God and
that his glorified humanity, on which divinity and power had been
conferred, was no more than a glorious creature, and that, though
human nature had to be employed in the work of our redemption,
God alone has the honor of it and it was altogether divine and his
doing.[11]

Most interestingly, Prat himself can be pressed into support of the
old reading. Referring to Eph. 1:23, in which occur the noun
pleroma, the participle *plerouménu* and also the expression *tà pánta èn pãsin,* Prat writes that the sense of "completing" for the participle and of "complement" for the noun is "as simple as it is
natural."[15] He proceeds to discuss whether the participle should be
taken in the transitive voice, so as to "obtain the antithesis: 'The
Church is the complement of him who completes all things.' " But he
concludes that it is "preferable" to take the participle "in the passive
voice (who is completed) or still better in the reflexive (who completes himself)." Defending this construction, he continues: "There
is no objection to the accusative *tà pánta,* for this is an adverbial expression signifying 'in every way, entirely' (Herodotus, i, 122; v, 97;
Xenophon, *Anab.* II, i, 1: *oiómenoi tà pánta níkàn. CF.* Scott's
Lexicon)" Then Prat adds:

It is well to consult the erudite article of J. Armitage Robinson,
"The Church as Fulfilment of the Christ" (in *The Expositor,* fifth
series, vol. viii, 1898, pp. 241-259). The author compares our text
with Col i, 24. . .He regards the expression *Tà pánta èn pãsin* [in
our text] as a sort of adverbial expression, similar to the English
"all in all" or to the Classical Greek *pantapasin,* but with more
emphasis, and he invites us to compare I. Cor. xii, 6; xv, 28; Col.
iii, 11.† Finally, he quotes in favour of his exegesis the ancient

---

† The phrases for comparison are "the same God which worketh all in all," "that God may be all
in all," and "Christ is all, and in all." *New Testament,* according to the received Greek text,
together with the English Authorized Version (Cambridge, 1899).

Latin version [of the latter part of Eph. 1:23]: *supplementum ejus qui omnia et in omnibus impletur,* also the first Syriac version, the Coptic version, St. John Chrysostom, and above all the very acute commentary of Origen, which the biblical catenae have preserved to us.[16]

In view of Prat's warm recommendation of Robinson's reading—a reading that enlists as an example the very formula (1 Cor. 15:28) under consideration here—one cannot attach great importance to his use of *en tous.* One may look on it as a tentative passing thought.

As for "everything to everyone," it takes Saint Paul's formula outside the pantheism question, because the preposition *in,* which would be pertinent to that question, is missing. Hence, it cannot but get equated to the sense "of paramount or exclusive importance."

Incidentally, as a result of Prat's citation new light is shed on the pantheism question. If that issue is valid, what is one to make of the formulas from Col. 3:11—*tà pánta kai èn pãsin Christos* "Christ is all, and in all"—and from the latter part of Eph. 1:23 in the Ancient Latin version—*omnia et in omnibus?* One gets a banding together of sheer pantheism and pantheism à la Teilhard, as if they had to be vitally interconnected. "God is all" and "God all in all" are shown up as indivisible. But, of course, the whole issue of pantheism in Paul's utterance of this type is irrelevant.

Teilhard seems to have wrested Paul's phrase out of its true setting of significance and tried to render the violence plausible by calling in the aid of a grammatical nuance. His entire attempt to clinch the issue of Christian pantheism by way of Paul's pleroma is misguided.

His deprecation of the essential oneness of things and his casting about for any means to buttress himself in it stems from his idea that if there is oneness there can be no differentiation and that without differentiation there can be no love. He lacks the insight that the original Vedanta had and that Sri Aurobindo summarizes in some old notes found among his papers:

> God is the All and that which exceeds, transcends the All; there is nothing in existence which is not God but God is not anything in that existence, except symbolically, in image to His own consciousness. . . . He is always one in His being, yet both one and separate from His symbols, and in that differentiated oneness able to stand quite apart from them. . . . It is the privilege of spirit that though indivisible in its pure being, it is freely self-divided in its conscious experience and can concentrate itself in many states at a time. It is by this tapas, by this varied concentration of self-knowledge that Divine Existence creates and sup-

ports the world and is at once the same God and Nature and World, Personal and Impersonal, Pure and Varied, Qualitied and without qualities, Krishna and Kali, and Shiva and Brahma and Vishnu, man and animal and vegetable and stone, all aspects of Himself and all symbols. We need not doubt therefore that we, recovering our divine reality, shall not be bound to a single condition or aspect. . . . We too in our ultimate divine realisation, when we have become one with our divine Self, may and should be able to stand out as the self at once of all things and beings, yet differentiated in the symbol, so as to enjoy a blissful divided closeness such as that of the Lover and Beloved mingling yet separate in their rapture; and may and should even be able to stand away from God with a sort of entire separateness holding His hand still, unlike the pure dualist, but still standing away from Him so that we may enjoy that infinity of human relation with God which is the wonder and beauty and joy of dualistic religions. To accomplish this is the full or Purna Yoga and the Sadhak who can attain to it is in his condition the complete Yogin.[17]

Notes

1. Teilhard de Chardin, *Activation of Energy*, p. 221.

2. *Religion of Teilhard de Chardin*, p. 332 n. 15.

3. Teilhard de Chardin, *Activation of Energy*, p. 225.

4. Henri de Lubac, *Teilhard de Chardin: The Man and His Meaning*, trans. René Hague (New York: New American Library, Mentor Omega Book, 1967), p. 40.

5. *Christianity and Evolution*, trans. René Hague (London: Collins; New York: Harcourt Brace Jovanovich, 1971), p. 151.

6. N.M. Wildiers, *An Introduction to Teilhard de Chardin*, trans. Hubert Hoskins (London: Collins, Fontana Books, 1968), p. 20.

7. H.D. Lewis, *Philosophy of Religion* (London: English University Press, Teach Yourself Books, 1965), p. 199.

8. *Encyclopaedia Britannica*, 1960, s.v. "pantheism."

9. Teilhard de Chardin, *Christianity and Evolution*, p. 59.

10. Lucien Cerfaux, *Le Chrétien dans la théologie paulienne* (1962), p. 212 as quoted in Henri de Lubac, *Teilhard de Chardin: The Man and His Meaning*, trans. René Hague (New York: New American Library, Mentor Omega Book, 1967), p. 28 n. 6.

11. *Concise Oxford Dictionary*, 5th ed., s.v. "all." Cf. *Webster's New International Dictionary of the English Language*, 2d ed., s.v. "all in all": "everything."

12. *Claude J. Peifer, O.S.B., First Corinthians, Second Corinthians*, New Testatment Reading Guide (Coleville, Minn.: Liturgical Press, 1960), p. 56.

13. James Hastings, ed., *Encyclopaedia of Religion and Ethics*, 12 vols. (Edinburgh: T. & T. Clark, 1946), 5:386.

14. Matthew Henry, *Commentary on the Whole Bible*, 6 vols. (London: Marshall; Edin-

burgh: Morgan T. Scott, 1953), 6;590-591.

15. Férnand Prat, *The Theology of Saint Paul,* trans. John L. Stodd, 2 vols. (London and Dublin: Brown, Oates and Washbourne, 1945), 1:298 n. 2.

16. Ibid., pp. 298-99 n.2.

17. Sri Aurobindo, *The Hour of God* (Pondicherry: Sri Aurobindo Ashram, 1959), pp. 31, 38-40.

9

The Formula
"Union Differentiates" and
the Nature of Love

Now a short comment would be in order on Teilhard's linking of love with differentiation. Like "God all in all," a recurring note in him is: "Union differentiates." Zaehner also mentions it: "As Teilhard says, 'union differentiates' in the sense that 'in every organized whole, the parts perfect themselves and fulfil themselves' "(p. 39).[1] Teilhard's drift at its highest is that, if God is All, there can be no relation of love between him and souls, and that in the love union with God as in every authentic union the uniting parts not only reach their own perfection and fulfillment but also possess a fundamental distinctness of being from God. Criticizing pantheism, Teilhard, as already noted, says first that there can be no Other in it, at least no higher Other, with whom one can effect unification. Then he observes: "Nor can there be any 'union,' when the term of conjunction is strictly single. Union presupposes, up to the very limit of its perfection, duality beneath unification. Otherwise it completely changes its nature and loses all its attractive force."[2]

Surely, no more than a half-truth acts the dictator in such a statement. What is the true character of love? Teilhard has some fine things to say: "Love seeks. . .for contact with beings. . .lovers, driven on by passion to melt into one, to form but one, imagine that one can penetrate into the being of the other."[3] Still he keeps harping on the impossibility of love without an eternal difference of selfhood, without an increase of distinct personalization in proportion to the increase of melting into unity, forming an inalienable contact and association.

No doubt, the love that lies at the basis of union requires a relationship between different terms. Yet, if there were only difference, there could never be the mutual draw, the pull of the one toward the other, the urge to take the other into oneself and to be taken oneself into the other. Not only contact and association or even a flawless fitting together can be the motive-force of love: the motive-force must be also — and immeasurably more — an inner commingling, an inmost passing of each into each, an identification in the midst of relationship. Love in its core implies an intense coming together of separate terms that feel they are really one. Essential identity is the foundation of love: existential diversity is its superstructure. The rationale of love is a secret oneness striving to realize itself in a play of "manyness." In the supreme experience of love between the soul and God, the rapturous relationship is shot through and through with the ecstatic sense of identity. The truth about union is far deeper and richer than Teilhard's conception. It should be defined: "Union is the differentiation of a basic unity, union differentiates the one *into* the many rather than the one *from* the many." And in the full or integral spiritual realization of union, there should be room for a total awakening of the small self to its own divine reality of infinite Selfhood no less than room for an intimate play of God-as-the-One with God-as-the-Many.

Even apart from the true character of love, the formula "union differentiates" calls for a non-Teilhardian interpretation. The full sentence from which Zaehner has culled a portion is: "In any domain — whether it be the cells of a body, the members of a society or the elements of a spiritual synthesis — *union differentiates*. In every organized whole, the parts perfect themselves and fulfil themselves." I am afraid Teilhard lumps side by side systems that cannot be accurately compared. The members of a society as at present constituted are an organized whole dissimilar to the cells of a body. They gather together and cooperate, but they do not form, as do the cells, an integrated structure manifesting the striking phenomenon called *organic unity*. The word *organic* is in common use in various contexts, but in the present one it has a special and unique import deriving from the biological peculiarity of an *organism*. The cells do not merely gather together and cooperate and thereby contrast with an aggregate or a summation of parts, like a physical object. Each cell acts with the rest as if it were itself an aspect of an indivisible whole, as if it were that very whole on a small specialized scale. Organic unity is, to all intents and purposes, a whole self-differentiated, a whole self-concentrated into various parts—a whole, therefore, that appears to preexist and that, by its preexisting presence, brings together the parts to cooperate. Each part behaves as though the whole were actually within it in a subtle manner, permeating and activating it. There is an internality of relation between the parts and the whole and, as a result, between part and part. No such relation exists in a present-day society but something of the kind should be expected with "the elements of a spiritual synthesis"—in an intensified and heightened form when the organized whole involves a Being who, whether one is a pantheist, a Christian, or an Aurobindonian, is the primal support of all beings. There it is necessary to repeat what has been said apropos of the nature of love, and add that short of a differentiation of a basic unity—short of a multiple singleness—there is at most a fitting together into a system of external relations as in a machine, or a loose external-internal organization of common purposes as in a society, but never a union in the true and appropriate sense. Teilhard's argument is misconceived.

Teilhard has asserted that throughout nature the principle of union by differentiation and of differentiation by union operates. Quite true, but that does not mean an absence of basic unity at work. Teilhard has himself hit on the truth when he writes about the result of elements' uniting: "Everything is something more than the elements of which it is composed. And this something more, this soul, is the true bond of its solidity."[4] What he calls "soul" is the principle and power of unity lying at the basis of the union of multiplicity. By the presence of the same binding "soul" in every element, a unification of different elements is effected. If it were not there, there would be no real synthesis, what Teilhard designates "complexity and centration," where there is a new emergence, a "something more," which is not a mere collection of parts but the underlying cause of their combination, the guiding center of their complexification—in a word, their hidden, all-pervading raison d'être. More operative or less, more or less perceptible, there must be, in every genuine union, what I have marked as organic unity in a body composed of cells.

A universe in which organic unity is being developed or evolved in

a variety of forms must be a universe single in essence and substance
of being but one that deploys itself diversely by a manifold power of
consciousness: everywhere unity in diversity would tend to manifest
in an ascending series of what Teilhard describes as material complexity going hand in hand with conscious centration. Teilhard's
law of "complexity-consciousness" requires an Aurobindonian
universe.

I do not think Zaehner would disagree. His own ultimate position
is eclectically Christian. It is not Christian as opposed to Hindu or
Mohammedan but as particularized in a certain way from a general
ground that can make room for all religions. Throughout his book
one feels a spirit of accord; he tries again and again to show
parallels, affinities, identities. As Spalding Professor of Eastern
Religions and Ethics at Oxford, in succession to Sir Sarvapali
Radhakrishnan, his knowledge and sympathies are vast, and in this
respect he is as un-Teilhardian as can be and as near being Aurobindonian as is possible for a convert to Roman Catholicism and an ardent yet not uncritical champion of Teilhard. Both his particular
penchant and his general outlook are well displayed in one of his introductory passages:

> For what, after all, does mysticism teach us? Broadly speaking
> it teaches us that all things are one in God who is the Centre on to
> which all "centres" converge. This is not just a Christian inter-
> pretation of an experience which, as all agree, is ineffable: we
> find it in such unaligned authors as Rousseau, Balzac, and
> Teilhard de Chardin, and we find it in the Upanishads, the Gītā,
> Rāmānuja, and Sri Aurobindo. Its earliest formulation, perhaps,
> is this from the *Brihadaranyaka* Upanishad (2,5,15):
> "Just as the spokes of a wheel are fixed together on to the hub
> and felly, so are all contingent beings, all gods, all worlds, all vital
> breaths and all these selves fixed together in this Self."
> Let no one think that I regard all mystical experience as being
> ultimately the same. All that I have written shows that I do not;
> and I have not changed my mind. Nor should I now be lecturing
> on Sri Aurobindo and Teilhard de Chardin if I had. All I would
> say now is that the convergence of human personalities on to the
> hub and felly of a divine centre is one of the main themes of
> mystical experience, and it is the one consistently emphasized by
> both Aurobindo and Teilhard. (p.3)

Zaehner, in another book of his, comes out unmistakably in support of my standpoint: the Aurobindonian universe needed by

Teilhardism.[5] There he elaborates the love-mysticism of a certain
Hindu system or sect that he mentions in his present book: "Very few
of us feel as a living reality that unity in diversity suffused by love
that not only Christianity proclaims but also the Śaiva Siddhānta
and the Vedānta according to Rāmānuja which have grown up independently on Indian soil" (p. 113). Drawing upon "Fr. M.
Dhavamony's definitive and sympathetic study, *Love of God according to 'Śaiva Siddhānta,'* " Zaehner writes:

> As one of the texts puts it: "Just as the two words *tāl* and *tālai*
> combine into one word *tatalai*, the *bhakta* is mystically united to
> the Lord as one. If the *bhakta* and God were identically one in
> substance, then no union would be possible between them, for
> union presupposes two beings; if they were to remain two, there
> would be no fruition; hence in the mystical union they are neither
> identically one nor two." "The condition of such a bhakta," Fr.
> Dhavamony adds, "must be a combination of duality and non-
> duality; after release the soul is not merged into the supreme Be-
> ing (there is no non-duality); yet they are not separate (no duality
> either). Hence the mystical union does imply both duality and
> non-duality but at different levels of being and [of] experience."
> To express this experience words can only mislead, for such
> words as "one and many," "dual and non-dual," are only ap-
> plicable to sensible things as the twelfth-century Andalusian
> Muslim mystic, Ibn Tufayl, points out: between liberated souls,
> or "separate essences" as he calls them, and God there is both dif-
> ference and identity: there is oneness of spirit but difference in
> degree, God being cause, the soul effect. . . .
> In the experience of union with God the sense of unity
> predominates over that of separateness, but to interpret this as
> absolute identity Ibn Tufayl calls a "misgrounded conceit"
> *(shubha)*, and both the author of the Bhagavad-Gītā and the
> Śaiva Siddhānta would agree with him, for where there is love
> there must be both duality and unity. This may be incomprehen-
> sible to the intellect: to the lover it is self-evident.[6]

What renders Zaehner's reference and comment and conclusion
especially pertinent to the Teilhardian context is his further exposition:

> For the Śaiva Siddhānta salvation means a gradual growing in-
> to God. "Let my unchanging great love grow towards him," one
> of the most important texts says. This "growing into God" takes
> place in four stages, each of which corresponds to some specific
> form of religious activity. . . . In the last phase God and the soul

are inextricably united in knowledge and love. This is called *sāyu-jya*, "yoking together" or "interpenetration" which, as the texts repeatedly point out, is not simple identity: it is. . .a conscious realization of a oneness with and in God which yet does not abolish the existence of the soul. The essence of the experience is love saturated in knowledge, and it is symbolized by the union of bride with groom.* It is a melting away into the divine Being—a simile that is used time and again. . . .Now the mystic no longer lives, acts, and enjoys the supreme bliss, but it is Śiva who lives, acts and enjoys within him. This seems to echo the words of St. Paul: "It is no longer I who live, but Christ who lives in me," [Gal. 2.20], so close is the Śaiva Siddhānta to the Christianity of St. Paul and St. John.[7]

Zaehner continues:

United with God [the soul] is united to all other beatified souls in something not unlike what Christians call the Communion of Saints.
Theologically the Śaiva Siddhānta stands closer to Christianity than any other Hindu system or sect.[8]

In another place, after saying of the Śaiva Siddhānta that "of all the religions and sects of India it approximates most closely to Christianity," Zaehner remarks: "All that is lacking is the Incarnation."[9] Conversely, one may observe: "Of all the religions and sects outside India Christianity approximates most closely to the Śaiva Siddhānta. All that is lacking is the comprehensive concept of God." After listing the three categories under which the Śaiva Siddhānta classifies existence—"the Lord, the herd, and fetters"—Zaehner offers this concept:

The Lord is Śiva who alone is God, the Lord of all things, endowed with wisdom, love, and grace, wholly transcendent and wholly immanent, wholly independent of all that is not he. He has his centre everywhere, his circumference nowhere; he is the inner principle of all things, self of all selves. He is the soul of the soul, indwelling it just as the soul indwells the body. He is a God in trinity—he is love, he is the Absolute (*Śivam* (neut.)), and he is creative power *(śakti)*. Love, however, is the essence of his nature, for it is love that makes all things cohere. This follows from the mythological representation of Śiva who unites within himself

---

* *Cf.* p. 168: ". . .for the Śaiva Siddhanta, marriage is the highest form of union because the most intimate; and this union, as with St. John of the Cross and the mystics of the Eastern Church, means nothing less than deification."

both the male and female principles, both the *lingam* and the *yoni*. Śiva is the union of the two. God is inseparably united with his creative power as the sun is with sunlight. In his essence he is ever at peace, but through his creative power he never ceases to work. As one of the texts puts it: "Śiva generates Śakti, and Śakti generates Śiva. Both in their happy union produce the worlds and souls. Still Śiva is [ever] chaste and the sweet-speeched Śakti is [ever] a virgin. It is only the true lovers of God who comprehend this mystery."* The Śaivite trinity, then, is one of male and female and the love that unites them, each deriving from the other in an eternal ebb and flow. Yet the Śaiva Siddhānta insists as much as does the Christian mystic that this union and this "generation" are essentially chaste.[10]

Through the insight of the Śaiva Siddhānta, Zaehner puts himself on the side of Sri Aurobindo and exposes the defect of the Christian notion of love and union as well as of Teilhardism insofar as it coincides with that notion. But, as everywhere else, Teilhard is not of one piece here, and he does not completely cut himself off from an Aurobindonian universe of the manifold One, the unitary Many. The born pantheist in him is bound, here as elsewhere, to break out and render ambiguous his final message. Indeed, on occasion, he writes no differently from any believer in the Universal focusing itself in individual centers, any upholder of the single Self of selves, any adherent to the Superperson whose partial projections are all personalities. Thus, when envisaging the change of outlook resulting from a vision of things ahead where "we may descry an ultimate state in which, organically associated with one another (*more closely* than the cells of a single brain) we shall form in our entirety a single system, ultra-complex and, in consequence, ultra-centred," Teilhard writes: "The world glows with a new warmth: that is to say, it opens wholly to the power of Love. To love is to discover and complete one's self in someone other than oneself, an act impossible of general realization on earth so long as each man can see in his neighbour no more than a closed fragment following its own course through the world. It is precisely this state of isolation that will end if we begin to discover in each other not merely the elements of one and the same thing, but of a single Spirit in search of itself."[11]

Here Teilhard begins with the usual Christian postulate of the eternally other—the selves external each to each—one's self and some-

---

*P. Nallaswami, *Śivajñana Siddhiyār*, Madras, 1913, 3.2.77. [This text is quoted again by Zaehner in *Evolution in Religion*, p. 104.]

one else's. But he simultaneously implies that the otherness, the externality, the "elsehood" is an appearance; for he speaks not only of completing one's self in someone other than oneself: he speaks also of discovering one's self in another. The completion comes of realizing a new shade, as it were, of the identical being that has assumed a particular shade in one. The usual Christian postulate is at once undermined. And immediately afterward follows the suggestion that the sense of the otherness, the externality, the "elsehood" is an error, seeing individuals as separate pieces closed in themselves and moving on exclusive tracks. The truth is that individuality is just a significant stress on a certain play of the Universal progressing toward a consummation in the multitudinous yet single spiritual Reality that it secretly is. There can be no two interpretations of a phrase like "elements of one and the same thing,. . . of a single Spirit" and the declaration that in these elements this Spirit is searching for its own self. All the more is the sole possible interpretation indicated by the preceding turn of thought about being "organically associated (*more closely* than the cells of a single brain)."

Even when Teilhard is most insistent on the Other, the One different from us, as the sine qua non of meaningful unification in love, an inner instinct of the fundamentally real pushes him beyond the Christian view. The Christian color he cannot quite — at least not always — avoid. But behind the dome of many-colored glass, the One White Radiance of Eternity is felt, in which that spectrum of separative personality has to dissolve, has to die in order most abundantly to live, or, rather, it has to pass into a submerging identity in order to realize love's experience of difference most authentically. Thus we get those beautiful and solemn words, which may be labeled one more "moment of truth" breaking out through every obstacle of preconception, particularly as they themselves begin with a mention of veracity: "In truth those will be saved *who dare to see* the Centre of their being *outside themselves*, who dare to love Another *more* than themselves and in some sense become this Other: which is to say, who dare to pass through death."[12]

Yes, there can be, for the aspirant, no escape from "some sense" in which the soul and the Other-seeming Divine are a single fact of mystical self-becoming.

The Aurobindonian universe of the manifold One, the unitary Many, shines out here and there in Teilhard in a more direct relation also to his formula "union differentiates." He is not quite without the realization that a social union cannot be compared to the soul's union with God and that the latter is the biological unity of an organism raised to the nth degree. Here it is highly suggestive that he speaks of the supreme union — or the Communion of Saints, in strictly Christian language — as the completion of the Body of Christ — in other words, a cosmic spiritual organism. The suppressed pantheist in Teilhard surfaces to make him write:

> Under the influence of natural evolution, community of work produces only a Whole whose texture is divergent, so that its parts can pull away and disintegrate at the whim of all sorts of accidents or impulses; again, the group of living beings that are the most united in their destiny, that is to say the human group, has not (or not yet?) advanced beyond the stage, in its unification, of an organized collectivity. On the other hand, souls that have attained holiness can envisage at the term of their development and confluence a solidarity of a very different nature.
>
> Grace, in fact, is more than the common environment or overall current by which the multitude is bound together into the coherence of one solid whole or one single impulse. For the believer, it represents, quite literally, the common soul that brings them under the infinitely benign domination of a conscious mind. The Communion of Saints is held together in the hallowed unity of a physical organized Whole; and this Whole — more absolute than the individuals over which it has dominion, in as much as the elements penetrate into and subsist in God as a *function* of Him and *not as isolated particles* — this Whole is the Body of Christ.
>
> Minds that are afraid of a bold concept or are governed by individualistic prejudices, and always try to interpret the relationships between human beings in moral or logical terms, are apt to conceive the Body of Christ by analogy with human associations; it then becomes much more akin to a social aggregation than to a natural organism. . .The Body of Christ is not, as some unenterprising thinkers would have us believe, the extrinsic or juridical association of men who are embraced by one and the same benevolence and are destined to the same reward. . . . It constitutes a world that is natural and new, an organism that is animate and in motion, one in which we are all united, physically and *biologically*. . . .
>
> Grace is not simply the analogous form found in a number of different immanencies, the life, uniform and at the same time multiple, shared by living creatures. It is the unique sap that starts from the same trunk and rises up into the branches, it is the blood that courses through the veins under the impulse of one

and the same Heart, the nervous current that is transmitted through the limbs at the dictate of one and the same Head: and that radiant Head, that mighty Heart, that fruitful Stock, must inevitably be Christ. Through grace, through that single and identical life, we become much more than kinsmen, much more, even, than brothers: we become identified with one and the same higher Reality, which is Jesus Christ.[13]

Teilhard has confuted himself out of his own mouth better than anyone else could have done. What does one have in these passages? A higher Reality with which all souls attain a common identification even though they know a differentiation from it in a Whole that is organized not like a human society on a grand scale but like a supreme biological unity, a natural animate organism constituted on cosmic lines, a universal entity carrying to the nth degree the living formations of the physical world, holding all its parts as functions of a single Divinity by whom they are interpenetrated and who essentially contains them in himself and whose differentiated identity or sameness they are. Surely, here in the Communion of Saints, in the Body of Christ, we have a beatific union not differentiating the one *from* the many but the one *into* the many.

Notes

1. Pierre Teilhard de Chardin, *The Phenomenon of Man* (London: Collins; New York: Harper & Row, 1960), p. 262.
2. Teilhard de Chardin, *Writings in Time of War*, p. 291.
3. Ibid., p. 170.
4. Pierre Teilhard de Chardin, *Human Energy*, trans. J.M. Cohen (London: Collins, 1969; New York: Harcourt Brace Jovanovich, 1971), p. 83.
5. R.C. Zaehner, *Concordant Discord: The Interdependence of Faiths* (Oxford: Clarendon Press, 1970).
6. Ibid., pp. 168-69.
7. Ibid., pp. 170-71.
8. Ibid., p. 171.
9. Ibid., p.164.
10. Ibid., pp. 164-65.
11. Pierre Teilhard de Chardin, *The Future of Man*, trans. Norman Denny (London: Collins, Fontana Books; New York: Harper & Row, 1964), pp. 92, 95.
12. Teilhard de Chardin, *Writings in Time of War*, p. 112.
13. Ibid., pp. 46-50.

10

Some Misconstructions by Zaehner of Indian Spirituality

Teilhard has an intense drive towards the mystical and a keen intellectual pursuit of the object toward which he drives. But his intensity is narrowed in several respects because his intellect tries to shut out certain instinctive movements of the mystic in him and to make options he considers necessary if not compulsory. No Teilhardian has equaled his merits, but most have escaped his defects. Among them we may count Zaehner as preeminent on the whole. Intellectually, he is more hyper-Catholic than Teilhard and certainly more ecumenical in the religious field. That, however, does not save him from some grave misconstructions of Indian spirituality as well as of Sri Aurobindo.

I may begin with his favorite quotation from the Brihadāranyaka Upanishad (2.5.15): "Just as the spokes of a wheel are fixed together on to the hub and felly, so are all contingent beings, all gods, all worlds, all vital breaths and all these selves fixed together in this Self." (p. 3). It is not fully interpreted by Zaehner. It does not only mean, as he makes out, a Center onto which everything converges. As the word *Self* must suggest, it also means that everything has its essential and inmost reality in one basic Existent and that everything is supported by this Existent and emerges or radiates from it. In addition, some central region in our being seems to be suggested, where all things find their sense of reality for us, go home to us and where we can reach by a profound inwardness or interiorization (as Teilhard would say) the Self of all. This Upanishad has often the turn "the Self that is within all" (e.g., 3.4.1), and the emergence or

208

radiation of everything from this Self is clearly illustrated in an
earlier stanza: "As a spider moves along the thread (it produces),
and as from a fire tiny sparks fly in all directions, so from this Self
emanate all organs, all worlds, all gods and all beings" (2.1.20).[1]
The various shades of significance, along with a pointer to some central region in our being, come out directly from three stanzas of the
Mundaka Upanishad (2.ii.5,6,1):

> He in whom are inwoven heaven and earth and the mid-
> regions and mind with all the life-currents, Him know to be the
> one Self. . . .
> Where the nerves are brought close together like the spokes in
> the nave of a chariot-wheel, this is He that moves within, — there
> is He manifoldly born. . .
> Manifested, it is here set close within, moving in the secret
> heart, this is the mighty foundation and into it is consigned all
> that moves and breathes and sees. . .[2]

Perhaps Zaehner fails to gauge the fundamental meaning of the
Upanishadic Selfhood, even though he has cited the Gītā (6.29):
"The Yogin sees his 'self in all beings standing, all beings in the self:
the same in everything he sees' " (p. 41), and even though he has
himself offered the Isha Upanishad's answer to his question about
"the abiding truth within," which he considers "the central message
of Hinduism" (p. 94). The question is: "And what kind of Self did
[the sage who turned his eyes inward] find?" And the answer is:

> When once one understands that in oneself
> The Self has become all beings,
> When once one has seen the unity,
> What room is there for sorrow, what room
> for perplexity?

And the verse just preceding the above goes, in Sri Aurobindo's
translation: "But he who sees everywhere the Self in all existences
and all existences in the Self, shrinks not thereafter from aught."[3]
    It is the deficient comprehension of the Self of the Upanishads
that throws Zaehner quite off the track when he faces another
revelation of the Brihadāranyaka (I.4.10), which he translates:
"Whoso thus knows that he is Brahman becomes the whole
[universe], even the gods have not the power to cause him to un-Be,
for he becomes their own self" (p. 18). With the two expressions "un-
Be" and "own self" glaring out, the sense is obvious. The knower of

Brahman realizes and cognizes, in terms of his own being, the single essential self-aware Existent who is all, and nothing can dislodge him from this omnipresent Selfhood that is his. The gods might think they have the power to make him forget what he is, but they too must fail, for he is even their essence of self, and how shall they dislodge what is their own selfhood? Can they obscure or obliterate the consciousness of Brahman that is the Being of all beings?

What does Zaehner have to say? His context is a passage of Teilhard's, which begins: "When a man has emerged into consciousness of the cosmos and deliberately flung himself into it, his first impulse is to allow himself to be rocked like a child by the great Mother in whose arms he has just awoken."[4] By "the great Mother" Teilhard means material Nature, which, according to him, is the objective of "all pagan pantheisms." The end of the passage runs in Zaehner: "The essential revelation of paganism [by which Teilhard means Hinduism and Buddhism as well as nature mysticism in general] is that everything in the universe is uniformly true and valuable: so much so that the fusion of the individual must be effected with all things, *without distinction* and *without qualification.*" Zaehner comments: "This is the mysticism of the earlier Upanishads" (p. 18). Then he makes his quotation from the Brihadāranyaka and gives his gloss: "This is to merge into the diffused state of primal matter, a state in which neither self-consciousness nor conscience has yet appeared: hence there is no sense of good and evil" (pp. 18-19).

Here there is, first, the gratuitous assumption that primal matter is the Upanishad's Brahman. When the Upanishad speaks of the knower of Brahman becoming the whole universe, it has in view the Self of all, and the universe concerned includes the gods who certainly cannot be considered matter. Next there is the assumption, equally gratuitous, that the Upanishad is describing a state so rudimentary that self-awareness and the moral sense have yet to arise, a state not only unconscious, but also devoid of conscience and capable indiscriminately of doing any evil without the least compunction. Zaehner has constantly on his mind the idea of an amoral or immoral component of Indian mysticism; he could not help referring to it even in the brief talk we had during his flying visit to the Ashram in 1969. And it breaks out in full force in what follows the interpretation that he gives to the Brihadāranyaka's verse. With another verse of the same Upanishad in mind, he continues:

To the man who has had this experience "these two thoughts
do not occur, 'So I have done evil, ' or 'So I have done good.' He
shrugs them off. What he has done and what he has left undone
does not torment him" [Brihadāranyaka Upanishad 4.4.22]. This
is the eternal temptation or the eternal glory (as some might say)
of Hinduism: for the man who is merged in cosmic consciousness,
in Brahman, good and evil no longer have any meaning. This is
quite brutally asserted in the Kaushitaki Upanishad (pp. 19-20).

Zaehner gives the assertion:

Indra did not swerve from the truth, for Indra *is* truth. So he
said: "Know me, then, as I am. This indeed is what I consider most
beneficial for mankind — that they should know me. I killed the
three-headed son of Twashtri, I threw the Arunmukha ascetics to
the hyenas. Transgressing many a compact, I impaled the people
of Prahlāda to the sky, the Paulomas to the atmosphere and the
Kālakānjas to the earth, Id did not lose a single hair in the process.
"The man who knows me as I am loses nothing that is his
whatever he does, even though he should slay his mother or his
father, even though he steal or procure an abortion. Whatever
evil he does, he does not blanch."

Then Zaehner asks:

But what is Brahman? Is it pure spirit, or is it merely undifferentiated matter?. . .Whatever it may be, this transcending of
good and evil in a state of undifferentiated oneness is typical of
Hinduism but not, significantly, of Buddhism. Even in the Gītā
(18.17) reaffirms the doctrine in no uncertain terms: "A man who
has reached a state in which there is no sense of 'I', whose soul is
undefiled — were he to slaughter all these worlds — slays nothing.
He is not bound." As Teilhard says, ". . .the fusion of the individual must be with all, *without distinction* and *without
qualification*," with what we generally regard as evil as well as
with what is obviously good.

Here is a pretty kettle of fish. I shall first clarify the intent of the
Brihadāranyaka. The verse from which Zaehner has culled the
passage about having done good or having done evil is followed by
another (4.4.23) that has the words: "This is the eternal glory of a
knower of Brahman: it neither increases nor decreases through
work. (Therefore) one should know the nature of that alone. Knowing it one is not touched by evil action. Therefore he who knows it as
such becomes self-controlled, calm, withdrawn into himself, endur-

ing and concentrated, and sees the Self in his own self (body); he sees all as the Self. Evil does not overtake him, but he transcends all evil. Evil does not trouble him, (but) he consumes all evil. He becomes sinless, taintless, free from doubts, and a Brāhmana (knower of Brahman)." Surely, the man who is self-controlled cannot be one who would indiscriminately indulge in evil and good. Nor can he who consumes all evil be irresponsibly capable of it. What is expressly said is that the knower of Brahman becomes self-controlled because no evil action touches him: there is no prompting to evil action within him. The same thing is said when we are told that no evil overtakes or troubles him. Indeed, how can it since the state he has reached is one that transcends or consumes all evil—that is, purifies and enlightens the passionate nature and brings about an utter freedom from egoism, freedom that is the infinity of the one Self in all? Evidently, what the preceding verse of the Brihadāranyaka—Zaehner's quotation—means is that the Brahman-knower, attaining the supreme Self, becomes free from the hold of all actions he has done, for he has left all his ignorant past behind and there is no remorse for the evil of his past any more than satisfaction for the good of days gone by. Mental torment for committing bad deeds or omitting good ones is no part of his liberated consciousness. Zaehner's suggestion that the knower of Brahman makes no distinction between evil and good is absolutely unfounded.

It is all the more surprising because the earlier portions that Zaehner has not quoted of the very same verse (4.4.22) are themselves enough to give it the lie. Referring to "that great birthless Self," they run: "The Brahmanas seek to know It through the study of the Vedas, sacrifices, charity, and austerity consisting in a dispassionate enjoyment of sense-objects. Knowing It alone, one becomes a sage. . . . The ancient sages, it is said, did not desire children, (thinking), 'what shall we achieve through children, we who have attained this Self. . .?' They, it is said, renounced their desire for sons, for wealth and for the worlds, and lived a mendicant's life. . . . This Self is That which has been described as 'not this, not this.' It is imperceptible, for It is never perceived; undecaying, for It never decays; unattached, for It is never attached; unfettered—It never feels pain, and never feels injury." It is after this passage that Zaehner's culling comes. Is it not absurd that sages, mendicants, and world renouncers, who keep a dispassionate and unattached attitude to sense objects and who practice austerity should be thought of as leaping into evil action without a scruple just because they are in a state of consciousness beyond the common lot of being ignorant and troubled, tempted by evil and uncertain in doing good? Besides, the passage Zaehner gives is precisely a reference to actions already finished: "What he has done and what he has left undone does not torment him." This pointer to the past is enough to weigh against Zaehner's case.

No doubt, there is a further aspect to the state of self-knowledge: this state "neither increases nor decreases through work." The same notion occurs in the portions before Zaehner's selection (4.4.22): "It does not grow better through good work nor worse through bad work." Being beyond the world of mutation, the world of conflicting opposites — being infinite and complete — the Supreme Self has no need of any work as such; nothing can add to it, nothing can take away from it; increase and decrease belong to the sphere of dualities like pleasure and pain, possession and loss, merit and demerit, good work and bad work. Yes, the Self is beyond good and evil in this sense of world transcendence and innate perfection. Nowhere do the Upanishads figure the knower of the Self as below either conscience or self-consciousness. He is above our ordinary moral struggles just as he is above our ordinary egoistic individuality. But, as the Brihadāranyaka pointedly says, he thereby "becomes sinless, taintless," which is the same as what Zaehner twice quotes Saint John as saying in his first Epistle (3:9):

> No one who has been begotton by God sins; because God's seed remains inside him, he cannot sin when he has been begotten by God.
>
> (Pp. 57, 107)

As for the Gītā, there is the identical teaching, Krishna's directive is toward a state free of sin, pure of evil. By knowledge of the Divine, even he who was at one time the worst offender can rise above them: "Even if thou art the greatest doer of sin beyond all sinners, thou shalt cross over all crookedness of evil in the ship of knowledge" (4.36).[5] And Krishna's promise to the lover of God is: "I will deliver thee from all sin and evil; do not grieve"(18.66).[6] The Gītā never tells us that the mystic sinks below the human level of conscience. No less than Buddhism, Hinduism enjoins work for the good of all creatures after realization of God has been obtained. The work may be static or dynamic: the God-realized man may stay in one place and help people by being their spiritual guru or he may shoulder an active undertaking in some walk of life. But work as a duty ceases for him, and he is not bound by any work: he has no personal reactions, for he is beyond the little ego that usually does work and that is attached to its results. And whether he works or not, the inner plenitude remains the same, and he is forever and infinitely free in the depth of his being where the Self of selves is known either as the universal Ground or as what the Brihadāranyāka, in an earlier part of the verse on which Zaehner has drawn (4.4.22), calls "the controller of all, the lord of all, the ruler of all, the protector of all." This relation of works to him is shown in the Gitā's: "When a man liberated, free from attachment, with his mind, heart and spirit firmly founded in self-knowledge, does work as sacrifice, all his work is dissolved" (4.23).[7] The inner freedom from the effect of works is emphatically put with an eye particularly to one's past actions when the Gitā says: "As a fire kindled turns to ashes its fuel, O Arjuna, so the fire of knowledge turns all works to ashes" (4.37).[8] And this very thought is differently expressed by the Gitā's declaration a man whose soul has passed beyond the world's "dualities" and is jealous of none and is equal in failure and success "is not bound even when he acts" (4.22).[9] The freedom from bondage to action is also one of the themes in the citation Zaehner has made with the aim of proving the Gitā's support to the doctrine that for the man merged in Brahman good and evil no longer have any meaning. Indeed, it is the master theme in the verse, but Zaehner has missed its bearing. In light of it, the meaning that comes through is: that acting without the sense of the small ego, of the common "I," acting from the ever-undefiled immutability of the Self, the Yogi "is not bound," he is as if he did not act at all, and even though he may slay the whole world's people he is not the slayer. Here is an extreme manner of reiterating the Ishā Upanishad's "Action cleaves not to a man."

But there is one important shade more. And this shade is what makes Zaehner stumble, for he misses the great revelation of Vedanta that the God-realized man does not act out of his own sense of good and evil, or in deference to society's conventions of virtue and vice or in obedience to some Shastra's distinction of right and wrong: he acts by an inspiration from the Divine Consciousness with which his soul has become one or else to which his being is completely surrendered. The call to such unity or such surrender, with its consequent inspiration issuing in action, is sounded in Krishna's: "Abandon all dharmas and take refuge in me alone" (18.66).[10] The inspired action may happen to be a terrible slaughter like the mighty battle of Kurukshetra in which Krishna asks Arjuna to take part with a liberated inner being. Not Arjuna but the Master of the Worlds to whom he has to give himself will then be the doer. A greater Good than any we can conceive with our normal standards will be the result of an action—be it ever so norm shattering—that is *truly* inspired by the more-than-mental Consciousness.

The shattering of norms brings me to Zaehner's excerpt from the Kaushitaki Upanishad. Two points must be made at the very outset. First, the exploits that Indra enumerates with a high pride in them are all concerned with supernatural hostile beings, as should be obvious from the three-headedness of the son of Twashtri, the sky to which the people of Prahlada and the atmosphere to which the Paulomas were impaled. Even apart from those clear clues, one knows from myth and legend, as R. E. Hume showed in the footnotes to his translation, that Indra is mentioning demons, Asuras.[11] In ridding the occult worlds behind the earth scene of devilish powers that extend their working to the earth scene as well, Indra is doing immense good and becoming all the more worthy of worship. Also, he adopts tactics suiting the diabolical character of his enemies, and in any case, the "ethics" of dealing with nonhuman evil doers who are devoid of conscience or the soul's inner touch, cannot be evaluated by ordinary standards. Next, there is a linguistic problem connected with the second part of Indra's assurances to his would-be worshiper. Zaehner translates them all in the present tense, implying that the man who serves Indra is given carte blanche to do anything, however evil. Hume's rendering has no sign of the present tense for the actual deed: it looks back from a poise in the present to what has already come to pass. It goes: "So he who understands me—by no evil whatever of his is his world injured, not by stealing, not by killing an embryo, not by the murder of his mother, not by the murder of his father; if he has done any evil (*pāpa*), the dark colour departs not from his face."[12] Here the direct implication seems to be that Indra's knower comes to a state of spirituality in which all his past Karma, be it ever so evil, has no force any longer: as the Gītà says, "the fire of knowledge turns all works to ashes" for him who has turned from his sins to the Divine. As Hume explains in a footnote, the God-realized man is no longer an individual consciousness, and whatever he may have done as an individual cannot relate to him or affect him in his liberated condition, his face does not become pale with the thought of even the most sinful past.

If one supposes Zaehner's present tense to be valid, then too the whole Kaushītaki excerpt has a lesson to teach. It is framed as a "shocker," an extreme mode of stating the inalienable purity and rightness of all that is authentically activated by the superhuman Light for the ultimate good of the world, no matter how heinous it may look in the immediate view. To the follower of this Light no loss can come; he remains divinely innocent even if he seems superficially to do evil. But it is important to remember that Indra is not asking anybody to engage in evil-looking deeds, to make it his special job to "slay his mother or his father. . . .steal or procure an abortion." He merely asserts that one who lives in the genuine knowledge of the nature of Indra does not act the prude or the puritan or the conventional moralist, but understands from the inside, so to speak, the unspotted spontaneity, the unimpeachable liberty of the divine consciousness. The quality of that consciousness is hinted at in the very first phrase: "Indra did not swerve from the truth, for Indra *is* the truth."

Zaehner, with his Christian background and modern humanitarian mind, seems to take Indra's "brutal" outburst as a call to horrible activities. In addition, he does not realize that an activity becomes horrible only when the divisive ego operates; where the divisive ego is in abeyance or is surpassed, one cannot bring the ordinary ethical yardstick to measure the work accomplished. It is by this yardstick that Zaehner also fails to gauge some aphorisms of Sri Aurobindo's (p. 38). Obviously he reads the Kaushītaki's Indra in the aphorism in which Sri Aurobindo has "dared to say": "God justifies Himself in the end even when He has masked Himself as a bully and a tyrant."[13] The crucial word *masked* seems ignored; it implies that God is never really what his face apparently suggests and that what appears to us as bullying and tyranny is a long-sighted superhuman deployment of overpowering energy to achieve a Good undreamed of by man.

Neither this aphorism nor the Kaushītaki, neither the Brihadāranyaka nor the Gītā blurs the distinction of good and evil in the ordinary world. Certain actions are, as a rule, to be avoided. Without such avoidance the whole movement of Indian Yoga would be shorn of one of its arms. But, for the arrived Yogi and for the ways of God with man, one has to suspend one's customary judgments. Does not Zaehner himself recognize the need for such suspension and recommend a higher consciousness's shocking norm transcendence when he describes how the Logos-made-man among the Jews "lived in flagrant opposition to all the received standards dictated by all the egoisms, both individual and collective, that had accumulated since the 'Fall' " (p. 74)? There is "the excoriating twenty-third chapter of St. Matthew. . .addressed to the religious establishment of the time, but addressed also to all the establishments, whether religious or secular, of all time."[2] In the "Jesus of the Synoptics" "we have a life which is the absolute antithesis of the kind of life the Jews expected from their Messiah," a life not only "of humility and self-effacement," "hardship and. . .spiritual anguish and near-despair," but also "of absolute and deliberate rejection of all the accepted social norms and of cant and humbug in all their manifold disguises (for was he not the friend of tax-collectors and prostitutes?)."[14] Zaehner was further reminded us "that Christ, the Prince of Peace, had also said. . . 'It is not peace that I have come to bring, but a sword' [Matt. 10.34]" (p. 112). One may look at the whole sequel to these surprising words: "For I am come to set a man at variance against his father, and the daughter against her mother, and the daughter in law against her mother in law. And a man's foes shall be they of his own household. He that loveth father or mother more than me is not worthy of me: and he that loveth son or daughter more than me is not worthy of me" (Matt. 10:35-38). A radical shattering of norms, if ever there was one, is here, and it is interesting that the victims of the norms shattering are some of those who figure in the Kaushītaki, one's most intimate relatives against whom any action would normally strike one as most culpable.

I may add that Zaehner elsewhere has noted a paradoxical trait even in Jesus' attitude to the problem of worldly life and interests. He writes apropos of Jesus' Church:

> From the beginning. . .she was a casuist; and for this at least she cannot be blamed, for the sayings of Jesus are themselves quite often not consistent. "Ye cannot serve God and Mammon" [Matt. 6:24], "You cannot be the slave both of God and money," Jesus had said. This, however, she has successfully done throughout her chequered career, and in this she could have claimed the authority of the Lord himself, for it was he, not she, who commended the unjust steward. You will all remember this most puzzling of all the parables—the incompetent steward who was dismissed for extravagance and who then proceeded to cook the accounts of his master's debtors. But "the lord commended

the unjust steward, because he had done wisely: for the children
of this world are in their generation wiser than the children of
light. And I say unto you, Make to yourselves friends of the mammon of unrighteousness; that, when ye fail, they may receive you
into everlasting habitations" [Luke 16:8-9]. Or, in a more
modern version:

"The master praised the dishonest steward for his astuteness.
For the children of this world are more astute in dealing with
their own kind than are the children of light. And so I tell you
this: use money, tainted as it is, to win you friends, and thus make
sure that when it fails you, they will welcome you into the tents of
eternity."

In these two things, then, at least the Church has been faithful:
she has wielded the sword and she has never hesitated to "make
friends of the mammon of unrighteousness." In neither case was
she totally disloyal to her master.[15]

Zaehner seems once to be on the verge of formulating the problem
of "beyond-good-and-evil" correctly. In a book later than the
present one, he discusses the Buddhist concept or experience of "Emptiness" and "Suchness," to which the Tao of the Taoists is akin.
Here, he says, "there is neither Nirvana nor *Samsāra* [the world]
neither Oneness nor multiplicity. Or, more positively, you could say
that it is a Oneness beyond all number or a 'Goodness' beyond good
and evil. 'Love and do what you will,' St. Augustine is alleged to
have said. A Zen master of the Tokugawa period said in a similar
vein: 'Die while alive, and be completely dead: then do whatever you
will, all is good.' "[16] The phrase "a 'Goodness' beyond good and evil"
hits the mark, and the Zen master's dying while still being alive indicates the transcendence of the ego that lives in the midst of
"dualities"—like and dislike, pleasure and pain, right and wrong,
all of them rigid reactions of a limited separative consciousness.
Freed from this consciousness, one is not below the right and wrong
of the ego stance but far above it. Saint Augustine saw in that
freedom a love in immediate touch with the true soul in man, as
distinguished from the ego—the soul that is infused with the Divine
Light. Proceeding from the selfless warmth of this Light, from the
golden glow of the heart's union with God, one would have no need
for common criteria of good and evil, for one would spontaneously
move in tune with the Supreme's purpose in the world and carry out
the works of a transcendent Goodness, whether understood of men
or not.

As a last word of clarifying sanity on the theme of "beyond-good-

and-evil" in relation to Hinduism, a passage from an early writing of
Sri Aurobindo's may be quoted. Expounding the attitude of the epic
Mahabharata's author, Vyasa, particularly with the figure of
Krishna in view, he writes:

> The drift of Vyasa's ethical speculation has always a definite
> and recognisable tendency; there is a basis of customary morality
> and there is a higher ethic of the soul which abolishes in its crown-
> ing phase the terms of virtue and sin, because to the pure all
> things are pure through an august and selfless disinterestedness.
> This ethic takes its rise naturally from the crowning height of the
> Vedantic philosophy, where the soul becomes conscious of its
> identity with God who, whether acting or actionless, is untouched
> by either sin or virtue. But the crown of the Vedanta is only for
> the highest; the moral calamities that arise from the attempt of
> an unprepared soul to identify self with God is sufficiently in-
> dicated in the legend of Indra and Virochana.† Similarly this
> higher ethic is for the prepared, the initiated only, because the
> raw and unprepared soul will seize on the non-distinction be-
> tween sin and virtue without first compassing the godlike purity
> without which such non-distinction is neither morally admissible
> nor actually conceivable. From this arises the unwillingness of
> Hinduism, so ignorantly attributed by Europeans to priestcraft
> and the Brahmin, to shout out its message to the man in the street
> or declare its esoteric thought to the shoeblack and the kitchen-
> maid. The sword of knowledge is a double-edged weapon; in the
> hands of the hero it can save the world, but it must not be made a
> plaything for children. Krishna himself ordinarily insists on all
> men following the duties and rules of conduct to which they are
> born and to which the cast of their temperament predestined
> them. Arjuna he advises, if incapable of rising to the higher
> moral altitudes, to fight in a just cause, because it is the duty of
> the caste, the class of souls to which he belongs. Throughout the
> Mahabharata he insists on this class-standpoint that every man
> must meet the duties to which his life calls him in a spirit of
> disinterestedness, — not, be it noted, of self-abnegation, which
> may be as much a fanaticism as the grossest egoism itself. It is
> because Arjuna has best fulfilled this ideal, has always lived up to
> the practice of his class in a spirit of disinterestedness and self-

---

† "Both of them came to Brishaspati to know from him of God; he told them to go home and
look in the mirror. Virochana saw himself there and concluding that he was God, asked no
farther; he gave full rein to the sense of individuality in himself which he mistook for the deity. But Indra was not satisfied; finding that there must be some mistake he returned to
Brihaspati and received from him the true God-Knowledge which taught him that he was
God only because all things were God, since nothing existed but the One. If he was the one
God, so was his enemy, the very feelings of separateness and enmity were not permanent reali-
ty but transient phenomena." Sri Aurobindo, *Notes on the Mahabharata* (Pondicherry: Sri
Aurobindo Ashram, 1956), p. 57.

mastery that Krishna loves him above all human beings and considers him and him alone fit to receive the higher initiation. . . .

And even the man who has risen to the heights of the initiation must cleave for the good of society to the pursuits and duties of his order; for, if he does not, the world which instinctively is swayed by the examples of its greatest will follow in his footsteps; the bonds of society will then crumble asunder and chaos come again; mankind will be baulked of its destiny. Sri Krishna illustrates this by his own example, the example of God in his manifest form.[17]

Notes

1. The Bṛhadāranyaka Upaniṣad, with the Commentary of Śankarācharya, trans. Swāmī Mādhavānanda, 4th ed. (Calcutta: Advaita Ashram, 1965).

2. Sri Aurobindo, trans., (Pondicherry: Sri Aurobindo Ashram, 1953), pp. 111, 109.

3. Ibid., p. 9. Sri Aurobindo's version of verse 7 is: "He in whom it is the Self-Being that has become all existences that are Becomings for he has the perfect knowledge, how shall he be deluded, whence shall be have grief who sees everywhere oneness?"

4. Pierre Teilhard de Chardin, Writings in Time of War, (London: Collins, 1968; New York: Harper & Row, 1973), p. 28.

5. Sri Aurobindo, The Message of the Gita as Interpreted by Sri Aurobindo, ed. Anilbaran Roy (London: George Allen & Unwin, 1953), p. 83.

6. Ibid., p. 278.

7. Sri Aurobindo, Message of the Gita, p. 78.

8. Ibid., p. 83.

9. Ibid., p. 77.

10. Ibid., p. 278.

11. R.E. Hume, The Thirteen Principal Upanishads (Oxford University Press, Geoffrey Cumberledge; Indian Reprint, Madras, 1954), p. 321.

12. Ibid., pp. 320-21.

13. Sri Aurobindo, Thoughts and Aphorisms (Pondicherry: Sri Aurobindo Ashram, 1958), p. 82.

14. Ibid., pp. 74-75.

15. R.C. Zaehner, Concordant Discord: The Interdependence of Faiths (Oxford: Clarendon Press, 1970), p. 368.

16. R. C. Zaehner, Drugs, Mysticism, and Makebelieve (London: Collins, 1972), pp. 124-25.

17. Ibid.

11
"Cosmic Consciousness"; Sri Aurobindo's "Supermind" and His Vision of the Divine Life

It would appear that for all his reference to Sri Aurobindo, no less than to Burke and the Sufis, Zaehner is often all at sea about Cosmic Consciousness. A further muddle comes of equating it with Brahman. Brahman, to Indian spirituality, is a host of things. Brahman is Cosmic Consciousness but also a consciousness beyond the cosmos. And in cosmic terms he is not just the world of matter. The Taittiriya Upanishad does have the statement: "Matter is Brahman" (3.2). But the statement is followed by four others: "Life is Brahman, Mind is Brahman, the knowledge beyond Mind (Vijnana) is Brahman, Bliss is Brahman" (3.3-6). Here the very constituent stuff of each level of existence seems to be called Brahman. But Brahman contains as well as constitutes, and he dwells within what he both contains and constitutes and he controls it too. He is the one Self and the single Lord, and beyond all levels of distinguishable existence he is the sheer Absolute. In relation to those levels he is at once the static Ground and the dynamic Energy. His Cosmic Consciousness is both the Universl Being and the Universal Becoming. As the former, he is the timeless and spaceless essentiality that is invariant in all; he is an infinity without dimension, wholly in an atom as in an Himalaya, entire in a moment as in the sweep of centuries. And, as such, he is not unconscious; he is sheer Consciousness, Consciousness from which all limits are removed, all name and form shed away. As the Universal Becoming he is a Consciousness spread out, an Infinite extended through all space and time, a perpetual continuity of active Consciousness where all the principles of dynamism in the universe are experienced as movements of one Consciousness. And the term *universe* connotes not merely the physical cosmos: there is the cosmos of Life, there is the cosmos of Mind. A triple universality of action is realized. All mind phenomena are felt as one Mind, all life phenomena as one Life, and Mind are known as a unity of endless and multiform conscious energy. The individual center from which the widening takes place grows no more than a focus point of a cosmicality of consciousness, and all other individual centers are recognized in general as variations of that center and instruments of the same cosmicality. Even an expansion of consciousness can take place, by which the whole universe is experienced as ensphered within oneself; this is the experience of what the Upanishads call Brahmanda, "the Brahman-egg." And in the Cosmic Consciousness new powers of perception and conception unfold; awareness by outward contact and inferential thought is replaced by an intuitive awareness by identity. Supernormal powers — clairvoyance, clairaudience, inspiration, revelation — develop as part of one's nature.

A proper reading of Sri Aurobindo should render clear all these diverse aspects of Cosmic Consciousness. And it should also disclose quite clearly — though Zaehner says Sri Aurobindo "is not always consistent about this" (p. 6) — that Cosmic Consciousness is not the ultimate condition of spirituality. For it is still a state of cosmic ignorance, half light, half shadow. There is a tremendous enlargement but not a radical conversion from ignorance to knowledge. One may be open to forces that are undesirable, that can make one a leaf in a storm, that at the same time can give a sense of inner liberation and a helpless outer drift on the modes of unillumined nature. But when the personality has been purified and calmed, the turn is toward the Cosmic Truth, and then the Supreme Divine takes charge of the liberated being and enlarged becoming — just as the ego self gives way to the World Self, the World Self gives way to the Supreme Self, and the active parts spring into luminous harmony with the Supreme Doer, the Lord of Creatures, the Mother of the worlds, the Ishwara-Shakti. And through one's inmost soul, which is a spark of the Transcendent's working out individual terms of the universe by a progression of rebirths in form after form, a passage is found to what is more than Cosmic Matter, Cosmic Life, Cosmic Mind. And through the Cosmic Truth as well as through the Individual Truth the aspirant is drawn toward the Vijnana Consciousness, the transcendent Creative Knowledge-Will that is the infallible expression of the Absolute, the ultimate Existence-Consciousness-Bliss (Sachchidanada) turned to an organized manifestation of the eternal mysteries of unity in multiplicity implicit in its indescribable depths.

It is in connection with the creative Knowledge-Will that the question arises: What is the Supermind that Sri Aurobindo speaks of? Zaehner identifies Supermind with Chit-Shakti, Consciousness-Force operating in the world, and he equates it with the Second Person of the Christian Trinity—the Son who is Logos, "the rational principle and, as it were, the blue-print of the universe"—as well as with Teilhard's "Soul of the World," the divine presence in the cosmos that grows from more to more until it reaches the coreflective collective state serving as the cosmic support of the final pleroma that is the transcendent Christ gathering up in himself the cosmos at the end of history (pp. 35, 38-39, 60, 104). Furthermore, Zaehner takes it to be Supermind's function to "reveal to the world that it has a common soul," and he associates Supermind with Cosmic Consciousness and "joy," as against "Overmind," that intermediary between the triple lower world and the transcendent "upper hemisphere": "Man is likely to get stuck in the 'lower' hemisphere which has Overmind as its ceiling, if there is no outpouring of Supermind, of cosmic consciousness and joy—of the Holy Spirit, we might say—to help it on its way" (pp. 31, 39). Finally, there is Zaehner's general interchange of the epithets *supramental* and *divine* and, by implication, the investing of Teilhard's Omega with the supramental divinity. Zaehner speaks of the common vision of Sri Aurobindo and Teilhard—matter's ultimate "convergence on to a centre of attraction which is supramental and divine" (p. 38).

Many of Zaehner's identifications and equations have a validity, but the validity is very general and mostly indirect. And surely Sri Aurobindo's Cosmic Consciousness is enough to reveal to the world "a common Soul": Supermind as such is not required here. Nor is Cosmic Consciousness something more than Overmind: Overmind itself, as the cosmic "ceiling," is indeed Cosmic Consciousness par excellence, the highest form of it. Zaehner everywhere has missed the specific character Sri Aurobindo ascribes to Supermind.

Chit-Shakti, Consciousness-Force, is certainly basic to all manifestation, but it has a varied spectrum and only the highest formulation of it is what Sri Aurobindo terms *Supermind*. In the radical sense Supermind is not a formulation at all; it cannot be put in the same universe of discourse as Matter, Life, Mind, or even Overmind. Supermind belongs to the Transcendent and is an eternal mode of it: the universe of discourse to which it belongs is Sachchidananda's. It is the mode in which the implicit truths of Sachchidananda stand forth in a supreme organized harmony of the One and the Many and constitute the creative Godhead from whom proceed the diverse ordered arrangements that are the several "planes" of cosmic existence, beginning with Overmind — the world of the Great Gods who are yet one God with many faces and fronts — and ending with the material cosmos evolving out of an infinite Inconscience by virtue of a push from within of all the higher powers "involved" in it and by virtue of a pressure from above of all these powers existing uninvolved and freely active in their own right on their characteristic planes. Supermind, along with Existence-Consciousness-Bliss, is also involved in the Inconscience, and the goal of our evolution is the manifestation of this divine quaternary under the action of Supermind from within and above.

To distinguish the specificity of Supermind, Sri Aurobindo writes:

Existence that acts and creates by the power and from the pure delight of its conscious being is the reality that we are, the self of all our modes and moods, the cause, object and goal of all our doing, becoming and creating. . . .

Still, when we have found that all things are Sachchidananda, all has not yet been explained. . . .We have the key of the riddle, we have still to find the lock in which it will turn, for this Existence, Conscious-Force, Delight does not work directly or with a sovereign irresponsibility like a magician building up worlds and universes by the mere fiat of its word. We perceive a process, we are aware of a Law. . . .

But why should we interpose any special power or faculty between the infinite Consciousness itself and the result of its working? May not this Self-awareness of the Infinite range freely creating forms which afterwards remain in play so long as there is not the fiat that bids them cease, — even as the old Semitic Revelation tells us, "God said, Let there be Light, and there was Light"? But when we say, "God said, Let there be Light," we assume the act of a power of consciousness which determines

Light out of everything else that is not Light; and when we say "and there was Light" we presume a directive faculty, an active power corresponding to the original perceptive power, which brings out the phenomenon and, working out Light according to the line of the original perception, prevents it from being over-powered by all the infinite possibilities that are other than itself. Infinite consciousness in its infinite action can produce only infinite results; to settle upon a fixed Truth or order of truths and build a world in conformity with that which is fixed, demands a selective faculty of knowledge commisioned to shape finite appearance out of the infinite Reality.

This power was shown to the Vedic seers by the name of Maya. Maya meant for them the power of infinite consciousness to comprehend, contain in itself and measure out, that is to say, to form — for form is delimitation — Name and Shape out of the vast illimitable Truth of infinite existence. It is by Maya that static truth of essential being becomes ordered truth of active being, — or, to put it in more metaphysical language, out of the supreme being in which all is all without barrier of separative consciousness emerges the phenomenal being in which all is in each and each is in all for the play of existence with existence, consciousness with consciousness, force with force, delight with delight. The play of all in each and each in all is concealed at first from us by the mental play or the illusion of Maya which persuades each that he is in all but not all in him and that he is in all as a separated being and not as a being always inseparably one with the rest of existence. Afterwards we have to emerge from this error into the supramental play or the truth of Maya where the "each" and the 'all" coexist in the inseparable unity of the one truth and the multiple symbol. . . .

This distinction between the lower and the higher Maya is the link in thought and in cosmic Fact which the pessimistic and illusionist philosophies miss or neglect. To them the mental Maya, or perhaps an Overmind, is the creatrix of the world, and a world created by mental Maya would indeed be an inexplicable paradox and a fixed yet floating nightmare of conscious existence which could neither be classed as an illusion nor as a reality. . . .

Supermind is the vast self-extension of the Brahman that contains and develops. By the Idea it develops the triune principle of existence, consciousness and bliss out of their indivisible unity. It differentiates but does not divide. . . .And it acts by the same operation on all the principles and possibilities which it evolves out of this all-constituent trinity. It possesses the power of development, of evolution, of making explicit, and that power carries with it the other power of involution, of envelopment, of making implicit. In a sense, the whole of creation may be said to be a movement between two involutions, Spirit in which all is involved and out of which all evolves downward to the other pole of Matter,

Matter in which also all is involved and out of which all evolves upward to the other pole of Spirit. . . .

This conception of the Idea points us to the essential contrast between our mental consciousness and the Truth-consciousness. We regard thought as a thing separate from existence, abstract, unsubstantial, different from reality, something which appears one knows not whence and detaches itself from objective reality in order to observe, understand and judge it; for so it seems and therefore is to our all-dividing, all-analysing mentality. The first business of Mind is to render "discrete," to make fissures much more than to discern, and so it has made this paralysing fissure between thought and reality. But in Supermind all being is consciousness, all consciousness is of being, and the idea, a pregnant vibration of consciousness, is equally a vibration of being pregnant of itself; it is an initial coming out, in creative self-knowledge, of that which lay concentrated in uncreative self-awareness. It comes out as the Idea that is a reality, and it is that reality of the Idea which evolves itself, always by its own power and consciousness of itself, always self-conscious, always self-developing by the will inherent in the Idea, always self-realising by the knowledge ingrained in its every impulsion. . . .It is Real-Idea. . . .

The world, therefore, is not a figment of conception in the universal Mind, but a conscious birth of that which is beyond Mind into forms of itself. A Truth of conscious being supports these forms and expresses itself in them. And the knowledge corresponding to the truth thus expressed reigns as a supramental Truth-Consciousness organising real-ideas in a perfect harmony before they are cast into the mental-vital-material mould. Mind, Life and Body are an inferior consciousness and a partial expression of that which strives to arrive in the mould of a various evolution at that superior expression of itself already existent to the Beyond-Mind. That which is in the Beyond-Mind is the ideal which in its own conditions it is labouring to realise. . . .

Above, the formula of the One eternally stable and immutable; below, the formula of the Many which, eternally mutable, seeks but hardly finds in the flux of things a firm and immutable standing-point; between, the seat of all trinities, of all that is biune, of all that becomes Many-in-One and yet remains One-in-Many because it was originally One that is always potentially Many. This intermediary term is therefore the beginning and end of all creation and arrangement, the Alpha and the Omega, the starting-point of all differentiation, the instrument of all unification, originative, executive and consummative of all realised or realisable harmonies. . . .

We have to regard, therefore, this all-containing, all-originating, all-consummating Supermind as the nature of the

Divine Being, not indeed in its absolute self-existence, but in its action as the Lord and Creator of its own worlds. This is the truth of that which we call God. Obviously, this is not the personal and limited Deity, the magnified and supernatural Man of the ordinary occidental conception; for that conception erects a too human Eidolon of a certain relation between the creative Supermind and the ego. We must not indeed exclude the personal aspect of the Deity, for the impersonal is only one face of existence; the Divine is All-existence, but is also the one Existent — it is the sole Conscious-Being, but still a Being. . .

In view of Sri Aurobindo's description of Supermind, one may say that the Consciousness-Force, Chit-Shakti, that one finds operating in the world is, in its definable origin, one aspect of Supermind at work, rather than, as Zaehner opines, that Supermind is the Chit-Shakti aspect of Sachchidananda going forth into world action.

Again, in view of Sri Aurobindo's identification of Supermind with the God-aspect, in distinction from the Absolute-aspect, of the Supreme Reality, and in view of his precise statement that it develops, without dividing, "the triune principle of existence, consciousness and bliss out of their indivisible unity," one may correct Zaehner's notion that the Christian Trinity can be equated with the Vedantic Sachchidananda (pp. 13, 38, 55, 103-4). Even in orthodox Vedanta there is the creative Ishwara answering in orthodox terms to Sri Aurobindo's Supermind. It is in Sachchidananda in its creative Ishwara aspect that the Christian Trinity of Three distinguishable Persons who are yet One Person has to be located. Existence, Consciousness, and Bliss as they obtain in the Ishwaric Supermind poise of the Transcendent may be seen as the Indian and Aurobindonian counterparts of the Father, the Son, and the Holy Spirit of Christianity.

Even here I must make a significant reservation, but I shall come to it after pointing out the philosophical inaccuracy of Zaehner's equation. Beginning with *Sat,* Zaehner states:

"Being" is the Absolute, the absolutely transcendent, but also the "Father, giver of the seed," as the Gītā (14.4) puts it, "the seer, the Father," who "sat on the high-priest's throne" [Rig-Veda 10.81.], "he who is the overseer in highest heaven" [Rig-Veda 10.129.7], God transcendent, the "Person than whom there is nothing higher, the goal and the all-highest Way" [Katha Upanishad 3.11]. The second aspect or "Person" in its original meaning of "mask" or "character" is *cit,* "consciousness" or "thought," the Logos or the rational principle through which all things cohere and are what they are in the context of an all-embracing unity. This is the principle of which it is written:

> In him were created
> All things in heaven and on earth:
> everything visible and everything invisible,
> Thrones, Dominations, Sovereignties, Powers —
> all things were created through him and for him.
> Before anything was created, he existed,
> and he holds all things in unity.
>
> [Col. 1:16-17]

But this Logos. . .is also the eternal life by which Paul lived and which he identified with Christ, the "more minute than the minute" which is yet "greater than the great" who is "hidden in the heart" [Katha Upanishad 2.20: Svetaśvatara Upanishad 3.20] of men. Last, there is the Holy Spirit, the God who is Love [1 John 4:8], the "seed" [1 John 3:9] from which the new Adam, the spiritual All-Man was born, substantial "peace and joy" [Rom. 14:17] — the *ananda* of the Hindu Trinity. What, place, then, does the Holy Spirit occupy in the total Godhead? Primarily he is the love that unites the Father to the Son, Being to the Logos. But this love is also creative, the equivalent of sexuality in the eternal world. (pp. 103-4)

Doubtless, it is possible to speak in general or popularly of Sachchidananda in terms of God the Father who is creative Will and God the Son who is the creative principle of ordering and unifying Knowledge and God the Holy Spirit who is love uniting and creating. But, philosophically speaking, Sachchidananda is the "essence" of reality, and none of these terms, which involve willing, knowing, and loving, can be equated to that essence: that essence can only be defined as Existence, Consciousness (or Consciousness-Force, Chit-Tapas), and Bliss. This point emerges in an analysis by Sri Aurobindo when a disciple asks: "You have written: 'Beauty is an expression, a form of Ananda.' In that case, is not Beauty itself part of the essence of the Divine, as are Ananda, Consciousness and Existence? If it is, should not one thing that Love, Knowledge, Force, Light, etc., are also expressions of Sachchidananda?" Sri Aurobindo replies:

The word "expression" means only something that is manifested by the Ananda and of which Ananda is the essence. Love and Beauty are powers of Ananda as Light and Knowledge are of Consciousness. Force is inherent in Consciousness and may be called part of the Divine Essence. Ananda is always there even when Sachchidananda takes on an impersonal aspect or appears as the sole essential Existence; but love needs a Lover and Beloved. Beauty needs a manifestation to show itself. So in the same way Consciousness is always there, but Knowledge needs a manifestation to be active, there must be a Knower and a Known. That is why the distinction is made between Ananda which is of the essence and Beauty which is a power or expression of Ananda in manifestation. These are of course philosophical distinctions necessary for the mind to think about the world and the Divine."[2]

Thus, philosophically, both the Son and the Holy Spirit, because of their being Knowledge and Love, cannot be given counterparts in Sachchidananda. Analogously, the Father too does not fall inside it. And when one reads the lines just preceding the passage Zaehner has quoted — the lines saying of Christ:

He is the image of the unseen God
and the first-born of all creation,[3]

and meaning that God the Father holds knowledge of Himself in that primal projection of His, the Son — when we read these lines and add their declaration to the one in Zaehner's passage that says that in the Son all things in heaven and on earth were created, then we at once understand how the Father cannot have in Sachchidananda His counterpart. For we find Sri Aurobindo writing: "The supreme supracosmic Sachchidananda is above all. Supermind may be described as its power of self-awareness and world-awareness, the world being known as within itself and not outside."[4] Again, Sri Aurobindo tells us: "I mean by the supramental the Truth-Consciousness . . . by which the Divine knows not only his own essence and being but his manifestation also."[5] For our ends we should aver that in the Supermind Sachchidananda manifests both itself and the world. Thus, not only the Son and the Holy Spirit but the Father as well belong to a plane of Sachchidananda's manifestation. But can we really put them all on the plane of its archetypal manifestation that is the Aurobindonian Supermind?

We cannot. This Supermind has a bearing very different from the Christian Trinity and even from the Vedantic Ishwara. According to Sri Aurobindo, there is in the Rig-Veda a vision of the Supermind and an attempt by the Rishis to reach it as an individual goal. The vision persists into the Upanishads, but already the presence of what he calls Overmind is beginning to be a power and the basic urge comes to be toward "the formula of the One eternally stable and immutable," though the level of the Many-in-One and the One-in-Many is not neglected. The Gītā, in its concept of Purushottama, the Supreme Being or Person, with his Para-Prakriti, his Higher Nature-Power, points toward the Supermind and lays great emphasis on work in the world through a relationship of the soul's love with the Supreme Being. But there is no direct awareness of the Supermind's specific character or special power; the Overmind's manifold grandeur of Cosmic Consciousness at its highest is in the forefront, and for all practical purposes the face of the Purushottama is haloed with it. Later Indian spirituality made no distinction between Supermind and Overmind and took the latter to be the ultimate dynamic Godhead. Sri Aurobindo says that Overmind is indeed a mighty delegate of Supermind, and it is hardly surprising that one should not look beyond it. Here too is a divine model of what is being worked out in the mental-vital-physical mold. But this model is not dynamic enough to transform that mold. That is why neither in the East nor in the West has there been the clear and effective sense of a world moving toward a divine perfection realizable in time and space themselves.

A vague sense could not help being there, for the flawless and omnipotent ideality of the Supermind is involved here. But some shortcoming in the Overmind has led to the conviction that, whatever one may achieve here, the final fulfillment is in the Beyond. Wherever that conviction reigns there exists the proof that the Supermind has not been truly and properly known. Supermind as God possesses the puissance to bring about in space and time a completely divine mentality, vitality, and physicality as evolved instruments of a soul fully awakened and developed into manifesting on earth a supramental play of the One and the Many, whose archetypal dynamism, along with the Absolute Existence, Consciousness-Force and Bliss, constitutes the "higher hemisphere," the transcendent Reality.

The Christian Trinity—like the Vedantic Ishwara who also was later described as a Trinity of Brahma the Creator, Vishnu the Preserver, and Shiva the Destroyer, three Divine Persons whose functions are not precisely identifiable with those of the Father, the Son, and the Holy Spirit—the Christian Trinity, never having been invested with the specific "puissance" I have spoken of as supramental, is not a vision of Supermind. It is a vision of Overmind in one of its grandest aspects.

I say "one of its grandest" because of the ideas associated with the role of the Son in world history: the Incarnation, the Resurrection, the Millennium, in which there would be a Kingdom of God on earth and Christ would rule over a community of Saints living in undecaying bodies like his own, either "resurrected" or "transformed." These ideas catch a bright shadow of the divine destiny that Supermind can bring about. No more than a shadow, however, for the new bodies would not be divine ones organically developed and thereby truly earth-fulfilling, nor would the Kingdom be anything except a golden-age interval, a sort of thousand-year resting house on way to the Beyond. And about it in general I may quote what Sri Aurobindo said in a letter about a similar dream of Indian religion: "The idea of a temporary kingdom of heaven on earth is contained in the Puranas and conceived by some Vaishnava saints and poets; but it is a devotional idea, no philosophical base is given for the expectation."[6]

Even with regard to the state of consciousness to which Christianity aspires in its millenarian hope Sri Aurobindo has some pertinent remarks in another letter. He finds there no exceeding of what Indian psychology terms *gunas,* the three modes or qualities of Nature: *tamas,* inertia and obscurity; *rajas,* energy and desire; *sattwa,* order and enlightened thought. He finds also an exposure still to the play of dualities—sin and virtue, attraction and repulsion, pain and pleasure, and so on,—because what is aimed at is still an enrichment and enlargement of the mere human person, the mental "I" or ego limited by life-force and body. And he does not find even in the extreme advancement possible within such a formula a key to a collective stability. Sri Aurobindo's comment runs:

There is no connection between the Christian conception [of the Kingdom of Heaven] and the idea of the supramental descent. The Christian conception supposes a state of things brought about by religious emotion and moral purification; but these things are no more capable of changing the world, whatever value they may have for the individual, than mental idealism or any other power yet called upon for the purpose. The Christian proposes to substitute the sattwic religious ego for the rajasic and tamasic ego, but although this can be done as an individual

achievement, it has never succeeded and will never succeed in ac-
complishing itself in the mass. It has no higher spiritual or
psychological knowledge behind it and ignores the foundation of
human character and the source of the difficulty — the duality of
mind, life and body. Unless there is a descent of a new Power of
Consciousness, not subject to the dualities but still dynamic which
will provide a new foundation and a lifting of the centre of consciousness above the mind, the Kingdom of God on earth can only
be an ideal, not a fact realised in the general earth-consciousness
and earth-life.[7]

On the subject of the Christian Trinity, it may be of interest to
note what Sri Aurobindo took it to signify. In his own spiritual
system the Divine has three aspects:

> It is the Cosmic Self and Spirit that is in and behind all things
> and beings, from which and in which all is manifested in the
> universe — although it is now a manifestation in the Ignorance.
> It is the Spirit, the Master of our own being within us whom we
> have to serve and learn to express his will in all our movements so
> that we may grow out of the Ignorance into the Light.
> The Divine is transcendent Being and Spirit, all bliss and light
> and divine knowledge and power, and towards that highest divine
> existence and its Light we have to rise and bring down the reality
> of it more and more into our consciousness and life.[25]

And about this triplicity of the Divine he declared to a somewhat
critical disciple:

> The distinction between the Transcendental, the Cosmic and
> the Individual Divine is not my invention, nor is it native to India
> or to Asia — it is, on the contrary, a recognised European teaching
> current in the esoteric tradition of the Catholic Church where it is
> the authorised explanation of the Trinity, — Father, Son and Holy
> Ghost, — and it exists in all spiritual disciplines that recognise the
> omnipresence of the Divine — in Indian Vedantic experience and
> in Mahommedan yoga (not only the Sufi, but other schools
> also) — the Mahommedans even speak of not two or three but
> many levels of the Divine until one reaches the Supreme. As for
> the idea in itself, surely there is a difference between the in-
> dividual, the cosmos in space and time, and something that ex-
> ceeds this cosmic formula or any cosmic formula. There is a
> cosmic consciousness experienced by many which is quite dif-
> ferent in its scope and action from the individual consciousness,
> and if there is a consciousness beyond the cosmic, infinite and
> essentially eternal, not merely extended in Time, that also must be

different from these two. And if the Divine is or manifests Himself
in these three, is it not conceivable that in aspect, in His working,
He may differentiate Himself so much that we are driven, if we
are not to confound all truth of experience, if we are not to limit
ourselves to a mere static experience of something indefinable, to
speak of a triple aspect of the Divine?

In the practice of Yoga there is a great dynamic difference in
one's way of dealing with these three possible realisations. If I
realise only the Divine as that, not my personal self, which yet
moves secretly all my personal being and which I can bring forward out of the veil, or if I build up the image of that Godhead in
my members, it is a realisation but a limited one. If it is the
Cosmic Godhead that I realise, losing in it all personal self, that is
a very wide realisation, but I become a mere channel of the
universal Power and there is no personal or divinely individual
consummation for me. If I shoot up to the transcendental realisation only, I lose both myself and the world in the transcendental
Absolute. If, on the other hand, my aim is none of these things by
itself, but to realise and also to manifest the Divine in the world,
bringing down for the purpose a yet unmanifested Power—such as
the supermind,—a harmonisation of all three becomes imperative. I have to bring it down, and from where shall I bring it
down—since it is not yet manifested in the cosmic formula—if
not from the unmanifest Transcendence, which I must reach and
realise? I have to bring it into the cosmic formula and, if so, I
must realise the cosmic Divine and become conscious of the
cosmic self and the cosmic forces. But I have to embody it
here,—otherwise it is left as an influence only and not a thing fixed
in the physical world, and it is through the Divine in the individual alone that this can be done.

These are elements in the dynamics of spiritual experience and
I am obliged to admit them if a divine work has to be done.[9]

The foregoing paragraphs constitute an excellent outline of Sri
Aurobindo's ultimate vision of Reality and Spirituality and, in addi-
tion, a sidelight on what he considered "esoteric" Christianity and
Mohammedanism. Beatrice Bruteau, in her penetrative book on Sri
Aurobindo, remarks in a footnote that she "is not aware of this in-
terpretation as the 'authorised explanation of the Trinity' by the
Catholic Church."[10] On the face of it, it seems impossible that the
Catholic Church, even in its esoteric moods, should countenance a
Cosmic Divine in the same sense as the Vedanta, though some
Catholic mystics like Meister Eckhart might imply it in certain of
their pronouncements. But the Aurobindonian view of the Trinity
catches the truth of Teilhardism as I have sought to free it from

Teilhard's own ambivalences and his coreligionist expositors' covering up of his "hyper-Catholicism." Sri Aurobindo, by referring to "spiritual disciplines that recognise the omnipresence of the Divine" and by identifying the Son with the Cosmic Divine, discloses the inmost sense of Teilhard's Cosmic Christ and lets a piercing light fall on Teilhard's attraction to pantheism through what, in a letter to Père Auguste Valensin, he calls "the urgency to venerate an omnipresence."[11] It is by arriving at the Aurobindonian view of the Trinity that Teilhardian Christianity can come nearest to being the spirituality of the future. What, of course, would still keep it at some distance is its lack of the intuition that would combine evolutionism with the sense of the earth-fulfilling Supermind's pressing from its free status above and pushing from its "involved" condition below.

Notes

1. Sri Aurobindo, *The Life Divine* (New York: Sri Aurobindo Library, 1949), 105-23.
2. Sri Aurobindo, *Guidance from Sri Aurobindo: Letters to a Young Disciple:* Nagin Doshi, 2 vols. (Pondicherry: Sri Aurobindo Society, 1974-1976), 1:240-41.
3. Cf. R.C. Zaehner, *Dialectical Christianity and Christian Materialism* (London: Oxford University Press, 1971), p. 90.
4. *On Yoga*, part 2 (Pondicherry: Sri Aurobindo International University Centre Collection, 1958), 6:261.
5. Ibid., p. 26.
6. Ibid., p. 89.
7. Ibid., pp. 142-43.
8. Ibid., p. 483.
9. Ibid., p. 484.
10. Beatrice Bruteau, *Worthy Is the World: The Hindu Philosophy of Sri Aurobindo* (Teaneck, N.J.: Fairleigh Dickinson University Press, 1972), p. 259.

12

The Demands of an Evolutionary World View; Teilhard's "Pleroma"

With the advent of modern evolutionism, the goal of an earthly perfection has taken an increasingly concrete body. Modern evolutionism, in its deepest drive, is the scientific reflex of the Supermind's light, which has been pressing upon the terrestrial consciousness and that has formed its double avatar, its joint announcer and realizer and organizer, in Sri Aurobindo and the Mother. Through modern evolutionism it has touched Teilhard—hence his scientific look forward to a collective evolution of man into a "super-consciousness" culminating in a divine manifold unity that he terms Omega Point. The element of inborn pantheism in his nature, feeling matter itself to be secretly a substance of divinity, tends him all the more to envisage a divine culmination within space and time. No doubt, the superconsciousness, born of what he designates the crossing of a new "critical threshold" that is not merely of "reflection," as when man appeared, but of "co-reflection," falls far below Sri Aurobindo's detailed and extensive account of Supermind embodied in a collective divine life. Still, the Teilhardian move is in the Aurobindonian direction. What spoils it is the grip that, for all his novelty, for all his "new religion," he allows traditional Christianity to have upon him.

He is right—and eminently Aurobindonian—in exceeding a pantheist evolutionism and holding that Omega is not just a cosmic potentiality in the future but a transcendent actuality here and now that will meet its own evolutionary form, the Soul of the World, when humanity will attain its maturity. If everything evolves the Divine, the Divine must be already there forever to serve as the magnet drawing upward and onward. Teilhard's concept of the "Prime Mover Ahead" completes pantheist evolutionism. But he falsified the latter and distorts the completing concept by saying that the maturity attained by humanity will coincide with an end of history, a cessation of time and space, a dematerialization of the cosmos into a pleroma à la Saint Paul, giving everything a fulfillment in the Beyond alone. Teilhard argues as though for a fulfilling "ultra-human" within the cosmos, but proceeds to identify the "ultra-human" with the "trans-human" in a noncosmic eternity.

Occasionally, the instinct of the evolutionist-cum-pantheist pulls him back from the identification and lends an earthly meaning to the next "critical threshold." Once more there is dissension within him and there are two voices speaking here as everywhere else. De Lubac notices, though grudgingly, the discrepancy:

> He may well on occasion have dreamed of "another" — relatively other — humanity that would arise at the critical point and take over from our own in a universe that had not yet arrived at its temporal term; and he may have attributed to this "other humanity" a "universal love" that would spontaneously introduce on earth the sovereignty of charity. But this chimerical element seldom enters into his thought. The thought itself is completely independent of it — even though he did not always, maybe, warn the reader against a chimerical interpretation. [2]

A critical point or threshold commencing a mankind strikingly different from what it is now, the members of the species *Homo sapiens* turned, as Teilhard elsewhere says, into "super-men" by being made "into elements governed by some higher soul," is obviously a pleroma within the cosmos.[3] And there seems no reason why the meeting of the transcendent Omega with its own evolutionary form should carry away the earthly ultrahuman immediately into the unearthly transhuman and put a finis to evolutionary existence in space-time rather than manifesting the transcendent in the spatiotemporal. If the point of maturity can coincide with the pleroma, it is just as logical to consider the pleroma manifesting in the spatiotemporal as to consider evolutionary space-time existence metamorphosed into the pleroma. But Teilhard mostly acted as though blind to this logic and could not steadily contemplate the truth, loyal to pantheist evolutionism's temper, of a cosmic millennium of the Spirit. De Lubac annotates the "dream" of that millennium with the dreamer's own words: "I have no personal illusions about the incredible element in my hypothesis."[4] And he adds: "Even in such rare passages, it could, moreover, be possible that Père Teilhard had in mind, without making it quite clear, the supernatural reality of the mystical body."

I am afraid that de Lubac is indulging in wishful thinking so far as the supernatural reality he speaks of is regarded as history ending. Teilhard nowhere drops as much as a hint that he is working along eschatological lines. De Lubac's earlier suggestion that Teilhard was writing of an event within the framework of a universe that would one day arrive at its "temporal term" is absolutely gratuitous. No "temporal term" figures in the essay from which he has quoted Teilhard's dream of "another humanity." The actual words, as given in the official translation, are: "*Another* mankind must inevitably emerge from this vision, one of which we have as yet no idea, but one which I believe I can already feel stirring through the old mankind."[5] And Teilhard goes on to relate the stirring he feels to his contact with any man, however "alien. . .by nationality, class, race or religion," who, like him, has opened his eyes and seen, through modern perspectives of the cosmos, the voyaging ahead of evolution. In such a brotherhood of vision, the Christian idea of a temporal term would be entirely out of place.

De Lubac also creates a false impression by failing to quote the sentences that follow what Teilhard says about his "hypothesis": "I find it indeed just as difficult as anyone to feel, or even to imagine, what sort of thing inter-human sympathy (between cosmic elements and other cosmic elements) could possibly turn out to be — even though the empirical laws of noogenesis oblige me to regard its appearance as probable, and even inevitable. With that reservation, however, I shall observe that the quasi-impossibility we still find in conceiving the establishment of a unanimity of man may well derive from our overlooking a certain factor which, if introduced into our calculations, is capable of producing entirely different results. By that factor I mean the quite recent sensitizing of our minds to the organic depth and convergent properties of time."[6] The sense would seem to be as follows: Feeling and imagination going by common experience fumble in unbelief as though one were in the realm of the quasi-impossible, but the case is different if one proceeds by insight into the evolutionary process and the impression it gives of more and more complex and unified organisms appearing irreversibly with the passage of time—cosmic elements converging upon ever greater centers of consciousness in the natural course of the ages. Such insight is bound to kindle the hope, nay, even the certainty, of a superorganism's arising with its interconnections established by love on a planetary scale. Teilhard's true position may be elucidated by another passage from the same essay: "The very first time we meet it, the idea of a super-human organism seems fantastic. Nevertheless, if. . .we are willing to entertain it, and then begin to examine it more deeply, it is surprising what order and clarity is introduced into our outlook on the universe by a hypothesis that at first seemed crazy."[7]

What renders the essay in question most definitive in its trend and not in the least pleromatic in the extra cosmic connotation is a certain linguistic turn that de Lubac ignores. Here Teilhard does not speak merely of "an ultra-human synthesis": he also refers to this "further degree of organization, and therefore of consciousness and therefore of freedom" as the actualization of a "possibility" and a "potentiality" represented and contained by "the plurality of thinking molecules," and this possibility and potentiality he defines as that of "a further trans-human synthesis of organic matter."[8] The "trans-human," like the "ultra-human," is now an earthly vision. It is a pleroma in the intracosmic and not the extracosmic connotation.

Nor is this fusion of the two terms, without implying the latter connotation, a unique aberrancy characterizing the present essay. Elsewhere, too, Teilhard has the phrase "the problem of knowing whether, and up to what point, it is physically (planetarily) possible for man to trans- or ultra-hominize himself."[9] There is also another context where one reads:

> It follows from what we have already said about the birth of the cosmic sense that the prime mover of human activity can only have been a reality possessing *universal dimensions*. . . .A total and totalizing end: nothing less could set the springs of our liberty in motion and bend them to it. . . .Not only for an elect minority but for the masses as well, it has become a commonly accepted "article of faith" that if there is any way forward for the world and salvation for the individual, they await us in the direction of some higher form to be attained by humanity. But how exactly are we

to picture the features of this super-humanity in which the world is to be epitomized?. . .The features of this whole subject of trans-humanity, which has been in continuous creation throughout the vicissitudes of the earth, perforce escape us.[10]

Here we have the already existent Omega and the evolutionarily emerging Omega playing into each other: they are the same reality under two aspects, holding our future fulfillment as at once a superhumanity and a trans-humanity. And neither aspect leads to an extracosmic consummation. All that the context carries us on to is the following suggestion:

> At two critical points human energy has already assumed the form in which we know it today: first the appearance of life, whence emerged the biosphere; then emergence of thought which produced the noosphere.
> Cannot a further and final metamorphosis have been in progress since the birth of love in Christianity: the coming to consciousness of an "Omega" in the heart of the noosphere — the circles' motion towards their common centre: the appearance of the "Theosphere"?[11]

A sort of divine "change of state" upon our planet itself is pictured for humanity; it is not made dependent on an exit from the planet into a timeless and spaceless beyond.

Yes, the instinct of the evolutionist-cum-pantheist in Teilhard sets him occasionally on an Aurobindonian tack. But, by and large, as de Lubac is happy to mark, the transhuman is the extracosmic supernatural side of the ultra or superhuman, and Teilhard himself, if religiously catechized, would be disposed to find any other view incredible.

Incredibility, however, would be quite out of place once one could challenge the precise argument by which Teilhard concludes that the condition he is describing must coincide with the end of history. His dialectic, in effect, may be framed thus:

There are two currents in cosmic history: entropy and complexity-consciousness. In science, entropy denotes the widely observed diminution, in all energy exchanges, of the utilizable form of energy. By the Second Law of Thermodynamics, utilizable energy grows less and less with time until a dead level of nonutility will be reached in the universe, a state of totally dissipated heat and, in consequence, utter disorganization. The Cosmos is bound to run down in the process of exchanging what one may call *tangential energy.*[12] This tangential energy pertains to the "without" of things. But there is also what one should term *radial energy*. It pertains to the "within" of things and brings about the complex arrangement of matter, the union of material factors to constitute a center of action: the complexifying and centrifying movement is radial or psychic energy. By means of radial energy "critical points or thresholds" are effected in evolution—notably the appearance of life out of prelife and mind out of animate matter. Here there is a current running counter to entropy. And every evolutionary leap is irreversible on the whole. Zigzags, even shuttles, occur on a minor scale, yet there is no definitive going back or reversal. This phenomenon one can designate *orthogenesis*. But for radial energy to counteract tangential energy's tendency toward entropy it must always be pushing forward. A stop anywhere will render its achievements a victim to entropy, to disorganization. Now if evolution attains its ultimate summit and nothing further is left to attain, a problematic situation exists. Entropy must begin to act since there is no further pushing forward in space-time; but what about the quality of irreversibility associated with every evolutionary leap? This quality cannot have force against the entropy-subjected state of evolutionary halt unless a push is made into a dimension other than space-time. Evolution must either break down by the law of entropy or else leave space-time for good and enter eternity.

Several issues are involved in Teilhard's argument. First of all, there is the issue of a finis to evolution. One may question the necessity to write a finis. And here one must ponder whether Teilhard can be justified in thinking of coreflective unanimity as the ne plus ultra of evolution.

De Lubac is inclined to query the very notion of a critical threshold that would lead to a mysterious "super-organism" whose cells would be individual persons. This subject need not be discussed. What is useful now is a certain Teilhardian posture framed by a remark of de Lubac's that claims to confound Teilhard out of his own mouth and thus disprove the legitimacy of talking in terms of a new critical crossover. De Lubac writes: "We have his own statement that the 'threshold of reflection bears in itself something definitive,' he asks, too, 'what advance could there be upon thought?' "[13] If Teilhard meant that on life's crossing the critical threshold of reflection, it has reached in general the final stage in the sense of having entered a phase of self-consciousness that will be the basis of all future achievement, he is on the right track. But he believes the rise of complexity-consciousness to have come to an end, so far as the human individual is concerned, with the advent of self-conscious mentality. The individual brain has attained its limit of organization. Over the last twenty thousand years, during which we have known it, it has shown no appreciable growth in complexity of structure or function.[14] Individual evolution as such, except for negligible modulations in the brain-box, has come to a halt. Still, says Teilhard, evolution along the human axis has not terminated. It has become—to use Julian Huxley's expression—"psychosocial." A development is taking place not directly in the individual but by way of the coming together of individuals. Socialization is the line followed by evolution. A grouping as of thinking cells is going on to form a collective Being, a sort of superorganism. Thus, for Teilhard, the individual cannot go beyond the reflective stage that accompanies the present complexity of his cerebrum. The individual in isolation has no future higher than of thought.

And to Teilhard, even in the collective evolution thought is not essentially overpassed. It grows totalized, magnified, "planetary," a huge "unanimity," but it is still thought. What Teilhard sometimes terms "super-consciousness" is yet nothing else than superthought: that is why he describes the next "critical threshold" as that of "co-reflection."

Now all this is a non-sequitur from the evolutionary premise. The human brain may not have shown any marked change in the last twenty thousand years, but has not Teilhard[14] himself in his less dogmatic moments admitted that "there is nothing to prove absolutely that important evolutionary assets (a more developed arrangement of the nerve fibres) may not still be held in reserve in our brain substance"?[15] And how can he assert that organic evolution has reached its ceiling in man, the animal group with the most expansive vitality, when he has, in one place, proclaimed: "In common with many observers, I am convinced that the modification of zoological forms continues to take place (in exactly the same way as the folds and cracking of the earth's crust) and that only their slowness prevents our seeing them. I am convinced, for example, that everywhere around us races are being formed at the present day, in preparation for the coming of new species"?[16] Moreover, the very proponents of a dead end for man speak, as even Teilhard has noted, of " some slight progress still to be expected in the direction

of an increasing brachycephalism and a further flattening of the
face" — two small yet not negligible clues to an organic process slowly
continuing.[17]

However, what is of primary consequence with man is not
zoological modification, and Teilhard himself has never been
backward in granting this. He holds that, with reflection, the evolution of consciousness acquires a greater "within," a deeper "interiority," a superior "centration," by which consciousness gains a
marked freedom from physical determinism, an active independence of the complexity counterpart. This being so, it is inconclusive to inquire for a development of the cerebrum in the last
twenty thousand years. What one has to ask is whether human beings have shown signs of a higher level of interiority than thought.
And there the evidence is overwhelming. In the mystical
phenomenon, thought often ceases and is rapt away in a luminous
beatific realization of the Superhuman, the Divine. Or if thought remains it is the passive instrument of a Light and a Bliss that are of
the nature of the Eternal, the Infinite. Surely, a Meister Eckart and
a Saint John of the Cross do not function in their mystical moments
as mere thinkers, mere reflective centers. Even in the less abnormal
phenomena of what we call *genius*, there are intimations of a conscious state beyond thought, above reflection, though thinking and
reflecting are mostly mixed up with them. A Plato, a Caesar, a
Leonardo, a Shakespeare, a Napoleon, an Einstein — restricting this
list to the Western hemisphere — have all a touch of the Superman.
Supermanhood comes in a distinctive form in giants of spirituality
like Buddha, Chaitanya, Nanak, Mirabai, Ramakrishna, and
Ramana Maharshi — to list some in the Eastern hemisphere only.
Superconsciousness, in the true sense, confronts us throughout
history: a "critical threshold" posterior in time to the one that introduced reflection into the evolutionary process is crossed by individual after individual, no matter if the crossing is partial and not
yet in the rare integral sense explained and considerably exemplified
by Sri Aurobindo. Teilhard is radically at fault in his outlook on individual evolution.

One may aver that in a broad sense complexity continues to
develop even physically. Mystical states do have an influence on the
body. Organic functions assume a supernormal aspect in many
phenomena. Teilhard should know how the bodies of saints and
mystics exhibit extraordinary properties under the stress of illu-

mined or ecstatic experiences. And what Sri Aurobindo defines as *Supermind,* possessed of the divine original or "truth" of the physical organism no less than of the vital being and the mental self, is bound to have in the course of its precipitation and emergence a fundamental transfigurative effect on the whole somatic system. By the very logic of evolution's developing a finer physical medium along with a finer psychological instrumentality, such a transfiguration must be on the cards.

Teilhard has frequently spoken of the importance of the person, the value of personalization. Evolutionarily, the importance and value has been focused in the individual, the human unit. No doubt, the collective is also of importance and carries value; it is the inalienable context and continent of the individual, but it is not more important, more valuable than he. Both are equal in the ultimate computation, but the individual is always the spearhead of evolution. Nor does the individual evolve just by a collective unity. Socialization however widespread, totalization however intense, unanimity however love-mooded and knowledge-motivated cannot by themselves effect a superior state of evolution. The individual has to follow the via mystica in himself, practice Yoga in his own distinct capacity. And it is only by evolving his true soul that feels itself to be a child of the Divine Father and Mother in a boundless family, only by realizing the one Self of selves and the unique Ground of all existences, only by entering the Cosmic Consciousness that interconnects all beings and things and that holds them as expressions of a single secret dynamic harmony, and most of all, only by getting into contact with the sovereignly illumining and unifying power of Supermind—it is only by compassing such mystic and Yogic states that the members of the human species can give rise to a true socialization, totalization, unanimity.

Teilhard, by postulating a full stop to individual evolution outside of a future collective development, has missed the essential potency as well as the essential significance of the individual. I have already noted Christopher Mooney's perception of Teilhard's underplaying of the individual vis-à-vis the race in spite of his care for the preservation of the personal in the universal. Teilhard's ultimate attitude toward the individual is in striking contrast to Sri Aurobindo's. Jacques Masui, French journalist and editor of art books and admirer of Sri Aurobindo, has gone to the length of remarking that here lies the fundamental divergence between Sri Aurobindo and Teilhard.

He says:

> Teilhard de Chardin was interested above all in the group, in mankind. Aurobindo was interested principally in man. There is here a certain paradox, since Père Teilhard had some fear of oriental thought which "depersonalizes." Now, the strange situation today is that it is the orientals who are concerned about the fate of the person, whom they see crushed by science and technology. They say—and Aurobindo said it first of all: "It is absolutely necessary, in the rather over-celebrated words of Bergson, to add to mechanicity mysticism."
>
> Yes, Teilhard de Chardin was more preoccupied with groups, and in one of his last writings—perhaps the last—he said this: "I do not know whether the present state of man is better or worse, but I am certain of one thing: it is that humanity is doing well, humanity is in good control"—that is to say, evolution moves towards its fulfillment, a fulfillment in which man and society find themselves united in a sort of unanimity, unanimity of which he does not speak much but which we feel in all his work, as also in that of Sri Aurobindo.[18]

It may not be inapposite to pause a little over the passage Masui has quoted from memory and to set it out in its original form in full. Orthodox editorship of Teilhard's writing has tried to give it a sense that does not really oppose concern about individuals to concern about the race. We must once and for all determine its true drift. Teilhard's words run: "If you tell me that as time goes on, man is getting 'better or worse,' I hardly know or care what the words mean. But if you tell me that mankind can be regarded at this moment as a species that is disintegrating or has reached its ceiling, then I deny it absolutely. And this for the very good reason that in virtue of the power and the actual method of operation of its technical mental unification, twentieth-century mankind, so far from trailing behind or falling back, represents itself as a system in the full vigour of *co-reflexion*, which is exactly the same as saying of *ultra-hominization*."[19]

The orthodox comment comes in a footnote to Teilhard's opening sentence. The footnote goes: "Whether a man be 'better' or 'worse' is in fact an ambiguous question. In any event, for Père Teilhard, as for every Christian, a man's moral value is a mystery of which God alone is the judge and to penetrate which is outside the competence of the scientist."

The comment is essentially off the mark. Teilhard not only says,

"I hardly know"; he also adds, "or care." What he means is that he is primarily concerned not at all with individual "moral" problems, which in any case are difficult to judge, but with the evolutionary growth of humanity into the state of coreflection or ultra-hominization. The race as a biological unit, not the individual as a moral unit, engages his attention and care in regard to the problem of progress.

The Jesuit priest Mooney, as already seen in an earlier chapter, understands Teilhard in the same way: "[Teilhard] says that by 'progress' he means not that man is becoming morally better but that as a species he is moving towards a higher state of complexity and consciousness." In Mooney's eyes, as in Masui's, the Teilhardian emphasis certainly falls on the group rather than on the individual person.

An analogous impression of Teilhard in general is also recorded by Emile Rideau, again a Jesuit: "Careful though he was to preserve the difference of individuals, it is fair to say that the problem of personal options and the eternal history of individual persons are blurred by an outlook that is primarily concerned with wholes."[20]

Sri Aurobindo's sights are trained on the individual more than are Teilhard's. The individual's evolution beyond thought is a possibility and an obligation on which Sri Aurobindo insists in season and out. And by his evolution within a cooperative assemblage of individuals and not cut off from them as in the old cave or cloister, the real evolution of society can occur. There is no mandate from the study of evolution to reverse this order. Teilhard has talked of convergence in evolution. Evolution is convergent in that the elements at play converge upon a center and create thereby an ever deeper and richer interiority of being. But the increasing centration does not mean that, at the human stage, evolution must bypass the individual and work exclusively on the collective level, with the individual centers benefiting as a result of the social convergence. What happens at the human stage is that social convergence goes on pari passu with convergence within the individual, but the former is the secondary phenomenon; the latter is the primary one and determines collective evolution.

In that evolution, too, the unified larger consciousness will not stop short at coreflection. Even Supermind will not mark the sheer terminus. The Divine is endless; a progression within the Divine must continue; vistas and prospects of perfection will keep opening up. The kind of necessity Teilhard posits for the collective being to break down by entropy is mythical. And even if the vistas and prospects of perfection did terminate, it would be arbitrary and irrational to think that an ultrahuman realization had not enough spirit-force to resist entropy. Teilhard has conceived all evolution as a countercurrent to entropy, a rise in complexity-consciousness against the drift toward disorganization. What is more, there is a general irreversibility. Are we to imagine that the summit of complexity-consciousness will forfeit the irreversible countercurrent and inevitably fall a prey to this drift? Will it not have consolidated a superconsciousness matched with a supercomplexity, which would stand against the tendency of disorganization? Radial energy at its sheer maximum should certainly be able to resist the drag of the common tangential energy. Even in the human stage of evolution, Teilhard takes psychism to be free of physical determinism to an appreciable extent. What may we not expect of psychism at its apogee? And let us not forget that the maturity accomplished is fit to make the evolving Soul of the World meet the transcendent Omega in its invincible eternity. The potentialities of the latter should be sufficiently active in advance in the former. How then should the Second Law of Thermodynamics have any decisive bearing? Obviously, a pressure from outside of science and logic and mysticism — some compulsion from a religious dogma — the demand of a doctrinal bed of Procrustes — has vitiated Teilhard's evolutionary and spiritual vision.

In that vision can even be found a "slant" on entropy that takes away the lethal look he gives it in deference to Christian eschatology. At one place he asks: "Are life and entropy the two opposite but equivalent faces of a single fundamental reality in eternal equipoise? Or radically has one of them the natural advantage of being more primal and durable than the other?"[21] Postponing a detailed answer, he says for the moment: "Later we shall show by a critical study of the conditions of human activity, that unless the universe contains internal contradictions, it seems to demand that life shall be guaranteed a boundless future; that is to say, it will escape the complete mastery of the forces of retreat. Life would not be liveable if it were not conscious of being, at least partially, irreversible, and therefore superior to the inverse attractions of entropy." Then Teilhard demonstrates that from "a universe whose primal stuff is matter" and whose "initial state. . .consisted entirely of determinisms" it would be "radically impossible to conceive that 'interiorized' and spontaneous elements could ever have developed."[22] "On the other hand, from a cosmos initially formed and made up of elementary 'freedoms,' it is easy to deduce, by virtue of the effect of large numbers and habitual behaviour, all the appearances of exactitude upon which the mathematical physics of matter is founded." This means that "a universe of 'spiritual' stuff has all the elasticity it would need to lend itself both to evolution (life) and to involution (entropy)."†[23] But if the *weltstoff* is spirit, how can entropy threaten it when it has manifested its spirituality at the maximum with the attainment of Omega Point?

Talking elsewhere of "the phenomenon of spirit," Teilhard affirms: "Since, very probably, these two contrary movements (that is to say vitalization and the dissipation of energy) are merely the opposite poles of a single cosmic event of which the positive or synthesizing term is the most significant, it is finally *the* outstanding cosmic movement, the movement on which everything depends and which nothing explains."[24] Surely, if finally even entropy must depend on and be explained by the phenomenon of spirit, "the dissipation of energy" cannot ever have the upper hand of "vitalization" at the latter's peak development as a "super-life," as "a common centre of total organization" coinciding with a God who is "the organic centre of [the world's] evolution"?[25]

Teilhard is hardly logical here. And wherever his forward look does not specifically bring in the world's end his language about things to come is always suggestive of endless evolution. In the quotations immediately above, there is the expression: "Life shall be guaranteed a boundless future." The essay on "the phenomenon of spirit" offers the statements:

> If the world is really bound as a whole for consciousness, nothing could possibly oppose the growth of spirit. . . .If, in fact, the pressure of spirit is on the one side irresistible, this is a sign that it must victoriously attain its natural goal. But if, on the other, this goal reveals itself as the infinite ahead, this is a proof that it must succeed in propagating itself interminably. . . . Theoretically, the phenomenon of spirit develops a magnitude

†Teilhard's "involution" here, meaning the fall of energy to a less organized level, must be distinguished from his own use of the term elsewhere in the opposite sense, as well as from Sri Aurobindo's several uses of it, the most common being to signify the concealed or submerged state preliminary to the disclosure or emergence or evolution of the various powers of the Spirit from apparently "inconscient" Matter.

that we think of as indefinitely perfectible, and consequently never self-saturated. *Functionally* it is sustained by its own growth, each degree of consciousness at a given moment existing only as an introduction to a higher consciousness: so that we cannot see how, from a mechanical point of view, its progress could be stopped. . . .And, in fact, *historically*, consciousness on earth has never ceased to expand. This simple observation should suffice to show us that, for the progress of the spirit, the universe is completely *free ahead*.[26]

If the "goal" of the spirit is "the infinite ahead" and if for this goal it is our "universe" and not an eternity beyond it that "is completely *free ahead*" and if the "magnitude" developed by spirit is "indefinitely perfectible" and "never self-saturated" and there is always "a higher consciousness" to be attained and if "consciousness on earth" has a history of unceasing expansion, how can we ever envisage natural conditions compelling the evolutionary spirit to escape from nature?

Even supposing that a coreflective unanimity or a totalization of consciousness such as Teilhard anticipates is the ne plus ultra of evolution on our planet, is escape from nature the sole means open for a step further? Let us remember that Teilhard has spoken of the "universe" and not merely of the earth as being "completely *free ahead*." Again, when he speaks of "the world as a whole" being "bound for consciousness," he has in mind the entire cosmos whose evolution has blossomed on earth into Life and Reflection. One cannot omit the vast dimensions of the cosmos and the possibilities of the universe in discussing our arrival at Omega Point on our globe. In 1950 Teilhard wrote: "We may assume that sporadically, in the course of time, numerous centres of indeterminacy and consciousness can and must have appeared in sidereal space, of which our own Earth is one. Although Life by its structure seems in certain ways to be highly exceptional, everything suggests that its pressure is exerted throughout the universe. And everything suggests that, wherever cosmic hazard has enabled it to hatch out and establish itself, it cannot thereafter cease to become intensified to the utmost, in accordance with an automatic process."[27] Nineteen fifty-three saw him affirming: "Considering what we now know about the number of 'worlds' and their internal evolution, the idea of a *single* 'hominized' *planet* in the universe has already become in fact (without our generally realizing it) almost as *inconceivable* as that of a man who appeared with no genetic relationship to the rest of the earth's animal population. At an average of (at least) one human race per galaxy, that makes a total of millions of human races dotted all over the heavens. . . .Then, our minds cannot resist the inevitable conclusion that were we, by chance, to possess plates that were sensitive to the specific radiation of the 'noospheres' scattered throughout space, it would be *practically certain* that what we saw registered on them would be a cloud of thinking stars."[28] In the same year, after asking "who will at last give evolution its *own* God?" Teilhard suggested that in Christ we should be able to find "the 'new' God for whom we are looking," provided he does not lack certain characteristics, and at once Teilhard tells us: "The first is this: that in a universe in which we can no longer seriously entertain the idea that thought is an exclusively terrestrial phenomenon, Christ must no longer be *constitutionally* restricted in his operation to a mere 'redemption' of our planet."[29] Both scientifically and religiously, a strain in Teilhard brings into view at Omega Point the entire universe that he has conceived to have been engaged from Alpha Point in evolving earth life. Further, he grants: "There is every reason to believe that should material contact be effected between two 'hominized' planets, they would be able, at least through their noospheres, to understand one another, combine and be synthesized with one another."[30] Thus, at the peak of our planetization, we may be destined to start being integrated within an organized complex composed of a number of noospheres. More and more noospheres in a practically infinite cosmos could synthesize with ours when we are launched on an Omega career after millions of years of Teilhardian evolution.

Mostly, Teilhard is disposed to reject this prospect, though something in him directly or indirectly takes it into account, at times, as when he speaks of Christ's third nature in addition to the two that are divine and human, respectively—"A cosmic nature," as a foot note in the context of other inhabited worlds explains, "enabling him to centre all the lives which constitute a pleroma extended to the galaxies."[31]

None of Teilhard's habitual attitudes are cogently and definitively argued. His picture of the world's end is forced. Sri Aurobindo's position is clear-cut. Supermind bears the perfect archetypes of our natural molds and, by both action from its state above and nisus from its own involved state below, makes evolution possible. Evolution is the process of complete development, in space-time terms, of the archetypal ideality of mind, life-force, and body organized around a perfected soul-person. This process is not only individual but also collective. A unified humanity, realizing the one Divine who is general in the race and particular in the individual, has to evolve. In the fully evolved being, there will be a variety of spiritual realizations—the inner psychic, the surrounding cosmic, the over-arching transcendent—and, corresponding to the realizations, a change in nature—a psychic transformation, a spiritual transformation, a supramental transformation. A complete self-fulfillment here and now, together with an attainment of all illumined reality beyond earth—this is the Aurobindonian objective, the legitimate consummation of evolutionary existence. The method of such consummation is what Sri Aurobindo calls Integral Yoga. Man, a self-conscious being, has to cooperate and collaborate in his own evolution. The reflective condition he has reached puts on him the obligation of deliberate endeavor, willed self-surrender to the Supreme in all his aspects and most of all to the aspect of the Divine Person whose projection is the embodied personal existence that each of us is. All nature is a secret Integral Yoga spread out over aeons and, since evolution starts with a total involution, a total seeming reversal of the Divine, the Integral Yoga of nature is beset with various difficulties, meanderings, setbacks. But through all vicissitudes the rise of consciousness in an ever more organized form is inevitable. With the appearance of man, this Yoga, by his deliberate and willed endeavor, can become an accelerated process. The practice of the Yogic acceleration under the guidance and influence of Sri Aurobindo and the Mother in an Ashram that balances the individual and the collective demands of life is what has gone on for over half a century with an expanding creativity in outer circumstances. A whole world ultimately progressing by an Integral Yoga flexibly adjusted without losing its essential truth is the vision animating the Ashram.

Notes

1. Pierre Teilhard de Chardin to Auguste Valensin, 8 August 1919, in *The Making of a Mind: Letters from a Soldier-Priest* (London: Collins; Harper & Row, 1965), as quoted in Emile Rideau, *Teilhard de Chardin: A Guide to His Thought*, trans. René Hague (London: Collins; New York: Harper & Row, 1967), p. 292.
2. Henri de Lubac, *The Religion of Teilhard de Chardin* (London: Collins; New York: Desclee, 1967), p. 218.

3. Pierre Teilhard de Chardin, *Human Energy*, trans. J. M. Cohen (London: Collins, New York: Harcourt Brace Jovanovich, 1971), p. 63.

4. de Lubac, *Religion of Teilhard de Chardin*, p. 358 n. 67.

5. Pierre Teilhard de Chardin, *Activation of Energy* (London: Collins, 1970; New York: Harcourt Brace Jovanovich, 1972), p. 74.

6. Ibid., pp. 72-73.

7. Ibid., p. 68.

8. Ibid., pp. 68-69.

9. Ibid., p. 369.

10. Teilhard de Chardin, *Human Energy*, pp. 137-38.

11. Ibid., p. 160.

12. Cf. Zaehner, *Evolution in Religion*, pp. 44-45, where he draws upon Claude Cuénot's explanations in *Teilhard de Chardin* (London: Burns and Oates, Baltimore, Md.: Helicon Press, 1965).

13. de Lubac, *Religion of Teilhard de Chardin*, p. 209. Quoted words are from Pierre Teilhard de Chardin, *The Phenomenon of Man* (London: Collins; New York: Harper & Row, 1960), p. 88.

14. Cf. Teilhard de Chardin, *Activation of Energy*, pp. 35-36.

15. Pierre Teilhard de Chardin, *The Vision of the Past*, trans. J.M. Cohen (London: Collins; New York: Harper & Row, 1966), p. 252.

16. Ibid., p. 123.

17. Ibid., p. 252.

18. Passage translated from the speech in French by Jacques Masui made in the *Échange de vues sur "L'Évolution de l'humanité selon Sri Aurobindo et le Père Teilhard de Chardin"* sous la Présidence de Dr. Louis Armand de l'Académie Française: le 4 Décembre 1965 à Paris, au Palais de L'UNESCO. A typed report of the seven speeches made is with the Sri Aurobindo Ashram.

19. Teilhard de Chardin, *Activation of Energy*, p. 380.

20. Rideau, *Teilhard de Chardin*, p. 249.

21. Teilhard de Chardin, *Human Energy*, p. 22.

22. Ibid., p. 23.

23. Ibid.

24. Ibid., p. 98.

25. Ibid., pp. 105, 109, 110.

26. Ibid., pp. 98-99.

27. Pierre Teilhard de Chardin, "From the Pre-human to the Ultra-human" in idem, *The Future of Man*, trans. Norman Denny (London: Collins, Fontana Books; New York: Harper & Row, 1964), p. 304.

28. Pierre Teilhard de Chardin, *Christianity and Evolution*, trans. René Hague (London: Collins; New York: Harcourt Brace Jovanovich, 1971), pp. 231-32.

29. Ibid., pp. 240-41.

30. Ibid., p. 231 n. 4.

31. Ibid., p. 239 n. 12.

13

Spiritual Teilhard and the Yoga of the Gītā; Teilhard's Late Contact with Sri Aurobindo's Thought

A full "Life Divine" on earth, à la Sri Aurobindo, prepared by mysticism and Yoga in the light of the all-perfecting Supermind, leading to entire transformation, entire divinization in the most literal and comprehensive sense, is very different from Teilhard's objective. Commonly, when he speaks of "divinizing," he means "consecrating" or "sanctifying." Even applied to the final stage of evolution, his "divinizing" and "transforming" would have another color. To say this is not to run down the Teilhardian divinization and transformation. One should not be misled by such prophecies as: "Under the combined efforts of science, morality and association in society, some super-mankind is emerging."[1] There is a mystical component in the typical Teilhardian push of the consciousness toward the evolutionary summit. That component may be suggested with fair adequacy by a few passages like the following, which may serve as a final confession of his faith and the determining matrix of his "Yoga":

> For the believer whose eyes have seen the light, souls are not formed in the world as discontinuous and autonomous centres, nor do they so leave it. Even more fully and more blissfully than in any pantheist dream, sanctified monads are atoms immersed in, nourished by, and carried along by one and the same unfathomable primitive substance; they are elements that are combined and given a special character by a network of intimate in-

terconnexions, in order so to constitute a higher unity. *While Christianity is a supremely individualist religion, it is at the same time essentially a cosmic religion*, since, when the Creation and the preaching of the Gospel have completed their work, Christianity discloses to us not simply a harvest of souls but a *world of souls*.

If we look at this world, we see that the fundamental substance within which souls are formed, the highest environment in which they evolve—what one might call their own particular Ether—is the Godhead, at once transcendent and immanent, *in qua vivimus et movemur et sumus*—in whom we live and move and have our being. God cannot in any way be intermixed with or lost in the participated being which he sustains and animates and holds together, but he is at the birth, and the growth and the final term of all things. Everything lives, and everything is raised up—and everything in consequence is one—in Him and through Him.

Worthily to describe the rapture of this union and this unification, the pantheists' most impassioned language is justified, whether unspoken in the heart or given expression by the tongue: and to that rapture is added the ecstatic realization that the universal Thing from which everything emerges and to which everything returns is not the Impersonal, the Unknowable and the Unconscious, in which the individual disintegrates and is lost by being absorbed: it is a living, loving Being, in which the individual consciousness, when it is lost, attains an accentuation and an illumination that extends to the furthest limit of what is contained in its own personality. God, who is as immense and all-embracing as matter, and at the same time as warm and intimate as a soul, is the Centre who spreads through all things; his immensity is produced by an extreme of concentration, and his rich simplicity synthesizes a culminating paroxysm of accumulated virtues. No words can express the bliss of feeling oneself possessed, absorbed, without end or limit, by an Infinite that is not rarefied and colourless, but living and luminous, an Infinite that knows and attracts and loves.

Souls are irresistibly drawn by the demands of their innate power, and still more by the call of grace, towards a common centre of beatitude, and it is in this convergence that they find a first bond that combines them in a natural Whole. The paths they follow inevitably meet at the term of the movement that carries them along. Moreover, grace, which introduces them into the field of divine attraction, forces them all to exert an influence, as they proceed, upon one another, and it is in this relation of dependence, which is just the same kind as that which links together material systems, that there lies the so astonishingly "cosmic" mystery (we might almost say the phenomenon) of the *Communion of Saints*.

Like particles immersed in one and the same spiritual fluid, souls cannot think or pray or move without waves being produced, even by the most insignificant among them, which set the others in motion; inevitably, behind each soul a wake is formed which draws other souls either towards good or towards evil.

There is an even more striking similarity with the organisms that life on earth forms and drives, in mutual interdependence, along the road of consciousness, in that souls know that the evolution of their personal holiness reaches its full value in the success of a global task that goes beyond and is infinitely more important than the success of individual men.[2]

Spiritual Teilhard in all his "complexity-consciousness," so to speak, is evident here. There is the love-hate relationship with pantheism. He is instinctively aware of the fullness and bliss of its dream and the impassioned language that this dream's realization evokes, but he intellectually visualizes with supreme inconsistency the pantheist experience as the disintegration and loss of the dreamer in an unconscious, as if such disintegration and loss could ever inspire so full and blissful a dream or get described in language of such passion. Again, while seeing the disintegration and loss as the result of absorption he still goes on to speak of the Christian as becoming, at his mystical height, absorbed and even lost in another kind and yet not disintegrating — as if a living and loving and luminous Infinite could make any difference. Surely, to be absorbed by and lost in anything or anyone must mean the disintegration of what undergoes the absorption and loss. The separate little personality must inevitably vanish. The process of disintegrating might be different, but the end would be the same. Nor is it clear how the process could differ when the dream of pantheism is acknowledged to be of fullness and bliss. And why are the pantheist's absorption and loss considered different when the plunge into the unconscious gives rise to a language of impassioned description just as the Christian's absorption and loss do? Furthermore, whatever the pantheist gets lost and absorbed in cannot be the unconscious when it is most joyously longed for and most intensely remembered. Lastly, if there is no real disintegration any more than in the Christian experience, the Pantheos must also be in some way an Other and not intermixed with the existences we know.

Teilhard's usual illogic and ambiguity, the result of secretly running with the hare and openly hunting with the hounds, is in evidence again. But he does succeed in putting his beautiful *élan* of spirituality across, and one gets the impression of a great genuine Yoga beyond mere science and morality and association in society. But the Yoga, grand though it is, does not go beyond extending to all mankind, in virtue of the general evolutionary push, one of the Gītā's Yogas, the Yoga of Bhakti (Devotion) for the Personal God who is also the Cosmic Divinity holding all things and beings—except that the Gītā explicitly views those things and beings as in one aspect the Transcendent's and Immanent's own projections and, in another aspect, as distinct from him. The supracosmicism, the manifesting power, the all-pervasion and yet the nonintermixture of the Lord come out in several stanzas: "He is called the unmanifest immutable; him they speak of as the supreme soul and status . . . .But that supreme Purusha has to be won by a bhakti which turns to him alone in whom all beings exist and by whom all this world has been extended in space. (8.21,22) By Me all this universe has been extended in the ineffable mystery of my being; all existences are situated in Me, not I in them. . . . All existences return into my divine Nature in the lapse of the cycle; at the beginning of the cycle I loose them forth. . . .(9.4.9) I am here in this world and everywhere, I support this entire universe with an infinitesimal portion of Myself. . . (10.42) His hands and feet are on every side of us, his heads and eyes and faces are those innumerable visages which we see wherever we turn, his ear is everywhere, he immeasurably fills and surrounds all this world with himself, he is the universal Being in whose embrace we live. (13.14)" The last phrase is reminiscent of the Pauline "In whom we live and move and have our being," which Teilhard quotes and goes on to reformulate as "Everything lives, and everything is raised up—and everything in consequence is one—in Him and through Him." And I may add that, however Teilhard may seek to guard himself against pantheism, some of his words, without diminishing the Divine Transcendence, echo the Gītā, which also keeps the Transcendence always in view. These words, corresponding to the Gītā's about all things being originally loosed forth by the Supreme Person from himself and returning to him at the end, are "the ecstatic realization that the universal Thing from which everything emerges and to which everything returns. . .is a living, loving Being."

To match the Gītā in one of its Yogas is no small feat of insight, and to give that insight a cast in keeping with the light brought by modern evolutionism in both its individual and its collective sweep toward a unified future renders Teilhard *the* Man of the Age in the West. But he is so in spite of himself; he continually interposes a veil between his illumination and his message. Even the illumination falls below the intrinsic demands of modern evolutionism turned spiritual. Not only does it miss all hint of the Supramental Yoga's integrality of consummation, but it also misses the possibility of accelerated progress that any Yoga collectively followed would bring. Does not Teilhard look only to a remote future of unification—a future millions of years away? In addition, for all his stress on advancement in the true spirit of evolution, his vision amounts finally to a denial of the evolutionary truth; it executes a sudden volte-face in favor of the otherworldliness that has characterized all preevolutionism and is the typical sign of every religious aspiration, whether Western or Eastern, that has lacked the clue of the Supermind. Teilhard did catch something of the clue, but he let it slip through his fingers. No doubt, he was not of the stuff of the supreme mystics and could never have realized even a moiety of Sri Aurobindo's spiritual experience. But he stood on the threshold of an intellectual and intuitive perception of what this experience signified. Had he not abjured, under the Christian religious climate, his innate pantheism on the one hand and his extraordinary evolutionary understanding on the other—had he not averted his face from Eastern mysticism without caring to enter into its manifold revelation that could have helped him to reconcile what he imagined to be opposites—he could have been the greatest Western index to the spirituality of the future. That he failed and that all he achieved was a blend of discordant tendencies most fascinatingly worked out, a many-sided exquisite ambiguity, with occasional bursts of his natural orientalism but on the whole weighted with a penchant too conventionally Christian—this is indeed the gravest tragedy of modern European science and religion.

But here also there was a sharp "moment of truth"—occurring in two phases—in which Teilhard saw his real role. It is connected with the question Zaehner raises in wondering how "Teilhard never came to hear of Aurobindo. . .whose thought so closely resembled his own" (p. 9). Actually, Teilhard did hear of Sri Aurobindo.

While Sri Aurobindo, who passed away in 1950 before Teilhard's works got published, could never have read Teilhard, Teilhard could have read Sri Aurobindo even as far back as 1914-15. For a French edition of Sri Aurobindo's monthly review, *Arya*, made its appearance for seven months under the title *Revue de grande synthèse*, and found its way to France. Teilhard, however, never knew any of its contents—until April 1949. In that month Jacques Masui wrote to Philippe Barbier St.-Hilaire of Sri Aurobindo's Ashram that he had acquainted Teilhard with the thought of Sri Aurobindo.

The next that was heard of Teilhard's contact with that thought was in 1954 from Eleanor Montgomery, who was in charge of the Sri Aurobindo Library in New York. Teilhard was living a few blocks away and he was brought by Masui to the library. Montgomery presented him with a copy of Sri Aurobindo's booklet *Evolution.*

This was just a year before Teilhard died. Prior to this time, there was a development whose witness again was Masui. The occasion was once more the meeting on 4 December 1965 in Paris for an exchange of views on the evolution of man according to Sri Aurobindo and Teilhard. In the course of very interesting reminiscences and reflections, he said that between 1946 and 1954 he had had talks with Teilhard and had often spoken to him of Sri Aurobindo. At last he had succeeded in making him read the first twelve chapters of *The Life Divine.* On returning them, Teilhard had remarked: "J'ai l'impression que c'est la même chose que moi, mais pour l'Asie" ("I have the impression that it is the same thing as myself, but for Asia").

This pregnant sentence is the first phase of the "moment of truth." On a straightforward approach, it can only mean that Teilhard and Sri Aurobindo share an evolutionism that sees in the future a spiritual completion of man fulfilling in a luminous earth life all the terms developed by nature of being and becoming. The completion would lie in a realized unity-in-multiplicity on all levels, the emergence of a harmonized collectivity of individuals into the Universal and Transcendent, a manifestation of the Transcendent and Universal in the whole of mankind in the process of time, a super-personalization of souls within a God who is a Superperson and the Center of all centers. One sole difference would be present between the Teilhardian evolutionism and the Aurobindonian—namely, Sri Aurobindo would have a Vedantic starting point while Teilhard would proceed from a Christian point de départ. And here comes for us the crucial question. The Vedantic starting point is the One Reality variously self-deployed. Can the Christian point de départ be taken as identical? It must, if Sri Aurobindo's evolutionism is "the same thing" as Teilhard's. The evolutionist

Christianity of Teilhard cannot, therefore, be equated with Christian orthodoxy turned evolutionist.

An approach subtle rather than straightforward would probe the closing phrase that declares Sri Aurobindo to be fit for the East and implies Teilhard to be suitable for the West. This phrase appears to bring in a significant qualifying note. Does it mean simply that for the West the One Reality has to be called Christ and explicated in a terminology linked with the Roman Catholic Church? Logically, it should, and then Teilhard's Christianity would indeed be a "new religion." But there is a touch of rejection in this phrase modifying the seemingly total acceptance in the preceding, as if the Aurobindonian evolutionism lacked in comprehensiveness and as if it did so not just because it expresses the identical truth in a terminology other than Teilhard's but because the Vedantic terminology fails to do justice to the truth and would not find favor with a West that has had the advantage of the Christian revelation.

Then there would not quite be the One Reality variously self-deployed; the many-sided monism of Sri Aurobindo would be absent, and the Teilhardian splitting of shades between "false" and "true" pantheism would return.

Does it actually return in appreciable force? It is difficult to make a positive pronouncement. In light of the sweeping impression of sameness recorded in the opening part of the statement, merely the ghost of a genuine dissidence appears to haunt the closing part. The ghost, however, is typical of the widespread Teilhardian ambiguity emanating from the born pantheist playing in and out of the intensely nurtured Christian. Its presence is perhaps the faintest here, and in the upshot, one may well adjudge Masui's quotation to be suggesting an Aurobindonian Christianity as the key to the core of Teilhard's ultimate message. Yes, the core, but not the environing matter which prevented it from radiating its full substance or even recognizing in itself all it contained.

And the same curious relation of the shining core with the veils around it is found in the second phase of the moment of truth. Masui recollects Teilhard's making another remark apropos of Sri Aurobindo: "Au fond Aurobindo n'a pas de pensée véritablement dogmatique. Peut-être est-ce une faiblesse, mais peut-être est-ce une force; car il fait bien reprendre les choses dans leur fondement pour aller très loin dans l'avenir" ("At bottom Aurobindo does not have a really dogmatic thought. Perhaps it is a weakness, but perhaps it is a strength; for it is indeed necessary to reconsider things from their basis in order to go very far into the future").

Masui himself confirms Teilhard's reflection on Sri Aurobindo. He has the remark founded on his own reading of the latter: "In fact, we do not find in Sri Aurobindo once more a dogmatic thought but a thought supported always on intuition and experience — the intuition and experience of all the attempts of man to understand himself." Masui touches here a double point — not only the intuitive and experiential nature of Sri Aurobindo's philosophy but also its comprehensive sweep, its regard for all lines of knowledge, its move to take up every side of human aspiration, its integrality of world vision. The very first chapter of *The Life Divine* sets forth the all-round objective of the evolutionary energy, of the conscious force secretly at work to harmonize apparent opposites. And the next two chapters deal with one fundamental pair of them — "The Denial of the Materialist," "The Refusal of the Ascetic" — and seek to reconcile in light of the very logic of progressive evolution the spiritual consciousness as the reality emerging in Matter and the material scene as the natural locus of Spirit's fulfillment through the evolutionary process. This combination of God and world is not underlined in Teilhard's second pronouncement, but it is implied in his first where he discerns an essential identity between himself and Sri Aurobindo. What this pronouncement throws into relief is a certain apparent distinction of the Aurobindonian philosophy from the Teilhardian. If Sri Aurobindo has a Vedantic starting point, it is because his own intuition and experience have validated it, and Vedanta is after all no more than a starting point for him; he goes beyond and ahead of Vedanta, develops its potentialities, introduces possibilities seen in his own sadhana, envisages realizations taking full stock of universal history and multifarious modernism. Vedanta is itself a free spiritual exploration in many directions rather than a fixed and faithful religion; but even its terminology, even its categories are not indispensable to Sri Aurobindo. He can afford to wash away all color of Vedanta in a recognizable form. Teilhard, on the contrary, constrains himself to be Christian — and not only Christian but also Roman Catholic. A number of dogmas that he considers crucial he cannot do without. He is often at pains to throw them into relief. In many respects the past holds him. However, face to face with Sri Aurobindo's utter freedom from dogmas, he is in two minds about his own posture.

On the one hand, he feels that it would be a lack in his thought to free himself from his Roman Catholic moorings and that it is a lack in Sri Aurobindo to have no such grip from the past. On the other hand, he feels such a grip to be a disadvantage in view of the future, and the Aurobindonian adventure to be the right thing for the age to come; that adventure allows one to do what one truly should — namely, to probe and plumb all things without preconceptions so as to reach their own basic nature and let this nature shape one's vision in the context of the new spirit that is abroad today and sallies toward tomorrow. Teilhard understands that unless one frees himself from dogma one cannot serve the vast time ahead, so full of a marvelous promise given by the revolutionary changes of inlook and outlook that the discovery of cosmic evolution has brought about.

Teilhard is here at the peak of his perceptiveness and truest to his own mission as innovator in the religious as well as the scientific thought of the West. And from this peak his attitude cannot help removing whatever reservation was expressed by him about Sri Aurobindo with the words "but for Asia." Here too, there is the reservation in the word *perhaps.* But the tinge of doubt it carries applies both ways. It is attached not only to "strength" — it is attached also to "weakness." Some little dubiety lingers — again the typical Teilhardian posture because of his double personality. Yet the sum total in the assessment of Sri Aurobindo is positive and the unspoken sense is that Sri Aurobindo may very well be for the whole world and not merely for Asia — even though Teilhard, the irreducible hyper-Catholic, cannot quite make up his mind to be different from what he is, a bit of a paradox with a new religion sending out its rays from his core through a fairly dense medium of Christian dogma.

How dense the medium was may be gauged from the fact that even in 1950 when he wrote "Some Reflections on Two Converse Forms of the Spirit" and in 1954 when he penned "Le Christique," he could declare his own loneliness of vision, his despair at discovering no published work in sympathy with his thought. Of course he was referring to the West, but he could surely have hailed a light from the East. And surely again he could have refrained from uttering, as he does even in that period, a sense of the inadequacy, the falsity, of Eastern mysticism.

Notes

1. Teilhard de Chardin, *Writings in Time of War*, p. 38.
2. Ibid., pp. 47-49.

14

Sri Aurobindo and the Modern World

It is over a hundred years since Sri Aurobindo was born (15 August 1872)—a hundred years of the world at its acme of modernism. One is apt to think of that century's master Yogi and of the science-minded world today as two separate and opposed forces. But the amazing fact is that one cannot understand what each of them represents without understanding what is represented by the other. A penetrating view will reveal Sri Aurobindo not as the antithesis of the modern age but as its very spirit. This age, seen in its many-sided whole, will show itself as secretly Aurobindonian. Sri Aurobindo will stand out as its source and focus of truth, its natural synthesizer and destined fulfiller, the master word for the spirituality of the future.

i

Sri Aurobindo's avowed mission was to lead the world a step further in its evolution—to establish a new status of human consciousness. The old Upanishadic cry

> From Darkness lead us to Light,
> From Appearance lead us to Reality,
> From Death lead us to Immortality

may be summed up in Aurobindonian terms:

From Mind lead us to Supermind,
From Man lead us to Superman,
From Earth lead us to Superearth.

These terms signify not merely transcendence, as in that great ancient mantra; they signify also a transformation by means of transcendence. To climb beyond is not the goal; the goal is to rise above and bring the Light, the Reality, the Immortality of the altitudes to the abyss. A divine faculty of self-knowledge and world-knowledge, a divine power of life within the human mold to discover and invent manifold means of self-fulfillment and world-fulfillment, a divine mode of physical existence ensuring radiant well-being for both self and world — these ultimately are what Light and Reality and Immortality connote for Sri Aurobindo.

But how can they become a perpetual part of our nature and of the world's if they are an omniscience, an omnipotence, an omnipresence pulled down from some supernal remoteness to be made sovereign in our midst, imposed upon our ignorance, our incapacity, our fragmentary finitude? There would be a binding together of contrasted orders of being, the higher holding and dominating the lower, a splendid foreigner from heaven subduing to his own norms and forms the annexed terrestrial native. The latter would follow a *dharma,* a law, which, though glorifying him, would still not be his own. And sooner or later he would chafe under the brilliant burden and tend to go back to his spontaneous imperfections. The heavenly conqueror would realize the futility of his superimposition on alien earth, and the soul of man, the Upanishadic seeker of Light, Reality, Immortality, would find its hunger for the Absolute unsatisfied by the compromise achieved. It would long to merge in the Beyond, the spiritually Perfect, and shun the material scene as a vain lure, a mixture of good and evil that leads to no final resolution. In the end this scene comes to be regarded as nothing more than Darkness, Appearance, and Death made colorful by some delusive magic, by what one school of Indian religious philosophy dubbed *Maya,* a mystification by which the Negative passes off as the Positive.

Throughout history the higher thought of man, fired by a vision of Spirit, has ended by a rejection of Matter. Even the most earth-affirming spiritualities have merely accepted the universe of time and space as a drama of test and travail, from which the soul must at last escape. The drama itself has been seen as reaching its termination at some point in the future. Even so cosmos-drunk and humanity-thrilled a thinker as the Roman Catholic priest-cum-scientist, Teilhard de Chardin, looks forward to a disappearance of his beloved universe at the point where a unified mankind attains its maturity; this point marks a forsaking of the universe by a totalized world, an ultrahuman product of evolution; the ultrahuman instantaneously becomes a transhuman and the whole immense environment of evolution vanishes as something that has served its purpose and grown thereby useless and null.

However, in Teilhard one catches a glimpse of a cosmic self-consummation: his ultrahuman, his totalization of mankind, his superevolution envisage the maximum prospect possible within a mixed context of modern evolutionism, orthodox Christianity, and a "cosmic sense" that has profound affinities with ancient Indian Vedanta, fervently deprecated though the affinities may be by Teilhard himself or his coreligionist commentators. And it is with that prospect on the one side and those affinities on the other that one can make a start in general to show Sri Aurobindo to be the very spirit of the age that superficially may strike one as his opposite.

For what do the Teilhardian prospect and affinities imply? Teilhard the Jesuit, as well as his Church-faithful expositors, may try to explain away the basis he lays down for his spiritual-scientific position, but this basis in its stark shape is nothing except those startling theses of his: "In a concrete [as distinguished from an abstract] sense there is not matter and spirit. All that exists is matter becoming spirit. There is neither spirit nor matter in the world; the stuff of the universe is spirit-matter. . . .If the cosmos were basically material, it would be physically incapable of containing man. Therefore, we may conclude. . .that it is in its inner being made of *spiritual stuff*. . . .Under the penalty of being less evolved than the ends brought about by its own action, *universal energy must be a thinking energy*."[1] Surely we are hearing echoes of the Ishā Upanishad's "Self-Being that has become all existences that are Becomings" and of its further statement: "The Seer, the Thinker, the One who becomes everywhere, the Self-existent has ordered objects perfectly according to their nature from years sempiternal."

Teilhard has often tried to take away with one hand what he has given with the other. He has made, in the interests of Christian orthodoxy, fine reservations that sometimes amount to hairspiltting. But again and again, as in the above quotations, the essential Teilhard leaps out.

And there, in his Vedanta in a modern evolutionist garb, is felt a touch of Sri Aurobindo as he rises from the original comprehensiveness of Indian spiritual thought into his "Integral Yoga" of a divinized mind, divinized vitality, divinized body, a supreme spiritual fulfillment here and now as a result of the evolutionary process that is the master motif of our scientific age. Sri Aurobindo goes far ahead of Teilhard's understanding of that process no less than our age's understanding of it. And, strange as it may seem, he does so by reading more deeply than does Teilhard the scientist the terms in which our age evaluates evolution.

The fundamental stress of modern science is on Matter, and its most idealistic dream is of a plenary human life on a fully organized earth. It never looks beyond the earth, and it envisions in Matter the seed of whatever highest state man is capable of. A Teilhardian world's end is a conclusion it can never accept, since it would be out of tune with its fundamental stress and the utmost dream of its idealism. A progression within the spatiotemporal framework without any finis is its general credo in spite of all threats of a "heat-death" trillions of years hence, and the progression it believes in is not only of a strengthened long-lasting body but also of a more capable vitality and a more subtilized mind. This, at first glance, is also the credo of Sri Aurobindo. The difference between the two credos, which strikes one on a deeper look, comes of Sri Aurobindo's clearer grasp of what modern science's Matter has really been doing toward the advancement of which modern science dreams.

I can best summarize this grasp by means of a paradox: the trend of evolutionary nature is governed by the logic of the "impossible." How does nature accomplish her decisive changes? What is the persistent problem solved by evolution? Out of apparently nonliving, inertly moving Matter there evolves its seeming contradiction: a series of living forms with their activities of response, instinct, desire, organizing the physicochemical. Out of living forms endowed merely with a seeking sentience and at most a practical intelligence but with no apparent thought power or self-awareness, one finds again a seeming contradiction evolving; a body that thinks and plans and evaluates, looks before and after, within and above, as well as senses, feels, and hungers.

Such is the story of progression up to now. What shall we expect by the logic of the "impossible"? Let us look at our own dominant urges differentiating us from the prehuman past and the all-too-human present.

We are in quest of complete knowledge, searching for unalloyed bliss and flawless beauty, endeavoring to possess an all-effective power, longing for lasting health and perpetual existence, crying for a universal unity and an infinite freedom. In brief, we are agog to find a manifold perfection that is a seeming contradition of the actuality that is ours. And, by the logic of the "impossible," we who strive and stumble and, for all our vaunted successes, are still condemned to Darkness, Appearance, and Death, are destined for what Sri Aurobindo calls "the Life Divine." Evolution, by its own paradoxical urge, must lead to the emergence of the Godlike Superman.

The epithet *Godlike*, having a literal bearing, hallmarks the Aurobindonian hope of the future. But the term *Superman* strikes the ear with the breath of a scientific prophecy; for its wafts toward us from the closing years of the nineteenth century, during which Sri Aurobindo was a student in England. In 1883 Nietzsche, building on Darwin's theory of evolution by "struggle for existence" and "survival of the fittest," sent out his dream of power and glory into the time ahead and proclaimed his new gospel:

God hath died: now do *we* desire — the superman to live.

I teach you superman. Man is something that is to be surpassed. What have ye done to surpass man? . . .

What is great in man is that he is a bridge and not a goal; what is lovable in man is that he is an *over-going* and a *down-going*. . .

I love those who do not first seek a reason beyond the stars for a going down and being sacrifices, but sacrifice themselves to the earth, that the earth of the Superman may hereafter arrive.[3]

A touch of Sri Aurobindo's accent is here, and Sri Aurobindo has himself praised Nietzsche's prophetic fire while laying bare the shortcomings of his Titan Superman, rudely heroic, egoistically grand, haughtily master racist. Indeed we catch in the mouth of this science-inspired Godless rhapsodist an anticipation of Sri Aurobindo's glimpse of a future that achieves the perfection that man the mental being lacks at present — an oblique hint of the Aurobindonian terrestrial "Godlike."

The Darwinist dreamer, however, never brought into intellectual light anything like the paradoxical urge that Sri Aurobindo disengages in the evolutionary process. This urge Sri Aurobindo names the Yoga of nature—the gradual preparation for self-exceeding and the sudden leap toward a new phase. But nature's push to be in "yoke" (which is analogous to the word *Yoga*) with the ever higher is from the subconscious or subliminal part of living things—until the human phase is reached. With the advent of a self-aware mind, nature demands that the evolving organism should cooperate with her urge. Evolution can no longer occur merely by a hidden drive in the midst of lucky accidents; man must set himself to the task. He must freely consent to his own change, collaborate with nature's trend. And man's collaboration, raised to its extreme pitch, is the Aurobindonian "Integral Yoga," consciously aiming by a concentrated effort of the entire being to accomplish in a short time the results that, with less clear vision and less inward pressure, might take millennia.

Here an important issue arises. Science holds that man, whom Sir Julian Huxley calls evolution grown conscious of itself, can work in unison with the evolutionary urge by exploiting and intensifying his mental faculties. Mind is the culminating stage of earthly development. Teilhard too speaks of "reflection" as the definitive turning point, and the future lies for him in a unification of all thinking units in a sort of superorganism of collective thought or "coreflection." Teilhard, unlike most scientists, is a mystic by temperament, but his is a mysticism mainly of thought scientifically maturing in integrated worldwide research and spiritualizing itself by an ever greater love-inspired concentration of mind on what he terms *Christ-Omega*, Christ conceived as a Cosmic Presence attracting evolution to a full mental flowering in the future by his stance as the gatherer of souls into eternity at the end of history. Sri Aurobindo's mysticism is not of reflectioin sublimated or consummated in a complex universality. It is a mysticism of the supramental. Just as the life-force marks a stage other than material energy, just as mentality forms a level above the life-force, so too the next grade must surpass mentality and bring a power sui generis, though not discontinuous with the preceding "planes." The panorama of evolutionary progression expects such supramental disclosure. What the logic of the "impossible" promises is indeed best comprehended under the aspect of the supramental.

Teilhardism, christening coreflection a "critical threshold" comparable in its definitive turn with the critical thresholds of life and mind, would seem to imply a similar aspect. And Sir Julian Huxley appears to incline still more toward it when he dares to look beyond Teilhard's "Point Omega" itself, his terminal state of coreflection. This eminent biologist remarks about Point Omega: "It might have been better to think of it merely as a novel state or mode of organization, beyond which the human imagination cannot at present pierce, though perhaps the strange facts of extrasensory perception unearthed by the infant science of parapsychology may give us a clue as to a possible more ultimate state."[4]

Thus from the scientific side there is an approach toward the Aurobindonian Supramental that, in its broad and general meaning, is after all the necessary conclusion of any impartial review of mystical phenomena in the world's past. The phenomena of sovereign genius also lead to the same conclusion. Even what one may dub the "crests" of common experience do so. In a striking passage Sri Aurobindo has summed up the vision of a mind-transcending power whose presence cannot but be attested by psychological facts:

The intelligence of man is not composed entirely and exclusively of the rational intellect and the rational will; there enters into it a deeper, more intuitive, more splendid and powerful, but much less clear, much less developed and as yet hardly at all self-possessing light and force for which we have not even a name. But, at any rate, its character is to drive at a kind of illumination — not the dry light of the reason, nor the moist and suffused light of the heart, but a lightning and a solar splendour. It may indeed subordinate itself and merely help the reason and heart with its flashes; but there is another urge in it, its natural urge, which exceeds the reason. It tries to illuminate the intellectual being, to illuminate the ethical and aesthetic, to illuminate the emotional and the active, to illuminate even the senses and the sensations. It offers in words of revelation, it unveils as if by lightning flashes, it shows in a sort of mystic or psychic glamour or brings out into a settled but for mental man almost a supernatural light, a Truth greater and truer than the knowledge given by Reason and Science, a Right larger and more divine than the moralist's scheme of virtues, a Beauty more profound, universal and entrancing than the sensuous or imaginative beauty worshipped by the artist, a joy and divine sensibility which leaves the ordinary emotions poor and pallid, a Sense beyond the senses and sensations, the possibility of a diviner Life and action which man's ordinary conduct of life hides away from his impulses and from his vision. Very various, very fragmentary, often very confused and misleading are its effects upon all the lower members

from the reason downward, but this in the end is what it is driving
at in the midst of a hundred deformations. It is caught and killed
or at least diminished and stifled in formal creeds and pious
observances; it is unmercifully traded in and turned into poor
and base coin by the vulgarity of conventional religions; but it is
still the light of which the religious spirit and the spirituality of
man is in pursuit and some pale glow of it lingers even in their
worst degradations.[5]

Yes, the Supramental cannot be denied and, after a spell of a
priori refusal, science more and more is being faithful through
parapsychology to its typical temper "to prove all things and hold
fast to that which is true," a temper, as these very words that Saint
Paul's show, is also at the core of "the religious spirit and the
spirituality of man." Where the one manifestation of this temper
differs from the other is in relation to the issue: Does the Supramental already exist or is it yet to be? Is it just waiting in its perfection to
unveil its face or has it to grow and get figured forth?

A number of scientists, carried away by the extremisms of a
Matter-emphasizing attitude, will not have it that the Supramental
is already there, its features discernible at a distance under different
expressions in the God of the religious and spiritual seekers. But the
thoroughgoing followers of science subscribe to the principle of
nature's unity and trace life and mind and whatever one may
designate *soul* to the beginning of things, however concealed they
may be and whatever time they may take to emerge in a
recognizable shape. For instance, there is the famous J.B.S.
Haldane, as representative a modern scientist as one could wish and
a Marxist to boot, and what does he say? "We do not find obvious
evidence of life or mind in inert matter, and we naturally study
them most easily where they are most completely manifested; but if
the scientific point of view is correct, we shall ultimately find them,
at least in rudimentary forms, all through the universe."[6]

This certainly narrows the gap between the materialistic and the
spiritual outlooks; there is in science the vision that life and mind
and whatever greater power is in process of expression are not late
products but coexistent with matter and disclosing themselves with
the increasing complexity and organization of material evolutes.
The space still remaining to be bridged between the two outlooks is
in the conception of the original state of these powers. Are they really rudimentary at the root of nature or is their rudimentariness a

mere cover? Here the Aurobindonian reading would be: If, by evolution's logic of the impossible, the future Godlike Superman is in the very nature of things, and if already there is a large body of experience testifying to the preexistence of a Light beyond the mind, then what appears to be in a primitive seed-state, just a scintilla, is actually a fullness covered up and slowly loosed forth under adverse conditions accepted by that preexistent supramental Light. This Light must be seen as operating both from beyond and behind, above and below, pressing down from the one poise and pushing up from the other. Such a view would best explain the emergence of the higher from the lower with inevitable surety and yet by an arduous and aeonic labor through trial and error, waste and vagary.

Rightly does Sri Aurobindo declare in a succinct appraisal of biological values:

> We speak of the evolution of Life in Matter, the evolution of Mind in Matter; but evolution is a word which merely states the phenomenon without explaining it. For there seems to be no reason why Life should evolve out of material elements or Mind out of living form, unless we accept the Vedantic solution that Life is already involved in Matter and Mind in Life because in essence Matter is a form of veiled Life, Life a form of veiled Consciousness. And then there seems to be little objection to a farther step in the series and the admission that mental Consciousness may itself be only a form and a veil of higher states which are beyond Mind.[7]

Involution and *evolution* — these are the key terms of the scientific spirituality that one may discern in our age as culminating in Sri Aurobindo. Rather, they are the secret indexes of truth in our age as discerned by the help of the Aurobindonian light. That light is the center of the *Zeitgeist* — nay, it is itself the *Zeitgeist* with a central focus and a various radiation all around — weak in one place, a little stronger in another, suggesting this or that aspect of the revelation for which Sri Aurobindo stands: Supermind, Superman, Superearth. And it is the fact of involution that is of primary significance. Evolution without involution would simply mean a development of higher forces without those forces being at the same time native to the material matrix. With involution, realization of God would be something essentially inalienable from Matter; it would be no foreigner glorifying earth but earth itself manifesting its hidden glory with the assistance of the uninvolved truth of its own being, which reigns as a Divinity in the mystic's Beyond. The great message of Sri Aurobindo is Supermind at the two poles of being: above Mind and below Matter. And such a double perfection waiting to be disclosed gives to modern science's fundamental stress on Matter its master meaning; for it ensures the spiritualization of material existence as no enforced unstable superimposition, but as a permanent part of the future because it would be the flowering of a natural *dharma*, a self-law.

ii

Not only does the materialism of modern science attain its grande finale in Sri Aurobindo's *weltanschauung* by having the supramental Divine inherent in the very atoms; the spirituality of ancient mysticism also gains a climax by discovering in the supramental Divine an inherent capacity of materialization, an all-transforming oneness with the very constituents of Matter. And it is by looking at the peak possibilities on either hand that one comes to seize the specific sense of Sri Aurobindo's Supermind. The word *supramental* is for him no blanket term for all that exceeds mentality, not even for all that has been known so far as the highest formula of what is beyond our thinking, willing, feeling, perceiving intelligence — the formula of God as framed by the world's spiritual leaders.

No doubt, the Vedantic vision is most affined to Sri Aurobindo's. India's spirituality stands nearest to him. His base and background cannot be anything else than the triple declaration of the Upanishads: "Brahman is all; all is in Brahman; Brahman is in all" — the essential One who is also a unified Multiplicity and a multiple Oneness. The Vedantic vision is "an absolute, eternal and infinite Self-existence, Self-awareness, Self-delight of being that secretly supports and pervades the universe even while it is also beyond it."[8] And in the Vedanta this truth of spiritual experience "has at once an impersonal and a personal aspect: it is not only Existence, it is the one Being, absolute, eternal and infinite."[9] This Being, who manifests and conducts the cosmos and who at the same time is its multitudinous Indweller and has various relations with all that is manifested, is Supermind in the directly operative connotation. Indian seers named this personal Divinity "Ishwara" in general and characterized him as "Satyam, Ritam, Brihat" (the True, the

Right, the Vast) or as "Prajna" (the Luminous Lord of the Causal Body) and "Vijnana" (the All-Knower of oneness and manyness). They saw too his Creative Consciousness as "Shakti" (Cosmic Energy) and "Para-Prakriti" (Supernature) and "Aditi" (the Goddess-Mother of the entire manifestation). All this largely rounded mysticism of India's greatest periods in the past is the natural inner context within which the Aurobindonian Integral Yoga has grown. But that Yoga moves further even than this mysticism.

For, according to Sri Aurobindo, the high promise with which that mysticism started was not fulfilled. Some secret of harmonizing the Eternal's Yonder and the Eternal's Here was missed. Consequently, there crept into the view synthesizing the Here with the Yonder the conviction that, however much the former might be irradiated with the latter, the two cannot be completely reconciled. The one has to be abandoned in the last resort for the sake of the other. And, if so, why not turn the last resort into the first? Quite a number of seekers asked that question. And some shadow of other-worldliness fell on all spiritual life. No scripture could be more a gospel of illumined action and of life acceptance than the Gitā, and yet there rings out from it the words: "Thou that hast come into this transient and unhappy world, turn thy love to Me" (9.32). These words echo in all the religions, no matter if they have a Church militant or look forward to a Kingdom of God upon earth.

The reason Sri Aurobindo gives for such an attitude even in the India of the Rig-Veda, the early Upanishads, the Gitā, the Tantric worshipers of the World Creatrix, and the Vaishnava devotees of Krishna the Master of the World Game (Lila) is that the Rishis and mystics and prophets and saints came to mix up in the Supramental what Sri Aurobindo calls Supermind proper and the delegated Supermind that he more accurately labels *Overmind*. It is Overmind that up to now has been taken as the supreme Dynamic Divine, beyond whom, or rather at whose back, there is only the sheer extracosmic Godhead—the East's Nirvana (infinite all-cessation) or Nirguna Brahman ("qualityless" eternity), the West's transcendent Alone or indistinguishable Ground.

The sign of Overmind's presence and dominance is that multiplicity comes into the front and unity remains in the rear, even though the unity is not lost. One notices, in the world, religion after religion arising, each claiming to be the sole truth; philosophy on philosophy taking shape, each making a world scheme to the exclusion of the others; theory clashing with theory of government and society. The fact that every one of the opposed formulas tries to embrace everything at the end of its single-track approach gives evidence of the unity at work from behind. There is the same evidence when in a more broad-minded and less religiously sectarian age a movement is set afoot to live and let live—a tolerant ecumenism. Even an attempt is made to bring together all conflicting dogmas and doctrines into a kind of universal Faith or Idea. But still multiplicity rules. Not that multiplicity is unnecessary and should be annulled; the richness of existence would vanish with its going. Yet it has to be exceeded, a new consciousness attained where we do not need to unify in the light of a truth standing in the rear; the unifying truth should be immediate, direct, as much a forefront reality as the many, the diverse, the different. A poise in which to be one is to be many and vice versa, a plane where unity and multiplicity are integrally at play, not as factors to be reconciled but as two simultaneous aspects of the identical—such a poise and plane is Supermind proper. In it the fragmentation of things that constitutes the basic problem of Ignorance, Incapacity, Instability is not worked upon from a certain distance, a certain outsideness, a certain otherness due to the unity being in the background and not level or flush with multiplicity. In Supermind the unity is operative in the very act of the fragmentation, is indeed the self-same force that fragments and creates the many, the diverse, the different that are essential to the opulence and plenitude of manifestation. Thus, what is now a mentality questing for knowledge, a vitality pressing toward effectuation, and a physicality driving in the direction of permanence, but all of them falling short of fulfillment and feeling some bar of ingrained finitude, would have in their nature itself the power of their own consummation—because they are already the fullness that they dream of and grope after. In short, they are Supermind hidden both below and above—Supermind coming into its own through evolution and thus automatically implying Superman and Superearth.

iii

Supermind has never before been reached and explored and brought down into human experience and organized there for a new creation. To make it a part of terrestrial realization is Sri Aurobindo's mission, and this mission accords by a preestablished harmony with the whole adventure of modern science — the holding of Matter in central focus, the finding of the evolutionary process by which Matter displays Life and Mind, the seeing of Life and Mind and what is beyond Mind in Matter as its inherent capacities. The superficial interpretation of modern science's discoveries was materialism. And that interpretation was badly required for a while in order to turn the eyes of man the visionary, the earth shunner, the spiritual absolutist, back to his earth mother and make him perceive in her the substance with which the true heaven of an evolutionary creature was to be built.

Sri Aurobindo has said that his fourteen years in England, from the age of seven to that of twenty-one, were spent in the heyday of Western materialism. In that period all mysticism was pooh-poohed as moonshine. But Sri Aurobindo says too that he foresaw the passing of such negative materialism and the coming of a greater day in which matter would have its glorification by the advent of a new power that would reconcile — nay, identify — the materialist's Here with the mystic's Yonder. He foresaw this day because the science-tempered modern world was precisely the base erected for his typical work by the same Supermind whose avatar he was. Materialism was the first appearance of the Supermind below, preparing the ground for the Supermind above to have its feet planted firmly forever as earth's own divinity. No world except our world today could have been ripe for the Aurobindonian Integral Yoga of total transformation.

And it is not only the theory of evolution that can be presented as proof. Along with it there have been movements of another kind to light up the earth scene with the subtle presence of Supermind as Matter's own self. The dizzying speed of transport, the lightning rapidity of communication, the almost instantaneous transference of sight no less than sound from place to faraway place, the supersonic jet and remote-controlled rocket, the worldwide radio and television network, and all these devices carried to their nth power in space exploration by which the moon and Mars and Venus become parts of any room on earth, the practical annihilation of dividing spatiotemporal factors — have we not here an accustoming of the physical consciousness to unity and omnipresence, the pervasion of our most external and material level of awareness by the one and infinite? In no other age was the day-to-day outward-looking mind of man suffused with a scientific translation of the mystic's sense of all as one and one as all, the single universal Self simultaneously poised at each point and active everywhere. No doubt, though science attempts to unify the world and knit together the cosmos, the impulsive and sensational nature of the human individual, even of the scientist himself, is an obstacle to its triumph on all the planes of our being. The double action of Overmind is still in force, but the pressure of the Supermind concealed behind it is felt more and more. One has only to awaken to Sri Aurobindo to realize what science's conquest of space and time is preparing us for in our bodily existence.

Then there is thermonuclear energy. So far the lordly sun, worshiped from time immemorial as the visible God of the physical universe, has stood aloof from us, although shedding upon our terrestrial being its golden grace, its power of radiant life and brilliant death. Now with the splitting of the atom and the discovery of the hydrogen bomb we have seized the secret of solar energy and are on the verge of changing the earth's face with the power that keeps the sun blazing almost inexhaustibly. The sun, as Sri Aurobindo has often reminded us, is the symbol of Supermind, the self-luminous creative Truth of the Infinite and Eternal. The "solar splendor" that he speaks of in a passage and that he describes as a power of illumination entering our intellectual consciousness by fits and starts at present has shown its physical reflection in science's thermonuclear development. Our age is being prepared to perceive in its outermost dimension the intimate presence of the grandest, the most prolific and productive force in the universe — force that is also light, force packed with potentialities of supreme knowledge. One cannot help recalling those lines from a poetic invocation by Sri Aurobindo:

Rose of God, great wisdom-bloom on the summits of being,
Rose of light, immaculate core of the ultimate seeing!
Live in the mind of our earthhood: O golden mystery, flower,
Sun on the head of the Timeless, guest of the marvellous Hour![10]

Wherever one turns one's eyes in the world today one can see the Aurobindonian Time-Spirit at work. This is but natural since it is the "marvellous Hour" that Sri Aurobindo has concentrated on, the establishment of heavenliness in "earthhood." Has he not declared: "No, it is not with the Empyrean that I am busy: I wish it were. It is rather with the opposite end of things; it is in the Abyss that I have to plunge to build a bridge between the two."[11] Matter and its labyrinthine depths are the field of Sri Aurobindo's supramental spirituality. If ever there has been a Yogi who could be called a Superscientist, it is Sri Aurobindo. The questioning mood, the experimental temper, the readiness for challenges and difficulties, the sense of objective effect, the turn for concrete practicality are always a part of his Integral Yoga. Quite characteristic is the letter he wrote to a disciple in 1933: "As for faith, you write as if I never had a doubt or any difficulty. I have had worse than any human mind can think of. It is not because I have ignored difficulties, but because I have seen them more clearly, experienced them on a larger scale than anyone living now or before me that, having faced and measured them, I am sure of the results of my work."[12] Equally typical is the letter of 1932 where he speaks on behalf of both himself and his coworker, the Mother:

> I must remind you that I have been an intellectual myself and no stranger to doubt — both the Mother and myself have had one side of the mind as positive and as insistent on practical results and more so than any Russell can be. We could never have been contented with the shining ideas and phrases which a Rolland or another takes for gold coin of Truth. We know well what is the difference between a subjective experience and a dynamic outgoing and realizing Force. So although we have faith (and who ever did anything great in the world without having faith in his mission or the Truth at work behind him?), we do not found ourselves on faith alone, but on a great ground of knowledge which we have been developing and testing all our lives. I think I can say that I have been testing day and night for years upon years more scrupulously than any scientist his theory or his method on the physical plane. That is why I am not alarmed by the aspect of the world around me or disconcerted by the often successful fury of the adverse Forces who increase in their rage as the Light comes nearer and nearer to the field of earth and Matter.
>   If I believe in the probability and not only the possibility, if I feel practically certain of the Supramental Descent (I do not fix a date), it is because I have my grounds for the belief, not a faith in the air. I know that the Supramental Descent is inevitable — I have faith in view of my experience that the time can be and should be now and not in a later age.[13]

Finally, a letter may be quoted in which, while showing how Yoga can bring up faculties unsuspected in one, he makes a statement that is most deeply in tune with the surface orientation of modern man's psychology, the apparent Godlessness of Matter-obsessed research. Sri Aurobindo, the born avatar of Supermind, utters his oneness with the evolutionary bipolarity of today when he goes further than his admission that at one time he was an agnostic:

> I had no urge towards spirituality in me, I developed spirituality. I was incapable of understanding metaphysics. I developed into a philosopher. I had no eye for painting — I developed it by Yoga. I transformed my nature from what it was to what it was not. I did it by a special means not by a miracle and I did it to show what could be done and how it could be done. I did not do it out of any personal necessity of my own or by a miracle without any process. I say that if it is not so, then my Yoga is useless and my life was a mistake, a mere absurd freak of Nature without any meaning or consequence.[14]

The essence of the scientific temper breathes here, in the secular starting point as well as in the insistence on and pursuit of a method, a process, a systematic growth, in spiritual consciousness, so that all may follow who have the courage, the curiosity, and the call to experiment with the unknown and to exceed themselves. Sri Aurobindo's nonegoistic, impersonal combination of the scientific approach with the spiritual quest should kindle a like blending in the world today. The Master Yogi has acted magnificently like a man of science; the mind of scientific modernism must realize that harmonious gesture in the cause of evolution and move toward the Master Yogi for the key to a consummation of its earth-centered idealism.

Already on 29 February, 1956, nearly forty-two years after Sri Aurobindo and the Mother first met (29 March 1914) and about five years after what is regarded as Sri Aurobindo's self-sacrifice (5 December 1950), the general manifestation of Supermind was announced by the Mother to have taken place at last in the earth's subtle atmosphere. This manifestation would, on the one hand, hasten the radical life-revolutionizing transformation of the individual's body and, on the other, push toward the materialization of the "Ideal of Human Unity" that is one of the leitmotivs of the modern world. Marx looked forward to that materialization in his own socialist terms when he wrote: "We shall have an association in which the free developing of each is the condition for the free development of all."[15] Teilhard strained his eyes in its direction when he affirmed his zeal "to promote in equal measure the mastery of the world and the kingdom of God."[16] Sri Aurobindo saw it coming, as he kept holding out always to his fellow men "the hope of the kingdom of heaven within us and the city of God upon earth."[17] Zaehner, in his study in Sri Aurobindo and Teilhard, returns again and again to the ideal of human unity and repeatedly quotes Marx about it no less than the two spiritual thinkers (pp. 4, 7). Sri Aurobindo, more than anyone else, strove for it creatively and concretely with his Integral Yoga of total earth divinization, which acts at once on the individual and the collective levels.

The hour has indeed struck for a response by the modern age to the Master Yogi's work.

Notes

1. Pierre Teilhard de Chardin, *Human Energy*, trans. J. M. Cohen (London: Collins, 1969; New York: Harcourt Brace Jovanovich, 1971), pp. 58, 120, 45.

2. Sri Aurobindo, trans. *Isha Upanishad* (Calcutta: Arya Publishing House, 1924), pp. 6, 7.

3. Friedrich Nietzsche, *The Philosophy of Nietzsche:* Thus Spake Zarathustra. Beyond Good and Evil. The Genealogy of Morals. Ecce Homo. The Birth of Tragedy (New York: Random House, Modern Library), pp. 320, 6, 8-9.

4. Julian Huxley, Introduction to *The Phenomenon of Man* by Pierre Teilhard de Chardin (London: Collins; New York: Harper & Row, 1960), p. 18 n.2.

5. Sri Aurobindo, *The Human Cycle* (Pondicherry: Sri Aurobindo Ashram, 1962), pp. 100-1).

6. J.B.S. Haldane, "Science and Ethics," *The Inequality of Man* (London: Chatto, 1932), p. 113.

7. Sri Aurobindo, *The Life Divine* (New York: Sri Aurobindo Library, 1949), p. 5.

8. Ibid., p. 295.

9. Ibid.

10. Sri Aurobindo, *Collected Poems* (Pondicherry: Sri Aurobindo Ashram, 1972), p. 584.

11. Sri Aurobindo, *Sri Aurobindo on Himself and on the Mother* (Pondicherry: Sri Aurobindo International University Centre Collection, 1953), p. 222.

12. Ibid., p. 223.

13. Ibid., pp. 377-78.

14. Nirodbaron, ed., *Correspondence with Sri Aurobindo* (Pondicherry: Sri Aurobindo Ashram Press, 1959), p. 49.

15. Karl Marx and Friedrich Engels, *Communist Manifesto,* as quoted by Zaehner.

16. Pierre Teilhard de Chardin, *Writings in Time of War* (London: Collins, 1968; New York: Harper & Row, 1973), p. 91.

17. Sri Aurobindo, *The Human Cycle*, p. 165.

Supplementary Note

The Ashram at Pondicherry

Sri Aurobindo does not aim primarily at giving the world a philosophical system, much less a religious creed. An intellectual exposition of his message is to him indeed a necessity for the world, particularly the West, though without too much of the technicalities of abstract speculation; so also in his eyes is a scheme of fundamental beliefs required, though with a freedom from cramping traditional dogmas and the sectarian proselytizing temper, but these are to be mere guide-posts and working supports. What he radically insists upon is a profound change of consciousness, an inner life of spiritual realization, a constant Yoga.

The word *Yoga*, deriving from the same root as the English *yoke*, means *union*, the coming together, the interpenetration, even the fusion, of the human and the superhuman. It implies a sustained methodized attempt at discovering one's true being, which is at the same time the single changeless Self of all and the ever-growing individual soul, a child of the Supreme Divine Person whose fullest manifestation it desires.

Sri Aurobindo calls his Yoga *Integral*, meaning thereby a spiritual adventure that leaves out no side of reality and that endeavors to establish the Infinite, the Eternal, the Divine in every part of our composite being, including the outer physical. The Integral Yoga is a life dedicated to the total transformation of all our existence in the light of what Sri Aurobindo terms the *Truth-Consciousness*, the creative Supermind.

The Ashram at Pondicherry is the field of this crucial experiment for man, individually and collectively, to pass to an evolutionary stage far beyond the mental, which is now nature's highest result. It

279

was founded in no hurry. In 1910 Sri Aurobindo, in answer to an inner call, left the turbulent scene of his leadership of India's fight against British rule and came to Pondicherry, then a French possession. He lived for sixteen years in this capital of French India without forming any recognizable spiritual center. He wanted to be sure of his ground. During those years, on every 15 August, the day of his birth and subsequently the day of India's Independence, he is said to have been asked by the few young men who lived with him whether he had found what he had been looking for. He had already gone through all the classical mystic experiences, yet his reply was always, "Ask me next year." Only in 1926, after a spiritual event that took place on 24 November he of his own accord let it be understood that the basis of his work had at last been laid and that he was ready to make the formal start of a Yogic center. To raise as quickly as possible the needed superstructure on the basis of what he described as the descent of the Overmind consciousness into the physical being itself, he retired into a background of "dynamic meditation" and put forward as the head of the new institution and the direct guru of his disciples his spiritual coworker, whom they had known by the name *Mira* and whom they now came to address as "the Mother."

French by birth and education, Indian by choice and predilection, and having followed on her own the same development of integral spirituality as Sri Aurobindo, she seemed the destined counterpart of one who had been Indian by birth but educated from his seventh to his twenty-first year in England. Again, while he had been poet and politician, she had grown up as painter and musician, besides being a born organizer. Together they represented the perfect nucleus for a Yoga intended to take up and solve the whole human problem. To those who have been intimately acquainted with them and their dealings with the disciples they have appeared to be avatars (incarnations) of the Divine Consciousness, who have yet assumed our common humanity in full. Thus, they could at once exemplify the problem and supply the solution. However, the avataric view is not obligatory, and the Integral Yoga can be practiced on its own merits and under the guidance of the copious literature emanating from Sri Aurobindo and the Mother. Indeed, an inward turn toward the personal channels of the Supermind's revelation is the swiftest path to fulfillment; but neither of the two channels has sought any spotlight on itself. It is the Truth embodied and expressed that has mattered. The principles of the Yoga and the discipline that they entail are the essentials put forward. To provide the best conditions for these essentials, the Mother, with Sri Aurobindo as her support from behind, built up the "Ashram."

The designation *Ashram* originally connoted the residence of a teacher with whom, as with a father, a number of pupils chose to stay, preferably from their teens. No asceticism as such was associated with the term. An Ashram was a scene of various activities as well of meditative insights; even the arts of war were taught there. Later in India's history, especially after the advent of Buddhism, a monastic color attached itself to the diverse groups of spiritual aspirants scattered all over the land. World renunciation became the cry of those who were dissatisfied with human life as it was. Sri Aurobindo's Ashram goes back to the formula prevalent in the great times of the Rig-Veda, the Upanishads, the Epics and combines an intense process of change of consciousness with a many-sided occupation in arts, crafts, sciences, vital services, and industries to help cultural and communal living. Stress is put on work, selected or allotted, as a means of self-perfection. "To work for the Divine," says the Mother, "is to pray with the body." All work is considered equal. And there is no hierarchy of officials and subordinates. Nor is there a premium set on exceptional ability. Skill and application, of course, are valued, but the thing of central importance is the consciousness in which the work is done.

Both the internal and external movements proceed in tune with something indefinable yet most concrete to all who have entered into the spirit of the evolutionary labour undertaken by Sri Aurobindo and the Mother. A vast, calm, luminous and inspiring "atmosphere" is felt, full of a deathless Presence that envelops and permeates everybody and everything. No doubt, Sri Aurobindo and the Mother have a worldwide reach; their realizations cannot be confined to local factors. Still, it is true that their influence is most directly active where they lived, where they did their Yoga for earth's evolution with their physical forms as its center of radiation and where the rosewood caskets containing their bodies have been laid in a vault in the courtyard of the main Ashram building with a simple monument over them to make a perpetual flower-strewn focal point of meditation.

There are at present nearly two thousand settled residents — men, women, children — and a floating population of several hundred visitors. The residents as well as the visitors hail from all over the globe. Among foreign countries, the United States seem to be particularly attracted.

Some of the facilities of the Ashram may be listed: agricultural farms, dairies, workshops, factories, printing presses, laundry, bakery, house maintenance, kitchens, dining-halls, tailoring, dispensaries (allopathic, ayurvedic, homeopathic, naturopathic), guesthouses and an educational center ranging from nursery to postgraduate levels. All of the activities have developed in an organic way rather than by artificial planning. Living and dynamic needs have created them, bringing together the right people and the correct technology.

In every sphere of Ashram life a complete equality prevails between men and women. Special care is taken to ensure good health and the development of the body for young and old. The rules and regulations for living are as few as possible. Great freedom is given to the individual to grow along the line of his own nature in purity and truth within the community with which he has to be harmonious and to adjust his possessions. Here an inner fraternity is the foundation of both liberty and solidarity.

Whatever the outer facilities, this is no easy life; it demands a ceaseless self-exceeding and can yield no genuine result without an ever-vigilant self-surrender to the Ideal set up by Sri Aurobindo.

Auroville

Auroville is the name given by the Mother to an extension of the experiment in evolution that the Ashram has attempted over the last several decades. This extension is situated on the border between Pondicherry and Madras. The name, from the French *aurore* (with a sub-suggestion from *Aurobindo*), means "City of Dawn." The Mother inaugurated it on 28 February 1968 with a unique foundation ceremony. Children from 124 nations and the states of India, carrying a multitude of flags, deposited, in a marble urn symbolic of human unity, handfuls of earth from their motherlands. Here countries divided by different ideologies put their token soils together, mingling republics and monarchies, democracies and communist regimes, secular governments and theocratic systems. All appeared to sow the seed of a single future beyond themselves, a day of Divine Consciousness expressing itself in a manifold of spiritual color.

The Mother drew up the Charter of Auroville:

1. Auroville belongs to nobody in particular. Auroville belongs to humanity as a whole. But to live in Auroville one must be a living servitor of the Divine Consciousness.
2. Auroville will be a place of an unending education, of constant progress and a youth that never ages.
3. Auroville wants to be the bridge between the past and the future. Taking advantage of all discoveries from without and from within, Auroville will boldly spring towards future realizations.
4. Auroville will be a site of material and spiritual researchers for a living embodiment of an actual Human Unity.

The project of Auroville has been sponsored by the Sri Aurobindo Society, an international organization that itself evolved under the guidance of the Mother and of which the Mother was the president. The role of the society has been to establish a first stable framework, legally and economically, and to handle the basic administrative tasks. It has served as the agency that brought Auroville under UNESCO sanctions in 1966, 1968, and 1970 and that collected grants and contributions through UNESCO, the Government of India, and foundations in West Germany, America and Canada as well as from individuals in India and abroad. It has been the guardian of Auroville's transitional capacities and is meant to be the fosterer of its internal initiatives.

UNESCO's Resolution, which not only the Western countries but also the Communist bloc supported in full, at the 14th General Conference in Paris, October 1966, may be cited.

The General Conference
Being apprized that in connection with the commemoration of the twentieth anniversary of UNESCO, the Sri Aurobindo Society, Pondicherry, India, a non-governmental organization affiliated to the Indian National Commission for UNESCO, proposes to set up a cultural township known as "Auroville" where people of different countries will live together in harmony in one community and engage in cultural, educational, scientific and other pursuits,
Noting that the township will have pavilions intended to represent the cultures of the world, not only intellectually but also by presenting different schools of architecture, painting, sculpture, music, etc., as part of the way of living,
Appreciating that one of the aims of Auroville will be to bring

together in close juxtaposition the values and ideals of different civilizations and cultures,

Expresses the belief that the project will contribute to international understanding and promotion of peace and commends it to those interested in UNESCO's ideals.

Auroville is planned for fifty thousand residents in the main town, twenty thousand in the model villages around, and thirty thousand in the subsidiary projects like World Trade Center, and so on. Over three hundred souls live in Auroville today in more than twelve communities devoted to a variety of enterprises. The residents, by the Census of 1975, are: Indian (81), American (59), French (47), German (41), British (14), Dutch (11), Australian (10), Italian (6), Swiss (5), Canadian (3), Swedish (3), Belgian (3), African (3), Mexican (1), Tunisian (1), New Zealand (1), Malaysian (1). Thirty-six children have been born Aurovillians.

Concentric circles with an outer diameter of two miles form the base of the town. A high plateau four miles from the sea marks the town's center. A green belt will surround the four zones into which Auroville is meant to be divided. These zones stand for the four fundamental aspects of man's activity: dwelling (residential zone), culture (cultural zone), social relations (international zone), and work (industrial zone). All the zones will converge upon the center of the city, "the soul of Auroville," the *Matrimandir* ("Shrine of the Mother"), where the new Consciousness that the Mother embodied will be symbolized by a large sphere, shining with golden discs and opening upward to the light; it will represent Divine Truth and Love and Harmony. The *Matrimandir* is not intended to be a mere impressive structure; every Aurovillian feels it to be impregnated with an inner force that will grow as it grows and that will suffuse the entire town and its residents.

Auroville is not just a town for collective existence laid out in the best manner of the modern constructive imagination. A town aiming at no more than an international community can be built at any spot on the earth. Auroville is closely linked with the goal of the Sri Aurobindo Ashram. It has indeed a more generalized framework, with life conditions permitting an intermediate phase between the human and the beyond-human. Its pressure on the being of impulse and instinct is not as rigorous as in the Ashram. But it must never lose sight of the ultimate objective. The Mother has clearly said that Auroville has consciously to assist the earth to evolve a new species, and for this "the best measure to take is to consecrate oneself entirely to the Divine." She has made allowances for certain human frailties for those who are not quite ready to leap into the future, but she has also insisted:

No big creation is possible without discipline
Individual discipline
Group discipline
Discipline towards the Divine.

But her finger points always to the necessity of "the inner discovery by which one learns who one really is behind the social, moral, cultural, racial and hereditary appearances." Although Auroville is broad-based, welcomes all men of goodwill, and rises above all religions no less than all politics and nationalities, one should never forget the Mother's pronouncement on the subject of individuals and groups who are willing to aid in Auroville's development: "They may not practise themselves but if they do not know about Yoga, how can they understand the purpose of Auroville?"

Finally, to the question "What is the difference between the Ashram and Auroville?" put in June 1968—that is, shortly after the foundation of the City of Dawn—there is the clear-cut reply by the Mother: "The Ashram will keep its role as pioneer, inspirer and guide. Auroville will be an experiment in collective realization."

Collective realization arising from the core of the Ashram's dream of the Life Divine can never be an easy achievement. Only the heroic in soul are beckoned toward it. But in proportion to the difficulty is the Supreme Grace offered to every sincere aspirant and promising him fulfillment. As a line in Sri Aurobindo's epic *Savitri* has it:

All can be done if the God-touch is there.

Bibliography

Aurobindo, Sri. *A Practical Guide to Integral Yoga.* Compiled by Manibhai. Pondicherry: Sri Aurobindo Ashram, 1955.

―――.*Collected Poems.* Pondicherry: Sri Aurobindo Ashram, 1972.

―――.*Essays on the Gita.* New York: Sri Aurobindo Library, 1950.

―――.*Evolution.* 5th ed. Pondicherry: Sri Aurobindo Ashram, 1950.

―――.*The Hour of God.* Pondicherry: Sri Aurobindo Ashram, 1959.

―――.*The Human Cycle.* Pondicherry: Sri Aurobindo Ashram, 1962.

―――.*Letters of Sri Aurobindo.* 4th ser. Bombay: Sri Aurobindo Circle, 1951.

―――.*The Life Divine.* New York: Sri Aurobindo Library, 1949.

―――.*The Message of the Gita as Interpreted by Sri Aurobindo.* Edited by Anilbaran Roy. London: George Allen & Unwin, 1946.

―――.*Notes on the Mahabharata.* Pondicherry: Sri Aurobindo Ashram, 1956.

―――.*On Yoga.* Part 2. Pondicherry: Sri Aurobindo International University Centre Collection, Vols. 6 and 7. 1958.

―――.*Sri Aurobindo on Himself and on the Mother.* Pondicherry: Sri Aurobindo International University Centre Collection, 1953. Vol. 1.

―――.*Thoughts and Aphorisms.* Pondicherry: Sri Aurobindo Ashram, 1958.

―――.*Guidance from Sri Aurobindo: Letters to a Young Disciple:* Nagin Doshi. 2 vols. Pondicherry: Sri Aurobindo Society, 1974-76.

―――.trans. *Eight Upanishads.* Pondicherry: Sri Aurobindo Ashram, 1953.

―――.Isha Upanishad. Calcutta: Arya Publishing House, 1924.

Braybrooke, Neville, ed. *Teilhard de Chardin: Pilgrim of the Future.* London: Darton, Longman & Todd, Libra Books, 1966; New York: Seabury Press, 1964.

Bruteau, Beatrice. *Worthy Is the World: The Hindu Philosophy of Sri Aurobindo*. Teaneck, N.J.: Fairleigh Dickinson University Press, 1974.

Cuénot, Claude. *Science and Faith in Teilhard de Chardin*. Translated by Noël Lindsay. London: Garnstone Press; New York: Humanities Press, 1967.

— — —.*Teilhard de Chardin*. London: Burns and Oates; Baltimore, Md.: Helicon Press, 1965.

Dasgupta, S. *A History of Indian Philosophy*. 5 vols. Cambridge: At the University Press, 1922-55. Vol. 2.

de Lubac, Henri. *The Religion of Teilhard de Chardin*. London: Collins; New York: Desclee, 1967.

— — —.*Teilhard de Chardin: The Man and His Meaning*. Translated by René Hague. New York: New American Library, Mentor Omega Book, 1967.

Études. May 1946. Paris

Gray, Donald B. *The One and the Many: Teilhard de Chardin's Vision of Unity*. London: Burns & Oates, 1969.

Haldane, J.B.S. *The Inequality of Man*. London: Chatto, 1932.

Hastings, James, ed. *Encyclopaedia of Religion and Ethics*. 12 vols. Edinburgh: T. & T. Clark, 1946. Vols. 5 and 7.

Henry, Matthew. *Commentary on the Whole Bible*. 6 vols. London: Marshall; Edinburgh: Morgan T. Scott, 1953. Vol 6.

Hume, R.E. *The Thirteen Principal Upanishads*. Oxford University Press, Geoffrey Cumberledge; Indian Reprint, Madras, 1954.

Huxley, Julian. *Memories*. London: George Allen & Unwin, 1973.

Lewis, H.D. *Philosophy of Religion*. London: English University Press, Teach Yourself Books, 1965.

Mādhavānanda, Swāmī, trans. *Brhadāranyaka Upanisad*, with the Commentary of Śankarācharya. 4th ed. Calcutta: Advaita Ashrama,1965.

Maloney, George A. *The Cosmic Christ: From Paul to Teilhard*. New York: Sheed and Ward, 1968.

Marx, Karl, and Engels, Friedrich. *Communist Manifesto*.

Masui, Jacques. Speech in French made in *Échange de vues sur "L'Évolution de l'humanité selon Sri Aurobindo et le Père Teilhard de Chardin"* sous la Présidence de Dr. Louis Armand de l'Académie Française: le 4 December 1965 à Paris, au Palais de L'unesco.

Monchanin, L'Abbé Jules. "Formes, vie, et pensée," in *L'Abbé Jules Monchanin*. 1960.

Mooney, Christopher. *Teilhard de Chardin and the Mystery of Christ*. London: Collins; New York: Curtis Brown, 1966.

Nietzsche, Friedrich. *The Philosophy of Nietzsche.* Thus Spake Zarathustra. Beyond Good and Evil. The Genealogy of Morals. Ecce Homo. The Birth of Tragedy. Translated by Thomas Common, et al. New York: Random House, Modern Library.

New Catholic Encyclopedia. Catholic University of America. 1967.

New Testament. According to the received Greek text, together with the English Authorized Version. Cambridge, 1899.

Nirodbaran, ed. *Correspondence with Sri Aurobindo.* 2d ed. Pondicherry: Sri Aurobindo Ashram, 1959.

Nouvelles Littéraires, 11 January 1951. Paris.

Peifer, Claude J., O.S.B. *First Corinthians, Second Corinthians.* New Testament Reading Guide. Coleville, Minn.: Liturgical Press, 1960.

Prat, Férnand. *The Theology of Saint Paul.* Translated by John L. Stodd. 2 vols. London and Dublin: Brown, Oates and Washbourne, 1945.

Rabut, O. *Dialogue with Teilhard de Chardin.* London and New York: Sheed & Ward, Stagbooks, 1961.

Rideau, Emile. *Teilhard de Chardin: A Guide to His Thought.* Translated by René Hague. London: Collins; New York: Harper & Row, 1967.

Rose, William, ed. *An Outline of Modern Knowledge.* London: Victor Gollancz, 1934.

Runes, Dagobert D., ed. *The Dictionary of Philosophy.* Bombay: Jaico Publishing House, 1957.

Schweitzer, Albert. *The Mysticism of Paul the Apostle.* Translated by William Montgomery, B.D. London: A. & C. Black, 1931.

Speaight, Robert. *Teilhard de Chardin: A Biography.* London: Collins; New York: Harper & Row, 1968.

Sproxton, Vernon. *Teilhard de Chardin.* London: SCM Press; Naperville, Ill.: Allenson, 1971.

Teilhard de Chardin, Pierre. *Activation of Energy.* London: Collins; New York: Harcourt Brace Jovanovich, 1972.

— — —.*Christianity and Evolution.* Translated by René Hague. London: Collins; New York: Harcourt Brace Jovanovich, 1971.

— — —.*The Divine Milieu.* Translated by Bernard Wall. New York. Harper & Brothers, 1960.

— — —.*The Future of Man.* Translated by Norman Denny, London: Collins, Fontana Books; New York: Harper & Row, 1964.

— — —.*Human Energy.* Translated by J.M. Cohen, London: Collins, 1969; New York: Harcourt Brace Jovanovich, 1971.

— — —.*Hymn of the Universe.* Translated by Simon Bartholomew. London: Collins; New York: Harper & Row, 1965.

— — —.*Let Me Explain.* Texts selected and arranged by Jean-Pierre Demoulin. Translated by René Hague et al. London: Collins, 1970; New York: Harper & Row, 1972.

— — —.*Letters to Léontine Zanta.* London: Collins; New York: Georges Borchardt, 1969.

— — —.*The Making of a Mind: Letters from a Soldier-Priest.* London: Collins; New York: Harper & Row, 1965.

— — —.*Man's Place in Nature.* London: Collins; New York: Harper & Row, 1966.

— — —.*The Phenomenon of Man.* Translated by Bernard Wall. London: Collins; New York: Harper & Row, 1960.

— — —.*Science and Christ.* London: Collins; New York: Harper & Row, 1968.

— — —.*The Vision of the Past.* Translated by J.M. Cohen. London: Collins; New York: Harper & Row, 1966.

— — —.*Writings in Time of War.* Translated by René Hague. London: Collins, 1968; New York: Harper & Row, 1973.

Wildiers, H.M. *An Introduction to Teilhard de Chardin.* Translated by Hubert Hoskins. London: Collins, Fontana Books, 1968.

Zaehner, R.C. *Concordant Discord: The Interdependence of Faiths.* Oxford: Clarendon Press, 1970.

— — —.*Dialectical Christianity and Christian Materialism.* London: Oxford University Press, 1971.

— — —.*Drugs, Mysticism, and Make Believe.* London: Collins, 1972.

— — —.*Evolution in Religion: A Study in Sri Aurobindo and Pierre Teilhard de Chardin.* Oxford: Clarendon Press, 1971.

Index

Absolute, Supreme, 24

Action: Christian solution of, 56; and Divine Consciousness, 214-15; and ego, 218; "free" and unattached, 171; freedom from bondage to, 214; and God, 56; and good and evil, 216-17; and Indian Yoga, 216-17; infinite consciousness and infinite, 225; Teilhard's notion of, 102-3; triple universality of, 222

Activation: imposed on universe, 56

Adam: and Christ, 121; and creation, 145; fall of, and Christ's appearance, 122-23; sin of, 149

Aditi and Supermind, 272

Alexandrian Fathers and Teilhard, 64

Alipore Jail, 30

Ananda: and Beauty, 228-29; and Holy Spirit, 228

Angela of Foligno, and Teilhard, 72

Anthropogenesis, 42, 143

Apocalypse and heavenly Jerusalem, 110

Aquinas, Saint Thomas, 123; Christ of, 121; and pantheism, 137

Aristotle, 143

Arjuna, 170, 215; and duty, 219-20

Arya, 30, 74-75, 76. 77, 256-57; Sri Aurobindo on, 74-75

Ashram, 22, 23, 32, 34, 70, 279, 281; and Auroville compared, 285; balances individual and collective life, 250; facilities of, 284, 285; as instrument of unity, 71; and Integral Yoga, 250; meaning of, 282; the Mother as center of, 73; natural locus of future world union, 73; and religion, 73

Asuras, 215

Athanasius, 141

August 15, 280

Augustine, Saint (of Hippo), 39, 64, 123, 166; "Love and do what you will," 218

Aura of Christ, 124

Aurobindo, Sri, 201, 279-81, 285; on the Abyss, 276; attitude toward happenings in the world, 33; attitude toward his work, 32-33; attitude toward science, 24; on Avatar, 127; Avataric status of, 72; avowed mission, 262; base and background, 271; on Beauty and Sachchidananda, 228-29; a being of highest spiritual consciousness, 72; belief in evolution, 19; and Bergson, 29-30; on Bergson, 30; on "beyond good and evil" in Vyasa, 218-20; born Avatar of Supermind, 277; combination of scientific with spiritual, 277; compared with Christ, 72; and consummation of evolutionary existence, 250; correspondence, 36; and Cosmic Consciousness, 222-23; on creation of perfect human order, 23; and credo of modern science, 265; on Day of Siddhi or Victory, 35; description of Supermind, 224-27; on difficulties and doubts, 276; early fourteen years in England, 274; evil for, 21; *Evolution*, 257; on evolution of consciousness, 77; on evolution of Mind, Life, and Matter, 270; evolutionary progression in, 267; on faith, 276; full "Life Divine" on earth, 252; fullness of spirituality in, 88; on fullness of Yoga, 23; and Gītā, 173-76; on giving up his body, 33; glimpse of future, 266; great message of, 271; on how Yoga can bring up unknown

Kingdom of God, 232; and power of evolution, 25; and process of psychogenesis, 63; Super-, 270-73; and super-earth, 263; Teilhard on, 248

East: religions of, 170-71; Teilhard on people of Far, 178; Teilhard and road of the, 178

Eastern Fathers, 151

Eckhart, M., 179, 233, 242; and Teilhard, 110, 111

Ecumenical movement, Teilhard and, 168

Ecumenism, 40

Ego: and action, 216, 218; divisive, 80; and Ignorance, 80; individual not an independent, 88; must be destroyed, 89; and Self, 214; -self and world-self, 222; and Supermind, 227; tamasic, rajasic, and sattwic religious, 231-32; and work, 214

Egoism, conditions for disappearance of, 23

Einstein, Albert, 102, 242

Encyclopaedia Britannica, on "pantheism," 192

Encyclopaedia of Religion and Ethics, The, 194

Energy: and entropy, 239; of love in Teilhard, 94; and matter, 102; radial and tangential, 246; secret of solar, 275; sun and thermo-nuclear, 275; Super-Person as evolutive, 119-20; tangential and radial, 102; Teilhard on human, 239; universe must be thinking, 264; vitalization and the dissipation of, 247

Entropy: and collective being, 246; and complexity-consciousness, 239-40; current running counter to, 240; and evolution, 240, 246; and life, 246; and spirit, 247; and super-life, 247; Teilhard's slant on, 246-47; and ultra-human realization, 246

Eucharist, and Cosmic Christ, 125

Evil, 18-21; and Christ, 46; cosmic consciousness and problem of, 84; and creation, 131; as final choice, 57-58; and Indra, 215-16; physical and moral, 44-45; as sign and effect of progress, 45; statistical, 45, 56

Evolution, 75; an apologetic based on, 94; has become "psycho-social," 241; becoming conscious of itself, 65; belief of Sri Aurobindo and Teilhard in, 19; ceiling of, 241; cephalization of, 61; Christ and, 53, 94, 267; Christ, Christianity, and, 21; Christ conducting cosmic, 56; Christ is God of, 146; Christ guides, 116-17; and Christ in Scotus and Teilhard, 122-23; Christ as ultra-humanizing principle of, 120; and Christianity, 65; Christifying of, 42; Church as axis of, 70; collective, Teilhard and, 235; of consciousness, 52, 77; of consciousness, Teilhard and, 242; consciousness of, for Teilhard, 59; and "co-reflection," 245; cosmic, 38; cosmic, and Christ, 138; and cosmos, 248; creation and, 131; as creation, incarnation, and redemption, 131; creative, 20; and Cross, 44; developing finer physical medium, 243; earth and power of, 25; and entropy, 240, 246; *finis* to, 240; fused with mysticism, 41; and Genesis, 98-99; and Gītā, 173: goal of, 224; God as force of, 119; God of, 59; and God's creative activity, 147; grown conscious of itself, man as, 267; and historical Jesus, 125, 126; how it works, 22; immanence and cosmic, 117; imperative to love, 159; and Incarnation, Teilhard on, 130; and increasing complexity and consciousness, 58; and individual, 241; individual and collective, 243-45, 249-50; individual, Sri Aurobindo and Teilhard on, 245; and involution, 247, 250, 270; irreversibility of, 246; leads to emergence of Superman, 266; of the life divine, 75; logic of the impossible and, 270; man collaborates in his own, 250; man collaborates with, 267; man as product of physicochemical, 63; of matter and universe, 182; of Mind, Life, and Matter, Sri Aurobindo on, 270; and modern science, 76; modern theory, background to Aurobindonian spirituality, 77; natural, 206; Neo-Logos as principle of, 158; none without suffering, 119; Omega Point of, 50; its own God, 249; and pantheism, 94; persistent problem solved by, 265; physics-founded religion of, 144; power of cosmic, 56; as process of

Krishna, 173-74, 272; on action, 214-15; cult, core of Gitā, 172; descent of, 35; on duty, 219-20; as incarnate God, 169-70; on sin and evil, 213; Sri Aurobindo's experience of, 30; worker in transcendental status, 171
Kurukshetra, 215

Lamare, Paul, 49
Latin Fathers and Saint Paul, 144
Leonardo da Vinci, 242
Lewis, H. D., 192
Life: appearance of, 239; concept of Divine, 76; cosmic, 223; critical thresholds of mind and, 267; divine, 34; diviner, 268; and entropy, 246; evolving, 65; and mind co-existent with matter, 269; new, of race, 74; passing new critical point, 143; science and plenary human, 265; super-, and entropy, 247; Teilhard on fidelity to, 85; transformation of, 75; trust in, 47; and universality of action, 222; and universe, 248
Līlā, 174
Logic: of the "impossible" and evolution, 270; of the "impossible" and Nature, 265-66; of the "impossible" and the supramental, 267; leaping, 65
Logos, 25; and Christ, 151-52; Christ and Alexandrian, 156; Christ as, 149; Christ as Divine, 150-51; in Christian philosophy, 157; Christic, 151-52; and *cit*, 227-28; definition and relation to Christianity, 156-57; and Fate, Providence, and Nature, 157; of Greek Fathers and Teilhard, 156-57; and logoi, 151; Neo-, principle of evolution, 157; and Philo of Alexandria, 157; Teilhard's and Christianity's, 157; transcendent, 152
Love: of another, Teilhard on, 205; between soul and God, 199; birth of, 239; of Christ and universe, 84; and Christianity, 70-71; destiny of individual and, 190; Divine, 32; energy in Teilhard, 94; in evolution, 23; of evolution, 158; foundation of, 199; mysticism of Śaiva Siddhānta, 201-4; pantheism and, Teilhard on, 190-91; sin as refusal of, 94; Teilhard and, 190-91; Teilhard's true character of, 198-99; unfound law of, 23-24; and

union, 198-99; and union, defect of Christian notion of, 204; union differentiates and nature of, 198-207

Mahābhārata, 219
Maloney, George, 158; on the Christ of Teilhard and his spiritual ancestry, 140-54; critique of, 149; critique of his linking Teilhard and Greek Fathers, 140; on mysticism of Saint Paul, Saint John, Greek Fathers, 149-51; use of "immanence," 151-52
Man: collaborates in his own evolution, 250; collaboration of, with evolution, 267; evolution becoming conscious of itself in, 65; as evolution grown conscious of itself, 267; modern way of recognizing God, 52; and Superman, 263; Teilhard's view of, 62-63
Manichaeanism, Teilhard avoids, 105
Many and One, 226
Martindale, C. C., 115
Marx, Karl: on association and free development, 277-78; on socialized and free society, 17
Marxian socialism, 17
Mass, Teilhard on, 111
Masui, Jacques, 243-44, 257-59
Materialism, 274; first appearance of Supermind below, 274
Matter: and advent of new power, 274; and ancient mysticism, 271; ascent to the Spirit, 23; and Brahman, 221; and Brahman in Upanishads, 210-11; and Christ, 137; conquest by the Spirit, 34; and its contradiction, 265; cosmic, 223; and cosmic Christ, 188; and creation, 99; and the Divine, 52; and energy, 102; inconscient, 25; infintesimals of, 106-7; infusion with spirit, Gitā, 172; interiorization of, 142; inwardly one with Spirit, 46; life and mind co-existent with, 269; makes Christ tangible, 53; master-meaning of science's stress on, 271; mathematical physics of, 247; monist or pantheist, 86; and mysticism, 210; and Nirvana, 178; -obsessed research and Sri Aurobindo, 277; quasi-, 183; and radial energy, 240; Redeemer dissolved in, 120-21; and science, 265; self of, Supermind as, 274; and Spirit, 50; spirit-, 264; Spirit and rejection of, 263; and Sri Auro-

304

THE SPIRITUALITY OF THE FUTURE

Teilhard's notion of Christ's, 57-58

Paul, Saint, 12, 21, 39, 53, 55, 118, 134-35, 140, 141, 193, 269; Acts, 116; Acts 17:28, 136; Christ of, 119; on Christ, 122; Christ of Teilhard and, 134, 145-46; Christian pantheism and Pleroma of, 195; and Christianizing pantheism, 192-93; Christology of Teilhard and, 144-45; Colossians, 129; Colossians 1:15-20, 132; Colossians 1:17, 133; Colossians, 1:17, 18, 132; Colossians 1:19-20, 135; Colossians 1:24, 195; Colossians 3:11, 195; Cosmic Christ of, 60; Cosmic Christ of, and Teilhard's, 128; Cosmic Christ, vision in, 70; and cosmicality of Christ, 132; Ephesians 1:9, 10, 135, 192; Ephesians 1:23, 195; and evolutionist pantheism, 85; "God all in all" and Teilhard, 190-97; and historical Jesus, 145; and Latin Fathers, 144; mysticism of, 149, 150; pantheism in, 115-16; Philippians, 136; Romans 8:19-22, 136; Romans 8:20, 21, 135; Romans 8:22, 114-15; and Saint John and Śaiva Siddhānta, 203; and Teilhard on Christ and Creation, 145; Teilhard on Pleroma of, 109-10; Teilhard's use of phrases from, 115-16

Paul VI, Pope, 40

Peifer, Claude J., 194

Person: collective, 50; and the human person, 94; Teilhard and, 243-45

Personality: and pantheism, 254; purified and calm, 222

Philo of Alexandria, and Logos, 157

Physics: effect on philosophy, 57; Teilhard's application to God's creative act, 101-4

Planetization, 249

Plato, 242; "forms" of, 146

Pleroma, 50, 55, 57, 117, 236; à la Saint Paul, 194; of Christ, 86, 95; and Cosmic Christ, 186; Cosmic Christ's, 86; earthly maturation of, 60; extended to galaxies, 249; intracosmic aspect of, 238; and Mystical Body, 158; Paul's, and Christian pantheism, 195; Teilhard and, 109-18; Teilhard on structure of, 110; Teilhard's, 236-38; true Christianity emphasizes, 103; within cosmos, 236

Pleromization, 152-58

Power, Divine, and human form, 127

Prajna, and Supermind, 272

Prakriti, and Gītā, 173-74

Prat, Férnand, 129, 141, 145, 146, 194, 195; on Colossians 1:15, 145; and cosmic role of Christ, 134-36; on cosmicality of Christ in Saint Paul, 132; on "God all in all," 191; *The Theology of Saint Paul*, 128

Progress: problem of, 245; Teilhard on, 109; of world guided by Christ, 115, 116

Psychic: realization, 250; transformation, 250

Psychogenesis, process of, 63

Puranas, 172, 173-74; and Kingdom of Heaven on earth, 231

Purusha: and bhakti, 255; and Prakriti in Gītā, 173

Purushottama, 230

Rabut, O., 66, 90, 92, 93, 114; on Teilhard, 113

Radhakrishnan, S., 201

Radial energy: and evolution, 240; tangential and, 240; within of things, 240

Ramakrishna, 242

Ramakrishna Mission, 22

Ramana Maharshi, 242

Ramanuja, 201; love in Vedanta of, 202; Vedanta of, 71

Real-Idea, 226

Reality, emergence of spiritual, 50

Realization: collective, 23; pantheism and religious, 86; of self, 86

Reason, and mind-transcending power, 268

Rebirth, 75; and evolution, 77; soul's, 77; Teilhard and, 77-78

Redemption: Christ and, 249; cosmic mystery of, 95; evolutionary, 45, 56; Teilhard and, 126, 152-54

Reflection, 42, 235; act of, 61; co-, 43, 63; collective, 43, 62; Teilhard and critical threshold of, 240-41; ultimate center of, 63; ultra-, 43; of universe upon itself, 63

Religion(s): and Ashram, 73; Christianity as individualist and cosmic, 253; of East, Teilhard on, 170-71; of evolution, 143-44; of future, 178; Hindu, 19-20; Hinduism not a, 72-73; "a hitherto unknown form of,"

181-82; and pantheist language, 90-91; the pantheism he sought to avoid, 108; of pantheism of Spinoza and Hegel, 179; on "pantheist" mysticism, 184: pantheistic *confessio fidei*, 84; and Saint Paul on Christ and creation, 145; Saint Paul, Greek Fathers and, 149-50; on Saint Paul and Pleroma, 109-10; and Pauline Christ, 55-56; on Saint Paul's pantheist context, 193: at the peak of his perceptiveness, 260; his penchant for pantheism, 110; on people of Far East, 177, 178; on personal and impersonal being, 105: personal interior experience, 43; and personalization, 243-45; *The Phenomenon of Man*, 49; on phenomenon of revelation, 130-31; on the "phenomenon of spirit," 247-48; on physical and organic cosmicality, 145; picture of Holy Trinity, 155-56; his picture of world's end, 249; and Pleroma, 60, 109-18; his Pleroma, 236-38; possibility of break with Church, 48-49; and power exercising creative union, 118-27; on pre-existence of Christ, 123-24; pressed to pantheistic Christianity, 117; "Prime Mover Ahead," 236; his prime significance to modern age, 167-68; principle of universal unity, 186; on progress, 95; and psychism, 246; his pure multiple, 106-7; pushed beyond orthodoxy, 118; and quasi-formal causality, 148; Rabut on his crypto-pantheism, 113; radial and tangential energy, 102; and rebirth, 77-78; his reconciliation of God Above with God Ahead, 75; relationship between God and world for, 147; on religion of the East, 170-71; religion of the whole, 107; his remark about *The Life Divine*, 257; remark apropos of Sri Aurobindo, 258-59; and remote future of unification, 256; replaces metaphysics of "Being" by that of "Union," 103-4; on Resurrection, 125; re-thought Christology, 57-58; his "revolution," 62; revolutionary religion, 58; and Scotus, 123; scriptural and traditional support for his view, 53; series of "equal terms," 95; on sin, 45; on sin of Rome, 48; on a single "hominized" planet

in the universe, 248; his "slant" on entropy, 246-47; "Some Reflections on Two Converse Forms of Spirit," 260; and the Soul of the World, 86, 183-89; on souls, 254; and Spinoza's pantheism, 110-11, 113, 126; on Spinozism, 108; on the spiritual, 109; and his "spiritual ancestry" regarding Cosmic Christ, 133-34; his spiritual modernism, 52; and "spiritual pantheism," 182, 188; *The Spiritual Possibilities of Matter*, 83; and spirituality of future, 256; on structure of Pleroma, 110; *The Stuff of the Universe*, 42, 62; on suffering and sin, 44; on a super-human organism, 238; on super-humanity, 238-39; and "super-men," 236; suppression of, 39; and Supramental Yoga, 256; synthesis between "above" and "ahead," 61; on "synthetic redemption of being," 104; "by temperament a pantheist," 91-92; and "theogenesis," 155-56; three stages on way to God, 186; on thought, 241; "tranquil ocean" of, 91; Transcendence in Gītā and, 255; and trans-human, 239; treatment of Body of Christ by, 95; and Trinitization, 155; on true character of love, 198-99; on true meaning of Mass and Communion, 111; on twentieth-century man, 63; two attributes of God in, 105-6; on two currents in cosmic history, 239-40; and the two pantheisms, 86; and two types of mysticism, 178-79; two voices of, 236; ultimate attitude towards the individual, 243-44; ultra-human and trans-human, 238-39; "uncompromising" evolutionism of, 93; his understanding of the "mobile-movement" couple, 101-4; understanding of his universal incarnationism, 132; his vision of Cosmic Christ and Greek Fathers, 159; union differentiates, 145; "union differentiates" and nature of love, 198-207; and union by dissolution and by differentiation, 86; union and unity, 199; and Universal Christ, 117-18; on Universal Christ and Omega-Point, 157; "The Universal Element," 182, 184; on universal element, 182-83; on universal physical element in Christ, 124-25; universalization of

Pauline Christ, 134; on universe as "the true Host," 113; on unknown form of religion, 55-56; urging revolutionization of immanence-concept, 156; use of language, 43; use of phrases from Saint Paul, 115-16; and Vedanta, 127, 155, 179-80; on Vedanta and Christianity, 178-79; and Vedantic "fusionism" in Christianity, 179; on Vedantic pantheism, 190; and Vedantic philosophy of Incarnation, 127; and Vedantic synthesis of cosmic and transcendent, 188; vision of cosmogenesis, 119; visions of creative union, 152-54; his *weltanschauung*, 61; on Whole whose texture is divergent, 206; and worldwide hypostatic union, 112-13; worship of two realities, 50; Zaehner's interpretation of, 78-82; Theogenesis, 155-56; Theosphere, 395; Theravada Buddhism, Teilhard attacks, 171; his Yoga, 255

Teresa, Saint, and pantheism, 137

Thought: and genius, 242; and interiority, 242; and mystical phenomenon, 242; Teilhard on, 241

Time: and cosmogenesis, 52; evolutionary, 23

Time-Spirit, Aurobindonian, 275

Transcendence: of God vis-à-vis creation, 148; pantheism and, 181-82; and pantheism in Teilhard, 180; and Pantheos, 156; in Teilhard, 112-16; in Teilhard and Gītā, 255; Teilhard's lack of sense of, 95; transformation by means of, 263

Transcendent, descent of, 127

Transcendental Divine, 232-33

Transformation: collective, 23; of cosmos, 247; Divine, 22; entire, 252; of human race, 27; individual, 23; inner, 23; by means of transcendence, 263; psychic, spiritual, and supramental, 250; Sri Aurobindo's meaning of, 31-32; of whole of life, 55; world ripe for total, 274

Trinitization, Teilhard and, 155

Trinity: of Catholic Church and Sri Aurobindo, 233-34; Christian, 25; and creative union, 153; God as, 26; Hindu, 21, 25, 27; and Īshwara, 227; and Mohammedan yoga, 232; and practice of yoga, 233; and

Sachchidananda, 227; Śaivite, 204; significance for Sri Aurobindo, 232-34; and Sri Aurobindo, 227; Sri Aurobindo's and Teilhard's view of, 233-34; and Supermind, 80, 223; Supermind and Christian, 229-31; Teilhard on, 131-32; Teilhard's picture of, 155; Vedantic Īshwara and Christian, 230-31

Truth-Consciousness, 226, 279; Sri Aurobindo on, 229

Tufayl, Ibu, 202

Ultra-hominization, 63, 244-45

Ultra-human, 55, 142; and evolution, 58; maturing of, 60; progression of human into, 57; realization and entropy, 246; and some transcendent supernatural, 62; and Trans-human, 236, 228-29, 264

Ultra-reflection, 43

UNESCO, 14th Conference, 282

Unification: and evolution, 145; evolution as progressive, 24; evolutive, of pure multiple, 155; future of, remote for Teilhard, 256; and Omega Point, 142; process of, 119; progressive, 153; progressive, of multiple, 131; supernatural and natural, 183

Union: and Being in Teilhard, 103-4; Christ and universal, 187; differentiates, 148; differentiates, Teilhard and, 198-207; by dissolution and by assimilation, 87-93 passim; hypostatic, 110; hypostatic, extended to universe, 125; hypostatic, and Incarnation, 126; love and, defect of Christian notion, 204; of multiplicity, 200; mystical, 202; pantheistic language of, 253; passion for, in religions of the East, 170-71; Pleromatic, 109; social and soul's with God, 206; Teilhard on love and, 198-99; Teilhard and world-wide hypostatic, 112-13; and unity in Teilhard, 199

United States, 282

Unity: biological and social, 207; the church as "focus of," 39, 70; in diversity, 201; divine, and the Multiple, 120; of God, 105; of God and multiplicity in Teilhard, 105; human, 21; human spiritual, 183; and multiplicity, 154; and multiplicity in Overmind, 272-73; and multiplicity in